MELROSE ABBEY

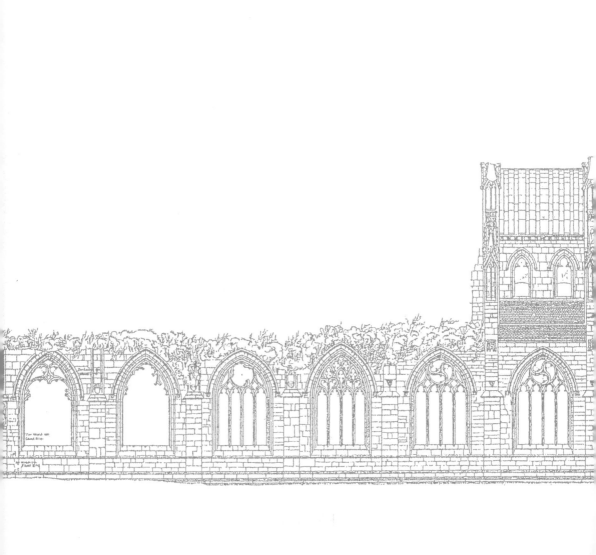

MELROSE ABBEY

RICHARD FAWCETT & RICHARD ORAM

TEMPUS

Frontispiece: Elevation of the south flank of the abbey church (Pinches, 1879)

The authors and publisher gratefully acknowledge a grant from Historic Scotland towards the publication costs of this volume.

All illustrations that are credited to 'Historic Scotland' are Crown Copyright, reproduced courtesy of Historic Scotland.

First published 2004

Tempus Publishing Ltd
The Mill, Brimscombe Port
Stroud, Gloucestershire GL5 2QG
www.tempus-publishing.com

British Library Cataloguing in Publication Data.
A catalogue record for this book is available from the British Library.

ISBN 0 7524 2867 5

Typesetting and origination by Tempus Publishing.
Printed and bound in Great Britain.

CONTENTS

PREFACE

This book has been written with the aim of providing a more detailed level of information for the interested general reader about an important property in state care than could be put together within the scope of either a guide book or an on-site display. It is one of a number of occasional publications aimed at contributing to the fuller understanding of major monuments maintained by Historic Scotland. However, there is no intention of attempting to offer an account that might in any way be regarded as an exhaustive study of the subject, and the authors will be fully satisfied if the book simply stimulates further debate on a complex of buildings that is particularly dear to their own hearts. The authorship has been divided between Richard Oram, who has written the essentially historical chapters (one and three) and Richard Fawcett, who has contributed the parts that deal with the architectural fabric (two and Appendix).

Melrose has, of course, an unusually distinguished monastic history. A community may have been established from Lindisfarne on a promontory within a loop in the Tweed as early as around AD 635, at the time that St Aidan was bishop of Lindisfarne. In 651, when Eata was its first abbot and St Boisil its first prior, it received its most famous recruit, St Cuthbert. That community is said to have suffered a devastating attack by King Cináed mac Alpín at some date before 858. While it is possible that monastic life was revived for a while thereafter, it was certainly defunct by about 1074, when an attempt to re-establish a monastery was made by two English monks, Aldwin and Turgot. Their unwillingness to accept the authority of King Malcolm III meant this venture was short-lived, though Turgot was later to enjoy the favour of Malcolm and his queen. Evidently a chapel dedicated to St Cuthbert, dependent on Durham, was built here at this time or soon afterwards.

The abbey that is discussed in this book was founded in 1136/7 by King David I, as part of his extraordinarily energetic campaign to bring the institutions of the Scottish Church into conformity with those of the rest of Western Europe. As the first house established for the austere Cistercian order in Scotland, and a daughter of Rievaulx in Yorkshire, it was a particularly important foundation, in which David took the closest personal interest. Indeed, it is likely that he had been planning its foundation for some years before 1136. Since the earlier monastic site would have been unsuitable for anything other than a small and essentially eremitic community, the new foundation was located instead on a spacious and low-lying site in the Tweed valley about 4km west of its predecessor. Enough of a first church had been built to be ready for consecration by 1146, and it must have been completed before the last decades of the century, when a western narthex, or Galilee, was added. It is also likely that some of the first conventual buildings had been constructed by around 1146, though a major campaign of providing more appropriate monastic buildings on a greater scale was in progress in the 1230s and '40s.

The abbey's location in the borders, close to the routes taken by English armies when invading Scotland from the later thirteenth century onwards, meant it was almost inevitable that the abbey should suffer, and it did so on several occasions. Robert I made substantial grants towards one phase of repairs in 1326. But the worst of these attacks was evidently at the hands of Richard II's armies in 1385, following which the decision was taken to completely rebuild the church, and probably some of the more important conventual buildings as well. Reconstruction of the church, which was started on a massive scale and to a very costly level of finish, progressed well for a number of years. But by the second half of the fifteenth century the pace was flagging, and by the time monastic life came to an end in 1560 it is likely that little more than about two-thirds of the great church had been completed, and that parts of the original church were still standing and at least partly in use.

Yet, despite its unfinished and now ruined state, the church is of the greatest interest for what it can tell us about changing attitudes to architec-tural design in Scotland in the course of the later Middle Ages, a period when Scottish patrons and masons were pursuing a far more independent approach to architectural design than had prevailed in the preceding centuries. It is therefore particularly fortunate that, although the monastic buildings were almost completely destroyed after the Reformation, and are now known through little more than fragmentary walls and excavated footings, so much of what was built of the church itself has survived. This high level of preser-vation is principally because a major part of the church, the monastic choir, was adapted for parochial worship in the early seventeenth century, and remained in that use until 1808. By then its enlightened owner, the third duke of Buccleuch, recognised the importance of what remained, and took steps to ensure its continued preservation. His successors continued the family's interest in the abbey, and it was the seventh duke who placed the abbey in state care in 1919.

ACKNOWLEDGEMENTS

Much help has been received from various individuals in the course of writing this book. Amongst those of whom particular mention must be made are: David Breeze, John Dunbar, Gordon Ewart, Sue Fawcett, Noel Fojut, Stuart Harrison, John Higgitt, Michael Hutson, A.A. McMillan, Christopher Norton, Allan Rutherford, David Simon and Sylvia Stevenson.

1
THE HISTORY OF
THE ABBEY

Reforming the medieval Church

Towards the close of the tenth century there emerged a reforming spirit within the western European Church. Reacting against the worldliness of the Church generally and its leaders in particular, groups of clerics began to seek a return to a purer, simpler form of religious life. At the heart of the movement was the abbey of Cluny in Burgundy, which gave its name to the whole process of reform. Monks from Cluny (Cluniacs) gradually extended their influence throughout all branches of the Church, mainly through their appointment as bishops, and gained widespread support from lay society in Europe. Cluniac ideals inspired many leading Church reformers of the eleventh century, most notably those who sought to exclude the interests of Kings and magnates from any role in the election of bishops and popes. This produced a major crisis between reform-minded clergy, bent on freeing the Church from what was often presented as ungodly interference, and secular powers who needed influence over the Church to underpin their government. In the Holy Roman Empire in particular, which covered most of central Europe from the Baltic Sea to northern Italy, bishops and archbishops were holders of great territorial power. There, the emperors had long enjoyed the right of investing these princes of the Church with the symbols of their office, and the prelates were accustomed to serve as councillors and officers of the emperors. The reform movement challenged the emperors' right of appointment, producing a long and bitter conflict known in history as the Investiture Contest. Despite various setbacks and reverses along the way, reforming popes were ultimately to triumph, aided by the active support of the Cluniacs. The influence of the order reached its peak in 1088 when Odo, cardinal-bishop of Ostia and former prior of Cluny, was elected pope as Urban II (1088-99).

The reform debate reached all corners of Christendom. In Scotland, the children of Malcolm III Canmore (1058-93) and his second wife, St Margaret, were all supporters of the Church reform movement. Margaret, who had been brought up at the Hungarian royal court in an intense atmosphere of religious fervour – Hungary had only recently been converted to Christianity and its King was an active supporter of the reformers – had been disturbed by what she saw as the spiritual backwardness of her husband's kingdom and set in motion a process of reform. Her programme was small in scale, but it started a chain reaction that was to transform the Scottish Church within half a century. Perhaps her greatest impact was achieved through her sons, for her one monastic foundation, a small colony of Benedictine monks sent from Canterbury to Dunfermline, appears to have been driven out of Scotland in the political upheavals which followed the deaths of Malcolm and Margaret in 1093. Margaret's chaplain and biographer, Turgot, however, tells of her impression on her sons and how she succeeded in literally beating into them devotion to God, understanding of their Christian duty as princes and future kings as well as ordinary men, and commitment to the spiritual regeneration of Scotland.

As Kings, Malcolm and Margaret's sons all showed varying degrees of commitment to the reformist principles of the time. The reigns of Edgar (1097-1107) and Alexander I (1107-24) saw the re-establishment of Benedictine monks at Dunfermline and the foundation of another Benedictine monastery at Coldingham, while Augustinian canons were installed in priories at Scone and St Andrews. During the reign of Alexander I, the youngest surviving brother, David, who had been given the rulership of a principality that covered most of the Southern Uplands south of the Lammermuir Hills encompassing Tweeddale, Teviotdale and Clydesdale, revealed what was to be the greatest commitment of all to the reform process. In about 1113, he founded a monastery at Selkirk in the heart of his lordship, and brought to it a colony of monks from the abbey of Thiron near Chartres in northern France. Thiron, founded by St Bernard of Thiron, was the head of what was growing rapidly into a new order of monks – the Tironensians – who followed a particularly austere interpretation of the rule for monastic life drawn up by St Benedict. David had been greatly impressed by the reports of the piety and austerity of Bernard's monastery and had attempted to visit him there, but arrived shortly after the abbot's death. David's interest, however, did not end there and he was to prove to be one of the greatest patrons of the fledgling order. He had been encouraged by his chaplain and confessor, John, whom he later appointed to the bishopric of Glasgow, and who may have served as an intermediary in negotiations to bring the colony to Scotland. David's new abbey at Selkirk, which he relocated to Kelso about fifteen years later, was the first monastery of any of the reformed monastic orders to be founded anywhere in Britain, and developed into one of the richest and most influential communities in Scotland.

In 1124, Alexander I died, leaving no legitimate son to succeed him as King. Instead, his last surviving brother took the throne, and as King David I (1124–53) he presided over an era of unprecedented growth and change in the kingdom of Scotland. A dynamic, capable and ambitious man, David transformed the basis of royal power in Scotland, redefined the relationship between the King and his great noblemen, and expanded his authority within northern Britain. That, however, was only part of his ambition, for David also aimed to remodel his kingdom's economy, which he achieved through the introduction of the first native silver coinage and by the foundation of burghs as privileged market centres through which all Scottish trade was to be channelled. The third strand of David's policies was the root and branch reform of the Church within his kingdom, building upon the foundations laid by his brothers in the heartland of the kingdom, and those which he himself had set in place in his own territories in the Southern Uplands. In many ways, this third dimension was the most important, for the impact of Church reform made itself felt in all aspects of the daily lives of the Scottish people, from the highest to the lowest. It not only brought about a transformation of the spiritual experience of the King's subjects, but the new class of literate clerics powered royal administration, enabling systematic record-keeping, which in turn underpinned the growth of kingly authority. The reformed Church, integrated as it was into the wider world of western Christendom, furnished the kingdom with fresh avenues of contact – economic and cultural as well as political – which accelerated the processes of social change set in train by David and his predecessors. The Church, moreover, acted as an important conduit through which new ideas and techniques were introduced to Scotland, in areas such as architecture, engineering, technical crafts, manufacture, crop-growing and livestock management. The demand of the Church for specialist skills and quality or exotic products served to stimulate the wider economy, and consolidated the commercial base upon which many of David's policies were founded. It was into this wider picture that Melrose Abbey was set.

The Cistercians

After becoming King, David founded no further Tironensian monasteries, his interest by about 1130 having switched to another of the new and rapidly expanding orders of monks, the Cistercians, who took their name from the first community of the order, founded in 1098 at Cîteaux in Burgundy. The community at Cîteaux, led by the English monk Stephen Harding, was to become the focus for a new wave of reforming zeal that was to sweep through the European Church in the early twelfth century. Rejecting the elaborate liturgies and concentration on intellectual pursuits that characterised the existing orders of monks, the Cistercian interpretation of the rule of St Benedict prescribed a life of extreme austerity and simplicity, set apart from the temptations of the secular world. It was based upon a routine in which labour and prayer were given precedence over the pursuit of learning and elaborate church services of the Cluniacs and Benedictines. In an age when austerity was equated with piety and spirituality, the Cistercians were considered as especially favoured by God and, therefore, quickly attracted the support of laymen who feared for the fate of their souls after death and who were looking for a spiritual 'insurance policy' that would secure salvation in the hereafter. The Cistercians' reputation as holders of a special direct relationship with God ensured the success of the order and drove its rapid spread throughout Europe as Kings and magnates scrambled to win the monks' spiritual favour. Within 55 years of the foundation of Cîteaux, there were 339 Cistercian monasteries, spread from Scotland to Poland. Although Cîteaux tried to put the brakes on such rapid proliferation, fearing that over-expansion would jeopardise the conformity to the rule set down in the eleventh century, by 1200 there were 525 Cistercian houses, and the number continued to rise throughout the Middle Ages.

Organisation was the key to the Cistercians' success. While Stephen Harding provided the inspirational ethos of the order, it was St Bernard, abbot of Cîteaux's colony at Clairvaux, who gave it an organisational framework that provided it with the means to set up and control a network of communities spread across Europe. Bernard of Clairvaux has been likened to a military commander, whose colonies of monks were the 'New Soldiers of Christ' sent as shock troops to carry the reforming ideal of Christianity to the corners of the continent. Like all armies, the Cistercians relied on a sound command structure that ensured coherence and cohesion. The system adopted was one referred to as 'filiation', where a 'mother-house' sent out colonies of its monks to found 'daughter-houses', which in turn would send out further colonies (**1**). The abbot of each daughter-house were subject to

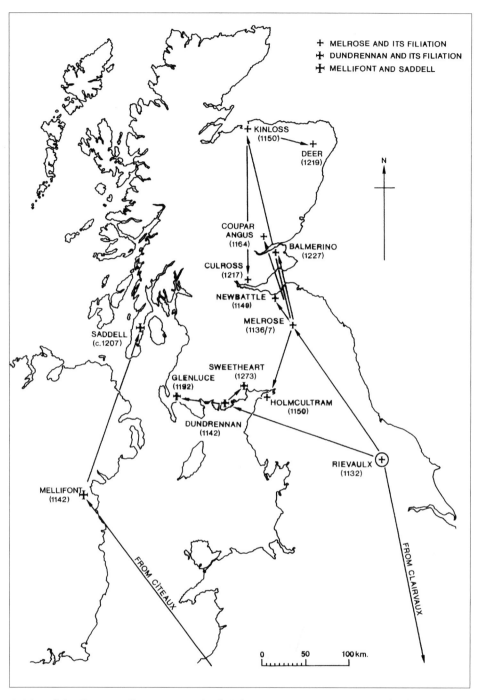

1 *Map of the Cistercian filiations in Scotland.* Sylvia Stevenson/Historic Scotland

the over-riding supervision of the abbot of the mother-house, back up the line all the way to Cîteaux, and each father-abbot in a filiation grouping was required to undertake annual visitations of his monastery's daughters. All Cistercian abbots, moreover, were required to attend the chapter-general of the order, held annually at Cîteaux. In practice, as the order spread to the peripheries of Europe, it was impractical for all to attend, and permission was given for representatives of a filiation to come, or for abbots of very remote houses to attend only every second or third year. This structure of filiation and the visitation system ensured that strict conformity with the rule was maintained, with visiting father-abbots having the authority to impose discipline and even to depose abbots who were considered to have failed in their duty to provide stability and discipline.

Each colony that was sent out contained experienced monks and new recruits. In theory, each new foundation was constructed to a blue-print that determined layout and internal organisation, with the result that a Cistercian monk from southern Italy arriving at a Cistercian monastery in Scotland, or wherever, would have found a broadly recognisable community following an ordered existence identical to that which he had left. Of course, there were variations in materials used for building and in the layout of some of the structures, usually dictated by the site selected for the abbey, but the Cistercian ideal for uniformity was otherwise adhered to quite strictly. That, however, does not mean that the order was fixed in its thinking, for the underlying principle within the medieval Church was, in theory, the notion of a Church *semper reformanda* (always reforming), modifying itself to prevent stagnation and decay. As a result, even the Cistercians adapted over time, although there were always to be those who hankered back to the original simplicity of the order's founders.

From the outset, the Cistercians projected an image of themselves as 'God's frontiersmen'. In their literature and art, they presented themselves as pioneers, toiling to make the wilderness and desert blossom into a new Eden. Certainly, their early monasteries were located in remote and inhospitable places, unpeopled and uncultivated, and it was only through physical labour that these settings were transformed into productive countryside. Their efforts were driven by two interwoven strands of reasoning. The first was a straightforward economic one: they needed to develop their estates to a level at which they could sustain themselves independently of the outside world, and which would permit their community to grow and send out new colonies without compromising the survival of the mother-house. Secondly, there was a spiritual motivation which subtly altered their economic instincts. Quite simply, they aimed to refashion the material world around them into a near-heavenly paradise. It has been said that their entrepreneurship was a logical extension of their religious culture: 'Land, like love, could be stripped of its secular connections and shaped to reflect the harmonies of divine creation' (M.G. Newman, *The Boundaries of Charity: Cistercian Culture and Ecclesiastical Reform*). This view was central to the writings of one of the great Cistercian scholars of the early twelfth century, Ailred, abbot of Rievaulx. In a treatise known as *The Mirror of Charity*, Ailred presented material and spiritual well-being as inseparable. Barbarity, cultural backwardness and inferior technology, all symptoms of material impoverishment, were equally symptoms of moral and spiritual degeneracy. For Ailred, the taming of nature was inextricably bound up in the process of civilising that would bring spiritual regeneration.

As harbingers of spiritual reform, the Cistercians were very much pioneers or frontiersmen. They were also cultural revolutionaries, who carried new techniques of land management and new attitudes towards land exploitation to all parts of Europe, where they established colonies. From the Cistercians' perspective, they were charged by God with the responsibility to maximise the return from their land. Dominion over the earth and all that is in it had been given by God to humanity – failure to harness that gift was to neglect God's bounty. Thus, in almost every area where Cistercian monks were planted, they undertook a widespread re-ordering of the landscape, even to the length of evicting the settled populations of property that they had been given. Of course, there is also much symbolism in the images that they employed. Making the desert bloom, or uncultivated land bear rich harvests, are as much parables for the winning of souls for Christ from the slough of spiritual waste as statements of fact. Nevertheless, wherever Cistercian colonists went, they took with them a new attitude towards management of the land and resources, which led them to reject the native systems that they discovered as primitive if not barbaric, and to cast their hosts as technologically inferior in the physical working of the land. This technological and economic inferiority was often also seen as a symptom of spiritual inferiority, linking once again Cistercian notions of their role as spiritual frontiersmen with that of pioneers on the limits of civilisation.

Cistercian colonisation carried the culture of the late eleventh-century Frankish West to the farthest corners of Europe. Within twenty years of the order's foundation the Cistercians arrived in England. In 1128, William Giffard, bishop of Winchester, brought a colony from L'Aumône in Burgundy to Waverley in Surrey. Four years later, the order reached northern England when a colony of monks from St Bernard's abbey of Clairvaux, the third daughter-house of Cîteaux itself, was established at Rievaulx in

Yorkshire. The colony, the second of a total of 80 sent out from Clairvaux, flourished quickly and in 1135/6 sent out its first colony, to Warden in Bedfordshire, where they had been given land by Walter l'Espec, a prominent north-Yorkshire nobleman. By early 1137, Rievaulx had grown sufficiently to send out a second offshoot to Scotland, where King David stood ready to act as its patron and protector. Preparations for bringing a Cistercian colony to Scotland may, in fact, have started very soon after the foundation of Rievaulx itself, for shortly before 1133 David granted the priory at Durham possession of the parish church of Berwick-on-Tweed in compensation for the church of Melrose, which he had given to the Cistercians. This church was not to become the site of the abbey, but lay at what became known as 'Old' Melrose some 4km down the river Tweed.

Old Melrose

Old Melrose had been the location of a much earlier monastery, founded in the mid-seventh century, but which had long ceased to exist by David's time (2). It had been one of the centres from which Bernicia, the northern part of the Anglo-Saxon kingdom of Northumbria which at that time incorporated the whole of what is now south-east Scotland, was converted to Christianity. The monastery was an offshoot of the abbey founded at Lindisfarne by St Aidan, itself a colony of St Columba's great abbey at Iona. Little is known of the history of Old Melrose, but in its early days it was home to a number of monks who were key figures in the spiritual life of Bernicia: its first abbot, Eata; its first prior, Boisil, whose name is preserved in the village of St Boswell's; the monk, Bothan, whose name is recorded in Bowden and in the dedication of Abbey St Bathan's in Berwickshire; but especially its second prior, Cuthbert, who became abbot of Lindisfarne, bishop, then the saintly protector of Bernicia. A later abbot, Aethelwald, became bishop of Lindisfarne in 721, ruling it during a period that came to be regarded as a 'golden age' in Northumbria's history.

Little seems to have disturbed the tranquillity of Old Melrose until the mid-ninth century, when the peace of the monastery was shattered in a tide of fire and blood as the Scottish King, Cináed mac Alpín, led a plundering raid through northern Bernicia. Melrose, we are told, was burned by the King's warband. It was just the first in a succession of blows to the monks, for within a few years the Danish conquerors of York ravaged Bernicia again. Nevertheless, in 875, there was still something here to offer shelter to the monks who had abandoned Lindisfarne in the face of repeated Viking

2 *Old Melrose, looking towards the Eildon Hills.* Fawcett

attacks, but there is no indication that the monastery continued to function for long after that. Indeed, the movement in the early 900s of Norse armies north and south along the line of the old Roman road known as Dere Street, which ran from York towards the river Forth near Edinburgh and crossed the Tweed at Newstead, had probably brought an end to monastic life at Old Melrose. There had been a short-lived attempt to revive it as a Benedictine community in the early 1070s by Aldwin of Jarrow and Turgot, former chaplain and confessor of St Margaret. The Durham monk, Symeon, described how they came to 'the former monastery of Melrose, at that time a solitude; and delighting in the secluded habitation of that place began to live there [as monks] serving Christ.' They had, however, acted without the permission of the Scottish King, Malcolm III, who had no wish to see foreign clerics take possession of a such a symbolic site in what was still disputed territory and, when they refused to swear fealty to him, he ordered that they be driven out. Malcolm's youngest son, David I, may have considered it half a century later as a possible location for a Cistercian colony, but the monks sent from Rievaulx to inspect the proposed site for their colony must have rejected it as unsuitable for the particular needs of their order. Instead, a more low-lying site by the river, with good access to water, agricultural land, pasture and building materials, was selected.

Although the Old Melrose site was not redeveloped as the location for the new monastery, the old church there continued in existence as a chapel, dependent on the relocated parish of Melrose. It also attracted special gifts and awards, underscoring its continuing importance as a minor cult centre. In the later thirteenth century, for example, Peter de Haig, lord of Bemerside, as compensation for certain 'transgressions' against the monks, agreed to pay them 10 salmon annually, plus half a stone of wax annually on St Cuthbert's Day (20 March) or 30 pennies, for the lights of the chapel of St Cuthbert of Old Melrose. The chapel is recorded as having been burned 'recently' by English soldiers when, in 1321, Simon de Wedale, bishop of Whithorn, granted an indulgence of 40 days to those who helped to rebuild it. In 1437, John Cavertoun, monk of Melrose, secured an indulgence from the Pope securing a remission of 21 years in purgatory for those who visited the chapel on St Cuthbert's Day. Thereafter, the lands of Old Melrose disappear from the records until 1564, when their tenant, Robert Ormeston, granted sasine in them to his son, John. By that date, the chapel seems just to have been a dim memory.

Foundation and early growth

According to the *Chronicle of Melrose*, a record composed at the abbey between the mid-twelfth and late-thirteenth centuries, the monastery was founded by King David on 23 March 1136, which by modern reckoning is 23 March 1137. Already by the time of the formal foundation, however, the King would have made arrangements for the material support of the new colony as well as ensuring the provision of suitable temporary buildings in which the monks could live and worship until the permanent stone complex was sufficiently advanced to house them. These arrangements would have had to have satisfied the abbot of Rievaulx before he would have permitted his monks to take up residence. What David had arranged was, in effect, a portfolio made up of blocks of real estate and a wide raft of economic rights and privileges that would have enabled the monks to support themselves in accordance with the strict rules of their order. These rules, for example, prohibited the monks from accepting control of parish churches, mills, or rental income from properties that they did not themselves work.

While many of the records of the abbey have survived, the original foundation charter given by David I has not. There is, however, a charter of around 1147 issued by the King which pulled together and confirmed all the gifts which he, his son, and leading members of the nobility had granted to

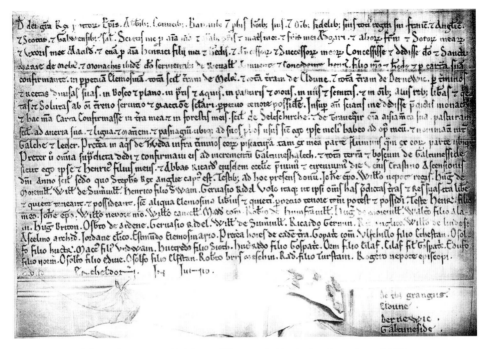

3 *A charter of the endowments of Melrose Abbey, probably dating from about 1147.*
Melrose Liber

Melrose by that date (**3**). From these, it can be seen that David's initial endowment of the monastery comprised a substantial block of 2,150 ha made up of the three royal estates of Eildon, Melrose and Darnick that stretched along the south side of the Tweed between the river and the Eildon Hills. This property was mainly well-drained land, suitable for arable cultivation, but with some marshy ground along the river and pasture on the north-facing slopes of the Eildons. In addition to this, David granted them generous rights and privileges in his land and forests of Selkirk and Traquair, including rights of pasture for their work animals, the right to take firewood and building materials, and the right to graze their pigs in the hilly district between Wedale (the valley of the Gala Water) and Lauderdale north of Melrose. Finally, he gave them the fishing rights in the Tweed along the length of their property, on both sides of the river. It was a generous provision, which gave the monks the basic means with which to support themselves and from which to secure materials for building the permanent complex of buildings that would replace the temporary timber accommodation to which they had come.

From the first, however, Melrose did not quite meet the strict conditions laid down by the Cistercian rule. Remote it may have been, but it was hardly an unpeopled desert and far removed from the snares of the secular world.

21

The landed endowment which David had provided consisted of three already established agricultural estates with settled populations. Indeed, the men of Eildon, Melrose and Darnick were named as witnesses to the King's grant. From its very foundation, then, the monks were lords of a dependent peasant population, from whom they were to draw rents and labour services. As the twelfth century progressed, this deviation from one of the founding principles of the order became more pronounced amongst Cistercian abbeys in general, and by the end of the Middle Ages the abbot of Melrose had become one of the greatest lords of southern Scotland.

The first abbot, Richard, presided over a period of sustained growth in the fortunes of Melrose. Support for the Cistercians was buoyant in the twelfth century and the abbey received a steady flow of generous gifts of land and rights from its royal patrons and from the wider nobility of southern Scotland. These gifts provided the funds and many of the materials for the first great episode of building at the abbey, whose progress was marked on Sunday 28 July 1146 with the consecration of the parts of the church that had been finished and its dedication to St Mary (**11** to **15**). The success of Melrose, however, was marked not just in material terms, for it is clear that the community itself had expanded rapidly under Abbot Richard's supervision. By 1140, the number of recruits was sufficient to allow Melrose to send out a colony of its own to found a new abbey at Newbattle in Midlothian, and by the end of that decade, plans were under way for the establishment of two further colonies. Despite the successes overseen by Abbot Richard, it appears that his relations with his monks had become increasingly bad. Later tradition describes him as learned and eloquent, but also as a quick-tempered and rigid disciplinarian who lost the respect and obedience of the convent. As a result, in 1148 he was deprived of his office by the abbot of Rievaulx and retired to Clairvaux, where he died the following year.

In place of Richard, the abbot of Rievaulx provided the sacrist of his own abbey, Waltheof. This appointment was highly significant for the abbey, for Waltheof was the stepson of King David, younger brother of Simon de St Liz, earl of Northampton, and half-brother of Earl Henry, heir to the Scottish throne and earl of Northumberland. Waltheof's abbacy was marked by continued sustained growth, building on the successes of his predecessor. On 1 January 1150, a second new colony was founded by King David and Earl Henry at Holmcultram in what is now Cumbria, and on 21 May that year, the King founded a third colony at Kinloss in Moray. High birth and deep personal piety might have marked Waltheof for yet greater office, but he consistently refused to be removed from his charge at Melrose, even turning down his election to the bishopric of St Andrews in early 1159. Waltheof's refusal, however, may have been influenced by an awareness of the nearness of his own end, for on 3 August 1159 he died and was buried in the chapterhouse of the abbey.

Prosperity and power

Waltheof's successor, William, a monk of Melrose, was elected by the convent on 27 November 1159, and was blessed two days later in the abbey church by Herbert, bishop of Glasgow. William's abbacy started well and the community continued to prosper under his rule, sending out its fourth colony in 1164 to Coupar Angus in Perthshire, where King Malcolm IV, Waltheof's half-nephew, had provided an extensive landed endowment. But relations between William and his brethren began to sour and the cause, surprisingly, was Waltheof. Rumours of miracles at the tomb of the second abbot had begun to circulate shortly after Waltheof's death and soon the peace of the abbey was being disturbed by pilgrims seeking the aid of what was widely believed to be a new saint. Abbot William sought to protect his monks from this intrusion into their secluded existence and attempted to silence talk of miracles. His actions, however, alienated the monks and in April 1170, his authority fatally undermined, he resigned the abbacy and was succeeded the same day by the prior, Jocelin.

The new abbot had few doubts about the sanctity of Waltheof, and in summer 1171, as described in the *Chronicle of Melrose*, he sought final proof:

> The tomb of our pious father, sir Waltheof, the second abbot of Melrose, was opened by Enguerrand, of good memory, the bishop of Glasgow, and by four abbots called in for this purpose; and his body was found entire, and his vestments intact, in the twelfth year from his death, on the eleventh day before the Kalends of June [22 May]. And after the holy celebration of mass, the same bishop and the abbots whose number we have mentioned above, along with the whole convent of the said monastery, placed over the remains of his most holy body a new stone of polished marble. And there was great gladness; those who were present exclaiming together and saying that truly this was a man of God…

The uncorrupted state of the abbot's corpse was believed to be conclusive evidence for his saintly status. Although he was never formally canonised, it is clear that he was venerated as a saint at Melrose and moves may have been made to secure wider recognition of his sainthood. As part of this, a *vita*, or *Life of Waltheof*, was written to provide a dossier of evidence for those who would consider his suitability for canonisation. Incorruptibility was regarded, however, as one of the clearest signs of sanctity, but even when Waltheof's tomb was re-opened in 1240, when the abbots' graves at the entrance to the chapterhouse were being moved to its east end, and his body was found to have decomposed, there was no decline in his cult. Indeed, onlookers at that time took away relics from the tomb, and the chronicler at Melrose in the thirteenth century was careful to record cures said to have been effected by these remains.

After only four years as abbot, Jocelin was appointed to the bishopric of Glasgow, the second most important spiritual office in the kingdom. In the words of the *Chronicle of Melrose*, the 'mild, affable, gentle and moderate' Jocelin was elected bishop at a council held at Perth on 23 May 1174 'by demand of the clergy and people' of the diocese of Glasgow, and 'with the consent of the King himself'. His election was not followed by his immediate resignation as abbot, and he appears to have continued to hold Melrose until his consecration at Glasgow. As a result, it was not until May 1175 that his successor, Laurence, a Melrose monk who had formerly been abbot of an unidentified and evidently short-lived Cistercian abbey in Orkney, was chosen. Elected on 14 May, he was consecrated by Bishop Jocelin at Melrose nine days later. Only three years later, however, Laurence, 'a man of marvellous humility and gentleness, and most learned in the divine writings', died, and in January 1179, Bishop Jocelin was again at Melrose to bless his second successor as abbot, Ernald.

In the person of Abbot Ernald, the status of the abbots of Melrose in the political life of Scotland was made explicit for the first time. The landed wealth and influence of the abbey gave its abbot a major prominence in royal councils, while his learning and position as an important abbot within the Cistercian network brought respect for his views and the employment of his services on diplomatic missions. In 1182, Ernald accompanied Bishop Jocelin and Osbert, abbot of Kelso, in an embassy to Rome on King William the Lion's behalf to discuss a raft of business ranging over the subjection of Scotland to English overlordship, the freedom of the Scottish Church from the jurisdiction of the English archbishops of York, and matters relating to elections to important benefices in the Scottish Church. According to the *Chronicle of Melrose*, they achieved all their objectives and, as a sign of favour to the King of Scots, Pope Lucius III sent a golden rose back with them.

After serving as abbot at Melrose for 10 years, in March 1189 Ernald was elected to the abbacy of Rievaulx, the mother-house of Melrose. His successor was Rayner, abbot of Kinloss, a former Melrose monk who had been abbot there for 15 years. Rayner held his charge until 1194, when he resigned, to be succeeded by his successor at Kinloss, Abbot Radulf (who in 1202 was elected to the bishopric of Down in Ulster). Throughout this period of relatively short abbacies, Bishop Jocelin had remained active in his support of his former abbey, offering it a degree of protection and guidance during times of uncertainty. Jocelin, indeed, maintained his connection with Melrose to the end of his life and may have withdrawn there to die in March 1199. The English royal clerk and chronicler, Roger, parson of Howden, who was also a canon of Glasgow, recorded that the bishop was buried in the abbey church on the north side of the monks' choir.

Jocelin's possible retirement to Melrose at the end of his life was not an isolated event. Prominent churchmen, royal officials and nobles often sought the spiritual certainty of assuming the habit of a monk shortly before their deaths, sometimes reflecting a desire to return to the simple life that they had been forced to leave through promotion, as in the case of Jocelin or his contemporary, Christian, bishop of Whithorn, who died and was buried at Holmcultram, or through anxiety to ensure the salvation of their souls through inclusion in the all-embracing prayers of the community. The second half of the twelfth century saw a flow of such retirements at Melrose, often by men whose patronage had added considerably to the abbey's wealth and prestige over the years. In March 1185, for example, Robert Avenel, lord of Eskdale in Dumfriesshire, who had given the abbey very extensive lands in the upper reaches of the valley, died at Melrose as a novice-associate, while in 1196 it was John of Roxburgh, treasurer of the diocese of Glasgow.

Not everyone could withdraw into the monastic life before death, but by the close of the twelfth century they could still benefit from burial and inclusion in the prayers and masses of the monks. Most who benefited in this way had either given generously to support the monks during their lifetime, or made provision in their wills for gifts to the abbey. In this way, they could secure the salvation of their souls in the hereafter. A martyrology or 'obit book', in which the names of dead benefactors were listed, is not mentioned specifically until 1333, but entries in the *Chronicle of Melrose* confirm that individuals were remembered in this way from the twelfth century. In 1188, for example, the *Chronicle* recorded that 'Richard de Morville, King William's constable, and his wife Avice, and their heir William, gave to God and St Mary and the monks of Melrose, in perpetual alms, the land that is called Park, as their charter testifies. May their propitious alms ever be in eternal memory!' The de Morvilles, however, were not buried at Melrose, although they were remembered in future years as patrons. One benefactor who was buried there was Philip de Valognes, the royal chamberlain, who died in 1215, and was taken to Melrose for burial in the chapterhouse. In 1219, his son William de Valognes died at Kelso and, although the Kelso monks tried to secure the burial in their abbey of so significant a figure, he was carried to Melrose and buried alongside the tomb of his father. That same year, Gervase Avenel, son of the Robert Avenel who died as a novice at Melrose in 1185, also died and was buried alongside his father. The number of such burials increased in the 1200s, with further members of the Avenel and Balliol families, as well as members of rising southern Scottish families such as the Crawfords, Maxwells, Normanvilles and Somervilles, being entombed in the abbey and bringing further gifts of property and rights to the community.

By the time that Abbot Radulf I was promoted to the bishopric of Down in 1202, the flow of gifts that the laity had brought to the Cistercians, in their desire to win the spiritual favours of the monks, had seriously eroded the founding principles of the order. After 1200, the rate and scale of new gifts began to diminish once men began to question the level of spiritual 'value-for-money' offered by the monks. Gifts of land and other property, which had been intended to promote the work of the Church and support the monks, served to turn the monasteries into highly organised land-managing corporations (**98**), where abbots became concerned increasingly with the running of the monastic estate rather than with the spiritual affairs of their communities. There are hints that Melrose was dabbling already in the 'futures' markets of the period and it has been suggested that the over-exploitation of its grazing rights at Hassendean in the 1190s (see pp.257–8) had been driven by a need to meet obligations to foreign wool merchants to whom they had sold the right to their wool crop in expectation of good yields. At around the same time, it emerges that Melrose was also standing surety for debts owed to Jews in England – including the famous Aaron the Jew of Lincoln - by important Anglo-Scottish noblemen, such as Robert de Quincy. Such behaviour was, again, wholly incompatible with the founding principles of the order and added to mounting criticism of monks in general. Dissatisfaction with the existing monastic orders saw the development of newer, still more austere groups, such as the Valliscaulians (named after their first community in the Val des Choux, or Valley of Cabbages, in Burgundy), who found brief favour in Scotland in the 1230s. From the 1220s, however, it was the new orders of friars, the Dominicans and, slightly later, the

Franciscans, who began to attract the support of lay patrons from the King down. Promising a high spiritual return for a low investment in material terms, they seemed to offer a better prospect for lay folk concerned about the destination of their souls after death.

At Melrose, there is no sign that the widespread dissatisfaction with the monks that was beginning to emerge across Europe had any impact on either the flow of gifts to the community in the early 1200s or on the spiritual health of the community itself. Indeed, despite a rapid turnover of abbots between 1202 and 1219, the convent appears to have remained stable and prosperous. Radulf I's departure in 1202 was followed by a run of six abbots in 17 years. Two of these, Adam (1207-13) and William de Courcy (1215-16), were promoted to greater things (bishop of Caithness and abbot of Rievaulx respectively), but the others had little time to make their presence felt during their short tenure of the abbacy. Hugh de Clipstone, for example, a Melrose monk, was elected in May 1214 and resigned at Cîteaux in November 1215, giving him an active period of barely a year as abbot. This was not, however, a period of instability or weakness in the life of the monastery, for its abbots continued to hold a key place in the councils of the Kings of Scots. In 1209, for example, Abbot Adam and the bishop of St Andrews spearheaded a Scottish diplomatic mission to King John of England seeking a treaty to end the growing antagonism between the kingdoms that had threatened to erupt into war. Adam's service in this business may have been the factor which drew him to the attention of the King and led in 1213 to his appointment to the see of Caithness, a territory where King William had faced repeated challenges throughout his long reign.

King William's close relationship with Melrose was maintained and, indeed, developed by his son and successor after 1214. Although the new King, Alexander II (4), spread his patronage widely, favouring both the Valliscaulians, for whom he founded a priory at Pluscarden in Moray, and the Dominican friars, he continued with his ancestors' special association with the Cistercians. In early 1216, the 18-year-old Alexander opened what was to prove a life-long association with Melrose when he and his chief advisors gathered there to meet the northern English barons who were seeking his protection against King John. Alexander, aiming to use the political crisis in England as an opportunity to regain control of the northern counties of England lost in 1157, and redress for John's various wrongs against him personally, received their homage in the abbey. Going even further, he had them renounce their allegiance to John and swear him fealty in the chapterhouse, 'touching relics of the saints', probably including Waltheof, for greater security.

4 *The seal of Alexander II.* © The Trustees of the National Museums of Scotland

The King's close interest in Melrose and employment of its monks as his agents in the political hotspots around his kingdom brought material returns for the abbey. In December 1229, the King and his mother jointly provided the endowment for the last of Melrose's daughter-houses, Balmerino, on the south bank of the Tay estuary in Fife. With its establishment, the last colony of Melrose or any of her older daughters, the Melrose filiation in Scotland was complete. There were also more direct benefits for the abbey in terms of its landholding. In 1235, Alexander gave the monks an extensive tract of upland in Ettrick which was to become one of the most valuable of their sheep ranges. At the same time, the King freed Melrose and the four granges immediately around it from his forest, an important economic concession which allowed the monks to exploit their lands in these areas more intensively, unhampered by the restrictions imposed by his hunting interests in the area. Alexander II's attachment to Melrose lasted into death. In the summer of 1249 he mounted a long-expected assault against the lordship of the MacDougals, who held land both in the Hebrides as subjects of the Norwegian crown and on the mainland as vassals of the King of Scots. In early July, he landed on the island of Kerrera in Oban Bay, making its sheltered anchorage his base for the final attack on MacDougal territory. There, however, he took a fever and died. In accordance with his will, his body was transported to Melrose for burial in the monks' choir.

Bishops and abbots

In the twelfth and thirteenth centuries, Melrose was the epitome of the tradition that Cistercian abbeys proved fertile breeding-grounds for well-qualified bishops. Jocelin in 1174 was the first in a long line of Melrose abbots and monks who were elected to the episcopate. The close relationship between the crown and the abbey probably played a major part in the process, for the bishoprics to which the Melrose monks were appointed were often in politically sensitive areas where the Kings of Scots needed to bolster their personal authority. Nevertheless, it should not be forgotten that their role was primarily a spiritual one and that they were selected for their personal spiritual qualities rather than their political leadership potential. The first appointment after Jocelin, however, was to one of the most troubled areas of the kingdom, Ross, where the King faced repeated challenges from supporters of the senior line of his own family, the MacWilliams. In 1195 Gregory, bishop of Ross, died and, in a council at Dunfermline, far removed from the politically unstable northern province, Reinald, a monk of Melrose, was elected. His appointment provided the crown with a dependable ally in an influential position, within a region where its authority continued to be challenged down to the 1230s. Reinald's promotion to the episcopate was followed eight years later by that of his former abbot, Radulf. In 1202 the papal legate, John de Salerno, left Scotland on a mission to Ireland, taking with him Abbot Radulf I. The legate clearly had plans for the abbot, who was duly consecrated bishop of the influential see of Down in Ulster, a region within which the Kings of England and Scotland were keen to establish closer controls. Behind him at Melrose, the speedy provision of William, abbot of Coupar Angus, as Radulf's successor hints at a well-planned operation. Like Jocelin before him, Radulf maintained close links with his former charge and in 1211 was present there to consecrate new abbots for five English Cistercian abbeys, who could not be consecrated in England because of a papal interdict in force there.

William's abbacy lasted less than four years and Patrick, the sub-prior of the convent, succeeded him, only to die the following year. His successor was Adam, the prior, a man later regarded as outstanding in his personal spirituality. After six years as abbot, in 1213 Adam was appointed to the bishopric of Caithness, a see as politically sensitive as Ross. There, he found himself caught in an unenviable position between John, earl of Caithness and Orkney, and the King of Scots, who was struggling to assert his mastery over this remote corner of his kingdom. Adam, however, did little to endear himself to the people of his diocese by his insistence on their absolute compliance with the laws of the Church and his determination to uphold his rights to teind and other revenues. In 1222, the festering hostility between bishop and people came to a head and, while the earl stood by and neither incited nor discouraged them, a mob attacked Adam at his residence at Halkirk, stoned him and burned him and his chaplain to death in the building. Alexander II took a swift and bloody revenge for the bishop's slaughter, and Adam was soon regarded as a saint, martyred for his determined defence of Church rights.

In 1235, Alexander II employed another Melrose monk as bishop in one of the most politically volatile areas of the kingdom, Galloway, where he had only succeeded in intruding royal power after the death of the last of the male line of its native lords. The King's nominee was Gilbert, master of the novices at Melrose, who until 1233 had been abbot of Glenluce in Galloway. In that year, for unknown reasons, he had resigned his charge in the chapterhouse at Melrose – highly unusual, since Glenluce was a daughter of Dundrennan Abbey – and took his profession there. His experience of the south-west, however, must have given him detailed personal knowledge of the political situation in the lordship of Galloway, and when Walter, bishop of Whithorn, a former clerk of the recently deceased ruler of the territory, followed his master to the grave late in 1235, the King moved quickly to establish him as bishop. Gilbert's election did not go unchallenged, the canons of Whithorn disputing the validity of his appointment and succeeding in forcing an investigation of the process in the court of the Archbishop of York. Nevertheless, realpolitik triumphed and Gilbert's election was confirmed in time for him to play an important role, along with Adam, abbot of Melrose, in negotiating an end to a dangerous rebellion in Galloway in support of the bastard son of the last lord. King Alexander's trust in Gilbert had been handsomely rewarded.

Promotions of abbots and monks of Melrose to important bishoprics, where they also served as agents and counsellors of Kings, served to strengthen the influence of the abbey within Scotland. Jocelin in particular maintained a close relationship with Melrose that benefited it materially and politically, while Radulf also clearly preserved ties after his departure to Down. Greater influence for the abbey, however, was maintained by the filiation system of the Cistercians which saw the continuing appointment of Melrose monks to the abbacies of the various daughter-houses established from the 1140s onwards. Even after around 1175, when most of Melrose's daughters were well established and producing monks of high calibre in their own communities, the mother-house continued to see its monks elected to vacant abbacies. In 1189, for example, Adam, sub-prior of Melrose, succeeded as third abbot of Coupar Angus, while in 1213 Alan, also sub-prior, was elected to the abbacy of Newbattle. This was a two-way process, for when Radulf II, abbot of Melrose, died in 1219, Adam returned from Newbattle to succeed him. And Melrose abbots could also rise within the system, with Abbot William de Courcy, himself a former abbot of Holmcultram, being elected to the abbacy of Rievaulx in 1216. In the 1230s, Melrose monks succeeded to the abbacies of daughters of its own successful daughters, Hugh, master of lay-brothers at Melrose, being elected abbot of Culross, and Hugh, prior of Melrose, elected to Deer. For the King, one of the most important extensions of Melrose authority in this way came in 1236 when the abbots of Dundrennan and Glenluce in Galloway were deposed and replaced by Melrose monks. The deposition of the two abbots, heads of houses which were not members of Melrose's filiation, has in the past been seen as an act of policy instigated by the King to remove two possible opponents of his recent political takeover of the lordship of Galloway, but the records of the chapter-general of the Cistercian order indicate that their removal was primarily occasioned by irregularities in the discipline at both monasteries. Of course, for Alexander II, the removal of two potentially hostile clerics and their replacement by monks from a dependable house was highly fortuitous. By winning the support of Melrose, and by extension its filiation, Alexander II provided himself with an extensive network of influence both throughout the political heartland of his kingdom and also in areas where his grip was less well established.

Golden years?

Alexander II's reign marked the opening of what was very much the high noon of the abbey's prosperity. From the 1230s onwards, Scotland enjoyed a long period of stability, interrupted only by the political uncertainty of the 10 minority years of the child-king, Alexander III. The political tension in the kingdom, however, does not appear to have had any significant impact on the economy, and Scotland benefited generally from the long boom in European trade that lasted through the middle decades of the thirteenth century. Melrose's trading interests blossomed in this period and the prosperity of the monastery was probably aided by the appointment of a highly able new head towards the end of Alexander II's reign. The new abbot, elected in April 1246 and consecrated in the abbey church on 17 May by William, bishop of Glasgow, was Matthew, the abbey's cellarer. His abbacy, which lasted 15 years, marked a decisive turning-point in the development of Melrose, with his reputation being made more by the material benefits which he brought to the monks than by his learning, piety or spirituality. His management skills and business acumen, it can be assumed, had been positive attributes which had earned him the highly responsible role of cellarer, the monk charged with management of the monastery's business affairs and household supplies. By the mid-thirteenth century, these same attributes would have been of great value in the selection of the abbot. An active acquirer of property and enforcer of the abbey's rights and privileges, he occupied an important place in national political life through the disturbed period of Alexander III's childhood (1249-58).

Like many of the leading churchmen in the kingdom, Matthew was a supporter of the Comyns against the government headed by Alan Durward. The Melrose monks in general seem to have favoured the Comyns, who were careful to cultivate the support of the Church by promising to safeguard ecclesiastical liberties that Durward and his allies were seen to threaten. The *Chronicle of Melrose*, one of our main Scottish sources for this critical period in the nation's history, is highly partisan, repeatedly painting Alan Durward in the poorest possible light, whilst praising Walter Comyn at every opportunity. But Melrose fulfilled more than a role as a propaganda centre for the Comyn regime, with Abbot Matthew being named in 1257 as one of the papal mandatories who published banns of excommunication against the oppressors of Gamelin, the Comyn bishop of St Andrews, who was being hounded by the supporters of Durward. In the same year at Cambuskenneth, in the company of the bishop of Dunblane and the abbot of Jedburgh, he solemnly excommunicated the leading members of the political faction that had seized power from the Comyns. The abbey also experienced a more active involvement in the tense manoeuvres that ended Alexander III's minority in 1257-8. It was there that Alexander assembled his army in 1257 as he began to flex his muscles and throw off both the controls of the rival magnate factions in Scotland and also of his interfering father-in-law, Henry III of England. A delegation from Henry met the young King at the abbey and escorted him for the discussions with his father-in-law that effectively marked the end of nearly a decade of political crisis in Scotland. It is unknown what part Matthew played in the end moves of the minority government of Alexander III, but it is likely that his position and experience gave him an important voice in the negotiations.

Four years later, Matthew's own rule ended in a flurry of uncertainty and controversy. The *Chronicle of Melrose* offers two different versions of the end of his abbacy. The first records that on 24 July 1261, Matthew, on account of illness, gave his personal seal into the keeping of the prior and resigned his office in the chapterhouse in the presence of his monks. Following that, the monks unanimously elected Adam, abbot of Newbattle, as his successor. The second version is less bland, stating that Matthew had been deposed *in absentia* in the chapterhouse at Rievaulx by his father-abbot, with no-one in Scotland consulted in the process. His deposition, it is claimed, was felt by the Melrose monks and lay-brothers to be wholly unjustified, although it was said that the abbot of Rievaulx had legitimate complaints against Matthew. What those complaints were is explained nowhere. The abbot of Rievaulx, however, did come to Melrose and personally released the monks, gathered in the chapterhouse, from their obedience and professions to Matthew. The chronicle account ends with a eulogistic lament for the deposed abbot, praising him not for his spiritual role as head of the community, but for the material gains which he had brought to his monks. These were listed, hopefully not in order of priority, as the 'pittance loaves' which the monks ate on Fridays in Lent, when they otherwise fasted on bread and water; the 'great houses' at Berwick (see below p.247); a number of cattle-stations and byres; the abbot's great chamber 'on the bank of the river' north of the cloister (**81**); and several other buildings.

Controversy dogged the abbots of Melrose throughout the next decade. In 1267, Matthew's successor, Adam of Maxton, was deposed in the general chapter at Cîteaux for a serious procedural breach. He had, it seems, failed to follow proper procedure in the deposition of Henry, abbot of Holmcultram, it being suspected, furthermore, that he had been improperly induced to depose Henry. As a consequence, both he and the monk whom he had appointed to succeed Henry suffered deposition, whilst Henry was restored to his abbacy by the general chapter. Adam's successor was John de Edrom or Ederham, master of the lay-brothers at Melrose. He proved to be an equally controversial choice, for in 1268 it is recorded that the abbot of Melrose and a large part of his convent were solemnly excommunicated at a council of the Scottish Church held at Perth, because 'they had broken the peace of Wedale by violently attacking the houses of the bishop of St

Andrews [there], had killed a certain clerk, and left many others wounded.'
This event was part of a particularly unpleasant dispute between the abbey
and the bishop over conflicting claims to grazing rights in the hill country
to the east of Wedale between Galashiels and Stow, which was to rumble on
into the fifteenth century (see below). The *Chronicle of Melrose* is, perhaps
understandably, silent about this episode, but it records John's resignation of
the abbacy in 1268 or 1269, presumably as a consequence of the disgrace of
his excommunication. His successor was Robert de Keldeleth, a monk of
Newbattle, who had previously been abbot of the Benedictine abbey at
Dunfermline and Chancellor of Scotland in the Durward government of
1249-51. He had resigned his abbacy following the overthrow of that
government, his own position having been hopelessly undermined by his
role in supposedly seeking letters from the pope legitimating Alan Durward's
wife, a bastard daughter of Alexander II, which would have made her heiress
to the young Alexander III. Leaving the Benedictine order, in 1252 he had
sought admission as a Cistercian monk at Newbattle and had spent 17 years
there in total obscurity. By 1269, his rehabilitation was clearly sufficiently
complete to allow him to assume the headship of a community that had
once been fiercely critical of the government in which he had figured so
prominently.

Of course, despite these successive crises of leadership at the abbey, the
daily affairs of the community continued to run with comparative smooth-
ness and Melrose monks continued to play prominent roles in national affairs.
One of the most notable of these monks was Reginald of Roxburgh, who
served the crown as a diplomatic envoy. In 1265, having secured effective
control over the Western Isles following the failure of the Norwegian expedition of 1263, Alexander III decided to open serious negotiations to secure
a treaty that would recognise his possession of them. A key figure in the
Scottish delegation was apparently Reginald, 'a man of glorious eloquence
and super-excellent resourcefulness'. According to the naturally partisan
Chronicle of Melrose, it was solely through Reginald's efforts that terms were
agreed and in 1266 he returned to Scotland in the company of the
Norwegian Royal Chancellor to settle a firm peace.

It is very unfortunate that the main source of evidence for the history of
Melrose in its early years, the *Chronicle*, peters out at the end of the 1260s,
probably with the death of the last of its regular keepers. Quite simply, no
new monk was interested in recording the affairs either of their house or of
the increasingly complicated world from which they could no longer keep
themselves detached. Unfortunately, the drying up of the chronicle coincides

with the start of what was to be one of the most traumatic periods in the history of the abbey and of Scotland generally, the years of uncertainty and crisis following the death of Alexander III and the beginning of the long wars with England from 1296.

After the repeated changes of abbot of the middle decades of the thirteenth century, the period 1269-96 fell under the abbacy of two men: Robert de Keldeleth (1269-73) and Patrick de Selkirk (1273-96). Other than the evidence for their management of the estate preserved in the charter book, we have little detail of their activities as abbot on a national or international level. Under Patrick, Melrose served as a depository for some of the moneys raised in Scotland by the papal tax-collector Master Boiamund di Viccia after 1274. It is likely that this role stemmed from Melrose's well-established trade connections with the Continent, for the abbey's chief monks would have possessed the knowledge and experience necessary for transmitting the money via merchants or banking firms to the papal coffers.

Little else is known of the affairs of the abbey until the 1290s, during the episode known later as the Great Cause, when thirteen claimants emerged as competitors for the throne of Scotland following the death of Margaret, Maid of Norway, the last direct descendant of Alexander III. In Spring 1290, Edward I of England, the great-uncle of Margaret, had cherished high hopes for a peaceful union of Scotland and England through the marriage of his son, the future Edward II, to the Scottish queen. Margaret, however, had died on the journey from Norway, dashing his hopes. With no obvious heir, however, the Scots again turned to him for aid in finding a new King. Determined not to lose a second time, Edward agreed, but on condition that the Scots accept him as their unquestioned overlord. Faced with the unpalatable choice of potential civil war between the rivals for the throne or accepting the overlordship of a King whose other commitments would probably prevent him from ever interfering too heavily in Scottish affairs, the leading clerics and nobles of the kingdom gave their grudging acceptance of Edward's terms.

Edward sought to exercise his new-found powers as overlord of Scotland at every opportunity while continuing to cultivate influential figures who could aid his designs. Churchmen as well as nobles were in receipt of royal favours, and the abbot of Melrose was no exception. On 28 August 1290, for example, he gave Patrick and the monks freedom from distraint, protecting their lands and property from seizure in legal judgements. Through 1291, as proceedings at Norham and Berwick dragged on, he issued letters of protection for Patrick and his monks, enabling them to continue with their trading operations. Edward's cultivation of the abbey did not secure him their long term favour, however, for Patrick de Selkirk was amongst the Scottish clerics who supported the Franco-Scottish treaty of 1295 against the English King. As a consequence, when war between Scotland and England broke out at the end of March 1296, Edward I ordered the sheriff of Northumberland to seize the abbey's lands in Northumbria and expel their men and servants as adherents of the 'rebellious' King John Balliol.

Wars and recovery 1296–1333

Following the collapse of Scottish resistance early in the summer of 1296, Edward I undertook what has been described more as a triumphal progress than a military campaign, reaching as far north as Elgin before returning to Berwick to draw a line under his conquest. In late August 1296, he ordered the formal submission of the political and social leadership of Scotland to his authority to be registered on parchment in the document later known as Ragman Roll, so called because of the ragged fringed appearance given by the tags to which the seals of the named men were attached. Amongst those recorded as swearing fealty to Edward was Patrick, abbot of Melrose. Patrick's submission, like that of most Scots, was probably short-lived and, as the cause of the captive King John revived under the leadership of first Andrew Moray and William Wallace, then, after 1298, of the Comyn family, the Scottish Church mobilised its resources and efforts in support of the struggle against Edward. The Church, however, did not offer simply material aid from its extensive lands, but it also provided active diplomatic aid. On 8 July 1299, Edward issued instructions to his officials ordering the interception and arrest of a Scottish diplomatic mission to France headed by William Lamberton, bishop of St Andrews, the abbots of Melrose and Jedburgh, and Sir John de Soulis.

Probably shortly after the surrender of the Scots in 1304, the abbot and convent of Melrose petitioned Edward I, requesting that he confirm all their charters, and sought his settlement of a dispute between the abbey and Sir Nicholas de Graham and his son, John, over land in Eskdale. It has been suggested that these petitions were a sign of pro-English sympathies at the convent, but Edward I had made it clear that submission would bring its rewards and even the leading members of the Scottish resistance movement, headed by the Comyns, had reached an accommodation with him. Quite clearly, the monks could see that their future lay in co-operation with the conquerors rather than in futile and largely symbolic opposition. At the same time, they requested a grant of timber from Selkirk Forest to restore buildings at the abbey which had been burned during the recent hostilities. The result was an instruction to submit their charters for inspection and a grant of 40 oaks from the Forest. Further signs of Edward I's willingness to secure the allegiance of so influential a monastery followed swiftly. By April 1305, the King was issuing a series of warrants to his chamberlain in Scotland ordering payment of moneys due to the abbot and convent. A clear sign of the importance attached to the abbot by the English authorities can be seen in September 1305, when he was named amongst the Scottish commissioners to the English parliament for drawing up the settlement for the future government of Scotland. The monks' relationship with the English administration in the south-east of Scotland developed further, and from May 1306 they were renting out storage space in fifteen granaries and four cellars for surplus grain from the English supply base at Berwick.

Like many leading members of the Scottish political community, there is no sign that the abbot of Melrose supported Robert Bruce's coup d'état of early 1307 in which he murdered John Comyn, lord of Badenoch, the leader of the Comyn family and of the pro-Balliol party in Scotland, and had himself inaugurated as King of Scots. It is often forgotten that most Scots still regarded John Balliol as the rightful King, and, despite the support offered to Robert Bruce by the bishops of St Andrews and Glasgow, there were also many who regarded Bruce as a bloody-handed, sacrilegious usurper and excommunicate for his murder of Comyn in the church of the Greyfriars at Dumfries. Furthermore, located as it was in a region over which the English administration in Scotland had its strongest hold, any declaration in favour of King Robert would have been impolitic to say the least. There is no clear evidence for when Melrose entered King Robert's peace, but the capture in early 1314 of Roxburgh Castle, the last English-held fortress in the Middle March of the border, gave the pro-Bruce Scots firm control over Teviotdale. Two years later, Robert was based at Melrose Abbey, from where he launched raids into Northumberland and down into the sphere of English control around Berwick. Despite the King's success in driving the English out of Scotland, and the scale of his victory at Bannockburn in 1314, he failed to force Edward II to the negotiating table. As a result, although it was chiefly northern England that suffered repeated devastation from Scottish raids or was bled dry of cash through payment of protection money to the Scots, the border region remained vulnerable to English campaigns, and Melrose was clearly regarded as a legitimate target for attack.

The later fourteenth-century churchman John Barbour, archdeacon of Aberdeen, described one incident at the abbey in his epic poem, *The Bruce*.

According to Barbour, as the English army headed south after their abortive 1322 campaign in Scotland, a camp at Melrose was planned and a company of several hundred armed men sent ahead to secure the place. Sir James Douglas, however, who was based in nearby Ettrick Forest, received intelligence of their advance and set an ambush at the abbey gates. Barbour paints a colourful picture in which Douglas sent one of the monks out of the gate to watch for the English, telling him to shout 'Douglas! Douglas!' when they arrived. The monk, described as 'sturdy and bold', wearing armour under his cassock and hood, carrying a spear and mounted on a horse, instead of just shouting, charged into the enemy followed by the rest of the Scots. The result was a total rout of the English force, with heavy slaughter and many captives taken. The fifteenth-century chronicler, Walter Bower, however, has a different story of the 1322 campaign. According to him, as Edward II's army retreated south from Lothian, they looted Holyrood and Melrose abbeys, and 'reduced [them] to the point of utter desolation'. He records that at Melrose the prior, a sick monk, and two blind lay-brothers, were killed by the English in their dormitory, and other monks were fatally wounded. To complete the picture of the barbarity of the looters, he described how the consecrated Host – the 'Body of Christ' as he termed it – was discarded on the high altar when the silver pyx in which it was kept was stolen by an English soldier. Like Barbour's account, Bower's report is highly partisan and cannot be substantiated. Perhaps significantly, the atrocities committed at Melrose described by Bower form an almost set-piece 'off-the-shelf' package, being almost identical to accounts of the behaviour of Scottish soldiers at Glenluce and Tongland abbeys in Galloway in 1235, or Galwegians at Holmcultram in 1216.

Throughout his reign, Robert I was heavily reliant on support from important elements within the Scottish Church, especially the bishops, but he also was careful to cultivate the backing of the main religious houses. Robert needed Church support to give legitimacy to his kingship and to shelter him to some degree from the charges of sacrilege that had been levelled against him since early 1307. It is clear that Robert always felt the need to have the spiritual salve for a deeply tortured conscience that could only be given by the masses and prayers of the monks. He was also careful to project his image as protector of the Church to stress his status as successor and inheritor of the throne of the Canmore Kings and their position as patron and protector as established by David I in the twelfth century. Melrose was of vital importance to Robert in all these areas. In the thirteenth century, the abbey had strong associations with the Comyn and Balliol families, his rivals for power within Scotland. Its support for him instead would have had great symbolic importance. Melrose, moreover, was perhaps the most closely associated of all the royal foundations with past Kings of Scots, therefore Robert would have been keen to stress continuity from the past through an active role as patron. Robert, though, was also keen to stress the recovery and renewal of Scottish independence under his rule, and the peace and stability that he had achieved after decades of turmoil. Conspicuous patronage of Melrose, a monastery that had suffered considerably from the actions of both sides in the war, and located close to the border with the defeated enemy, was an unmistakable trumpeting of the triumph of the Bruce cause.

Robert I's chief award to Melrose was the grant in March 1326 of £2,000 from the royal revenues within Roxburghshire, as a contribution towards the cost of building the abbey church *de novo*. The monks were to hold this privilege from the date of the grant until such time as they had received the £2,000 in full. This was one of the gifts that Robert, on his death-bed, urged his son to confirm to the monks and, as late as 1369, David II issued a confirmation of his father's award. Clearly, monies had trickled rather than flooded in, the collapse of Scottish royal administration in the region between 1333 and 1342 and again after 1346 having rendered collection impossible. With much of Roxburghshire still in English hands in 1369, it is unlikely that much cash ever reached the monks as a result of this ostensibly generous, but effectively inoperative, gift. When Robert II succeeded David II in 1371, while he confirmed most of the Bruce Kings' awards to Melrose, the £2,000 was not included amongst them.

In January 1327, at a time when Robert's health was failing, he began to make extensive spiritual provision for the weal of his soul after his death. Amongst the arrangements made was a grant of £100 annually to Melrose from the burgh ferme of Berwick, to be paid in two instalments each year. This was to pay in perpetuity for a daily 'pittance' or portion of rice made with milk of almonds or peas, to be known as the King's Serving, for monks eating in the refectory. Any of the pittance not eaten was to be served to paupers at the abbey gate, and the abbey was also bound by the King's will to clothe 15 paupers at Martinmas, to feed them with four ells of 'great and broad bread' or six ells of 'narrow bread', and issue each with one new pair of woollen socks. At the same time, instructions were issued to the chamberlain of Scotland and the provost and baillies of Berwick for payment to begin, while the sheriff of Berwick was instructed to distrain non-payers. The accounts of the provosts of Berwick from 1327 down to the fall of the town to the English in 1333 show regular payment of the £100 to the abbot.

Other gifts were of more general financial benefit to the monastery. In January 1327, at the same time as the charter for the pittance, Robert confirmed that all the lands in Carrick granted to the abbey by his ancestors, and all the lands in Kyle given by the Stewarts, were to be held in free alms and were to be free from all secular burdens, such as prises of goods and supplies, tolls on carts and other forms of levy, made for the King's works. This was an important concession, for it is likely that during the previous era of warfare such exemptions had been ignored by royal officials charged with maximising the supplies and resources available to the King. Later in the same year, he gave a similar exemption to the abbey in respect of its lands in Nithsdale.

At Cardross in Dumbartonshire on 11 May 1329, one month before his death and probably in sure knowledge of his approaching end, King Robert again issued a series of charters, writs and letters in favour of Melrose. The first was a general protection for Melrose, its monks, servants, properties and possessions, effectively restating its special place within the King's concerns. The second was a 'memo' to his son, the future David II, naming Melrose as the place where his heart was to be buried and enjoining the young prince to honour all his arrangements for the rebuilding of the abbey, as well as all his other gifts and confirmations to the monks.

Warfare renewed

The settlement of peace with England after 30 years of warfare brought instant benefits to Melrose. In October 1328, for example, the English government ordered that the payment of the pensions of various Scottish abbots, including William de Fogo at Melrose, from certain churches in England, should be resumed after years of suspension. Melrose, however, barely had breathing space to enjoy the stability which the 1328 treaty brought to the Anglo-Scottish border before warfare erupted anew. In 1332, Edward Balliol mounted an invasion of Scotland in a bid to win the crown from David II with the tacit support of Edward III of England, and in 1333 the English King brought an army north in support of Balliol. Following the defeat of the Scots in the battle of Halidon Hill outside Berwick, Edward III established Balliol as King Edward of Scotland and, in return for his aid, received from Balliol the award of the five south-eastern shires of Scotland. Melrose was again placed under English jurisdiction. After 1338, as Edward III's attentions shifted towards France, the English grip over the border shires began to slip and the Scots, mainly under the leadership of Sir William Douglas of Liddesdale and Sir Alexander Ramsay of Dalhousie, reasserted control over Teviotdale. In 1341, Edward III mounted a rare foray into

Scotland and based himself at Melrose for Christmas. Receiving news of the enemy's presence, Douglas raided the abbey and seized the King's provisions after a hard-fought struggle. He used the spoils to supply his own castle at Hermitage, whilst Edward spent a frugal Christmas without the rich food-stuffs that he had brought with him for the festivities.

Between 1342, when David II returned to Scotland from exile in France, and 1346, when the young King led his disastrous campaign into northern England that ended with his defeat and capture at Neville's Cross outside Durham, the Scottish hold over Roxburghshire had been consolidated. This position, however, collapsed in the winter of 1346-7 and an English garrison was re-established in Roxburgh itself. Melrose, once again, was forced to come to terms with the nearby presence of the garrison and, effectively, was returned to English overlordship. After David's release from captivity in October 1357, the King explicitly recognised this status quo by acknowledging that the abbey was 'of necessity in the peace of the English'. Thus, they were not to be stripped of their lands in Scottish-held territory as vassals of the English crown. David renewed that declaration the following year and, even more significantly, granted the abbot and convent a regality jurisdiction over the abbey and the portion of its estate immediately round about. This gave the abbot the right to try all legal cases, even those normally reserved for the royal courts, effectively exempting the abbey's properties within the bound of that jurisdiction from interference by crown officials. Much of the revenue from fines and forfeitures levied in the regality court would have found its way into the Melrose coffers, which would have provided a very significant source of income to the abbey. The profits of the regality court, indeed, would probably have been a major source of the revenues used from the 1380s onwards to rebuild Melrose. Possibly more significant was his grant to them in 1358 of the custom of all their wool exports, both from the clip of their own flocks and that received as teind from the churches that they held. Of course, this was an inducement to them to export their produce through Scottish outlets rather than through English-held Berwick, but it was still a major cash concession on David's part.

Through the 1360s and into the 1370s, the abbey found itself caught in something of a no-man's land between the authority of the Scottish and English crowns. David clearly considered himself patron of the abbey as his father's successor and was to base himself there on a number of occasions, as he travelled back and forward between Scotland and England in the course of his continuing negotiations aimed at finding a permanent end to the war with England. Edward III, however, equally considered Melrose to be under his protection and jurisdiction. Various solutions of compromise were tried, especially to find a means of resolving the conflict between the Percies and Douglases over their conflicting claims to lordship of lands in Teviotdale. These included share arrangements, where the revenues of the district were split between the Scots and English. Despite these efforts, the Scots continued to nibble away at the area under English jurisdiction. Nevertheless, as late as 1378, the government of Richard II of England was issuing letters of protection to the abbot and convent of Melrose, clearly still under the impression that it lay within its authority. By about 1380, the country around Melrose was largely under Scottish control although the abbey may still have acknowledged English overlordship. The difficult position in which the abbey was placed is emphasised in 1382 by King Robert II's re-grant of David II's concession permitting the monks to deal with the English 'of necessity'. This ambivalent position is also shown in a letter of September 1377, where Robert II, when making arrangements for a march day (a meeting on the border under truce conditions to attempt to resolve cross-border disputes) at 'Lillyat-Cros', a landmark roughly halfway between Melrose and Jedburgh, asked that the King of England's formal response be made via the abbot. Again, in negotiations in 1380 for a settled border line, the English demand was that it should follow the northern boundary of Berwickshire, down the Leader to Tweed but including the Melrose lands between Leader and Gala. The abbey, then, would have been placed firmly on the English side of the march.

Whatever the English view, by the late 1370s Melrose was very firmly in the Scottish orbit and was entering what was to become a very close relationship with the dominant noble family of southern Scotland, the Black Douglases. Douglas protection and patronage was to be very important for the abbey down to the mid-fifteenth century, but it could also be a two-edged sword as it drew the attention of the Douglases' English enemies. The association of the earls of Douglas with the abbey was emphasised by its choice as the place of burials by the first two earls, a choice that may have had as much to do with the symbolic staking of a claim to lordship in Teviotdale that their burial there signified, as with personal devotion to the monastery. In 1384, when William, first earl of Douglas, died at his castle of Douglas in Lanarkshire, he left instructions that he was not to be buried alongside his illustrious ancestors in the choir of the parish church there, but carried instead to Melrose for burial. His grave was located in a side chapel dedicated to St Bride, the patron saint of the Douglas family. There could be few stronger statements of the Douglas family's new-found domination of the Scottish side of the border. Four years later, the body of his son Earl James was brought to Melrose after his death in the battle of Otterburn and buried alongside his father. After 1388 the earldom passed to a different branch of the Black Douglas family, who, as earls, did maintain their patronage of Melrose but chose to be buried once more at Douglas or in the collegiate churches they had founded at Bothwell and Lincluden. The earls of Angus, descended from a bastard son of Earl James, also maintained close links with Melrose and were to be the avengers of the desecration of their ancestors' tombs by the English in the 1540s.

Despite the Douglases' numerous breaches of the Anglo-Scottish truce that had been set in place under the treaty of Berwick, open warfare between the kingdoms ended after 1357. Scottish provocation, however, led to a breakdown of the truce and in April 1384, John of Gaunt, duke of Lancaster led a major English army on a chevauchée, or fast-moving and highly destructive raid through south-east Scotland. On this occasion he spared the abbeys of Holyrood and Melrose, which lay in his path, but rather than chivalry or piety moving him to pity it was probably only the payment of a substantial 'ransom' such as that offered by the burgesses of Edinburgh for time to be given to them to remove their goods from the town, before he unleashed his troops on it. The raid also caused widespread damage across a broad swathe of country from Roxburghshire, through Berwickshire to Lothian, in which many of Melrose's estates were concentrated. Although the abbey itself may have been spared sacking on this occasion, it is therefore quite likely that Gaunt's invasion wrought havoc with Melrose's finances. Worse, however, was to come.

In August 1385, Gaunt's nephew, the 19-year-old Richard II of England, invaded Scotland. The campaign was particularly destructive, with Edinburgh being sacked as the climax of the advance, but the army also burned the abbeys of Dryburgh, Melrose and Newbattle as it headed north from Roxburghshire. The sack of Melrose appears to have been especially thorough, and was excused probably by the argument that it lay in a kingdom that had given its allegiance to the schismatic Pope Clement VII, based in Avignon, rather than Pope Urban VI, based in Rome, to whom the English adhered. It is unlikely to have been remorse for the actions of his army that prompted Richard to offer restitution to the monks four years later, especially since in the interval the Scots had soundly beaten an English army at Otterburn in Redesdale. Nevertheless, on 15 October 1389, he ordered the English Chancellor to issue letters allowing Melrose an abatement of two shillings a sack on the custom of Scottish wool exported through Berwick, for up to 1,000 sacks. The number of sacks in question, some 20 to 25 times greater than Melrose's annual production, indicates that the abbey acted as an agent on behalf of many other producers in Scotland. Three days later, the

King also instructed that the abbot, convent, their lay-brothers, and servants, should be given letters of protection for the duration of the three years' truce with the Scots, and safe-conducts to allow up to 12 of them, on horseback, to sell their beasts and produce in Northumberland and Cumberland, and to buy supplies and wine for their own use. Despite the recent escalation in violence along the frontier, it is clear that there was also a good deal of such peaceful cross-border dealing. Indeed, at around this date, Abbot Gilbert was asked to be godfather for the Northumberland nobleman, Gilbert d'Umfraville. It was clearly to encourage the monks to maintain such bonds and export their goods – and those of others for whom they were acting – through English-held territory, and especially through Berwick rather than the new Scottish wool-export centre of Edinburgh/Leith, that Richard II had given them their rebate. That hope, however, was to be short-lived.

It has often been said that it was Richard II's generous relief of customs on Melrose's wool exports that paid for the rebuilding of the abbey in the late fourteenth and fifteenth centuries. That, however, was most definitely not the case, for only a year after the award the rebate was cancelled on Richard's instructions. The monks, it seems, had sought to maximise their profit from the deal and attempted to export 200 sacks of wool more than their agreed limit. Evidently, many Scottish wool-producers had attempted to capitalise on Richard's generosity, or the monks had been very busy in buying up the clip from much of southern Scotland, for Edinburgh in the 1380s was handling around 1500 to 1700 sacks of wool per annum drawn from across the kingdom. What continued to be of greater significance to the monks was not this discount on offer at Berwick, which they were probably attempting to cream off from wool that they had either bought from, or were handling on behalf of, other Scottish producers, but the continuing exemption from all custom of their own wool. David II's grant of the custom on their wool had been confirmed to the monks by Robert II in 1386, and as recently as April 1389, when Richard II was making his own award, Robert Stewart, earl of Fife, the Chamberlain of Scotland and lieutenant on behalf of his father the King, sent instructions to the custumars of Edinburgh, Haddington and Dunbar restating the monks' exemption. For the remainder of the Middle Ages, Melrose benefited from the remission of custom on its own wool, a privilege that netted them over £57 in 1383-4 on wool exported through Edinburgh and still yielded over £30 in the 1460s.

As Melrose's channelling of its wool through Edinburgh so clearly reveals, by the 1390s, while still considered rightfully to be part of the English territories in southern Scotland, the abbey was effectively in the Scottish allegiance and was listed in 1400 as one of the Scottish places at which Henry

IV of England's demand for homage from the Scots should be proclaimed. In April 1401, in correspondence between the King and the earl of Northumberland regarding the duke of Rothesay's proposal to meet the earl at Melrose to discuss a treaty, Henry authorised the earl to go only 'if he can be sure of going and returning without fraud or injury from the Scots'. Melrose, clearly, by then lay beyond the sphere of English power around Roxburgh and Jedburgh. In July 1407, described as 'in Scotland', the abbey was granted letters of protection by Henry which guaranteed the safety of the monks, their servants, property and possessions, provided that they supplied the English garrison at Roxburgh with provisions at a fair price. Although the Scots were still in the allegiance of the schismatic Avignon-based popes, Henry was prepared to offer them the protection that Richard II had denied them in 1385, but he still accepted that their abbey lay outwith the sphere of his effective authority. Melrose's future in the fifteenth century lay firmly in a Scottish orbit.

Monks and abbots

It has been commented that the fourteenth and earlier fifteenth centuries were 'a bleak and undistinguished period' for the monastic orders in Scotland. From the perspective of the Protestant Reformation of the sixteenth century, it is easy to see the monks of the later Middle Ages as a self-seeking and self-satisfied group, content to live off the fat of their prede-cessors' efforts while avoiding the rigours of the original austere rule of their orders. Papal records from the time also show these same monks actively seeking to increase their earnings potential in the market for benefices that plagued late medieval religious life. Like members of the secular clergy, Cistercian monks sought promotion and advancement both within their own order and within the secular Church.

For some, hopes of promotion were pinned on securing quite basic legal status. Bastardy was formerly a bar to entry into the Church, with it being deemed theologically unsound for illegitimates to dispense sacraments and take even the most basic levels of holy orders. As the Middle Ages progressed, it became possible to secure letters of legitimisation from the Pope, which would grant retrospective legal legitimacy to the supplicant. The records of Scottish appeals for such letters show that entry into the Church was a favoured means of providing for the bastard sons of the lesser nobility. Even after securing such letters, the recipient would often seek more explicit state-ments of legitimacy as he sought promotion within the Church, for any

5 *A chapter seal of Melrose Abbey.* © The Trustees of the National Museums of Scotland

question raised about his condition of birth could lose him the chance of provision to a lucrative or powerful position. At Melrose, Brother David de Bennyn found himself in that position. In March 1380, he received confirmation of his legitimacy from Pope Clement VII, giving him 'more ample dispensation, having already been dispensed from illegitimacy of birth, being born out of wedlock, in order to receive holy orders, so that he may exercise all the functions of a monk and even accept the office of abbot, if elected.' David clearly cherished hopes for promotion, and in 1394 he was provided to the abbacy of Melrose, which he held for 28 years. In 1419, shortly after Scotland finally abandoned its allegiance to the Anti-pope Benedict XIII, Abbot David sought confirmation of his status from Pope Martin V, clearly fearing that a rival might challenge the legality of his dispensation from a pope whose authority had been rejected. Promotion and security in that promotion were the two factors that governed David's supplications to Rome. Similar hopes presumably motivated John Crawfurde, monk of Melrose, to make a similar appeal in 1436, but there is no record that he likewise rose to prominence within the order.

Melrose monks were active participants in the growing trade in benefices, supplicating at Rome for provision to lucrative offices. Three cases illustrate the problem well. The first concerns supplication for promotion within the Cistercian order. In September 1392, Pope Clement VII provided John Hailes, monk of Melrose, to the abbacy of Newbattle. The appointment appears to have stemmed from a supplication by John, for he was not welcomed at Newbattle, where the prior and monks refused to admit him. The second case relates to a monk holding a secular benefice. In 1432, a supplication by a secular priest seeking appointment to a prebend in the cathedral at Aberdeen, valued at £40 sterling, noted that for over four years it had been held by William de Foresta, monk of Melrose. For de Foresta to hold that benefice he must have doubly breached Cistercian rules, for it would have required him to spend considerable time away from the abbey and it would have provided him with a personal income, breaking the rule that monks should only receive their living in common. The third example relates to an attempt to secure promotion in a different order of monks. In 1435, Brother Richard Lundy supplicated Pope Eugenius IV to provide him to the office of prior of the Valliscaulian monastery of Pluscarden in Moray. In this he was ultimately unsuccessful, even though the Pope granted his supplication (for a fee), but in 1440 he was successful in securing provision to the abbacy of Melrose itself.

The picture, however, is not entirely one of spiritual decline and of monasteries filled by men who had no real vocation other than a desire for professional advancement. In February 1380, for example, one Melrose monk received papal permission to leave his monastery to study canon law abroad for up to seven years. Such university educations were still uncommon for monks, whose enclosed lives offered little opportunity to exercise the skills acquired in degree study. The monk in question, however, may have entertained ambitions of promotion and a career outside his monastery, for which his law degree would have provided enhanced prospects. A second Melrose monk received a similar concession in June 1417 from the Anti-pope Benedict XIII, whose authority was by then recognised in Scotland alone amongst significant European states. The award recognised that fact, but masked it by permitting him to study 'at a university, even if situated in schismatical territory and to communicate with schismatics', which meant basically that he could go to the main universities favoured by Scots in France or Italy, which had rejected Benedict's authority.

Under most monastic rules, it was rare for monks to spend any prolonged period away from their monastery. The discipline, stability and seclusion of the monks' routine were integral to the whole ethos of monasticism. Arrangements could be made for monks to spend time away from the monastery managing the monastic granges, but that existence was strictly regulated. It has been noted already that the abbots spent an increasing amount of time away from the abbey, usually involved in secular business, often on state affairs such as diplomatic missions. Their increasing involvement in business emanating from the papal court, however, also added to their time away from the community placed under their charge. By the 1300s, the abbots of Melrose were receiving several appointments each year as 'judges-delegate' to settle litigation that was subject to canon law, to oversee provision of clerics to benefices in secular and monastic churches around the country, and to arbitrate in disputes between other clerics. In the case of Abbot David de Bennyn, papal mandates involved him in a broad raft of business of widely varying types. In 1403, for example, he was appointed as a judge to investigate and settle various civil and criminal charges against John de Kettins, abbot of Coupar Angus. As father-abbot of Coupar Angus, David had the authority under the Cistercian rule to investigate and correct any abuses committed by John. Although John's 'impoverishing of the abbey, alienating its goods, allowing its monks to wander freely over the country and being known publicly to keep concubines' was common knowledge, he had refused David's right to visit the abbey and correct the abuses. This papal mandate gave him an authority that John could not deny. In 1409, Abbot David was given a papal commission to absolve two canons of Jedburgh who had killed a brigand, while in 1411 he was charged with approving on behalf of the Pope the granting of various liberties to the monks of Kelso by the bishops of St Andrews. He was also instructed in 1412 to reserve a benefice on behalf of a secular clerk who had successfully supplicated the pope for provision. With the exception of the Coupar Angus case, none of this business was of direct relevance to the monks of Melrose, but it provides an example of the increasing burden of responsibility and power that the headship of a major monastery involved in the later Middle Ages.

In the ecclesiastical hierarchy of medieval Scotland, the abbot of Melrose stood in the innermost circle, enjoying a status exceeded only by the senior bishops. In comparison to some bishops, the economic power at his disposal and the lordship over men he exercised vastly exceeded anything available to them. David II's grant of regality jurisdiction over portions of the monastic estate – a privilege progressively expanded by subsequent Kings – gave the abbots legal powers over their tenants that were the envy of all but the greatest lay lords in the kingdom. In August 1391, Abbot Gilbert de Roxburgh received a papal indult which granted to the abbot and his successors the right to wear 'pontificals' – a mitre, ring and pontifical vestments normally reserved for bishops – and to give solemn blessings at the end of mass, both in the abbey church and other churches dependent on the abbey. This was the spiritual equivalent of the secular grant of regality jurisdiction, confirming the status of the abbot of Melrose amongst the greatest churchmen in the kingdom.

Melrose in the fifteenth century

By the early 1400s, English influence in the borders area of Scotland had been reduced to narrow spheres around Roxburgh, Jedburgh and Berwick. Under the leadership of the earls of Douglas, the frontier had been pushed back by the Scots to more or less its pre-1296 lines, despite occasional dramatic reverses such as the defeat of a major Scottish army at Humbledon Hill near Wooler in Northumberland in 1402. Such defeats, however, never saw a collapse such as which had followed Halidon Hill in 1333 or Neville's Cross in 1346 and, while Melrose's position remained very exposed and vulnerable to raid, it remained firmly in Scottish hands. That position was never to be challenged for the remainder of the fifteenth century.

The location of Melrose, close to the blurred boundary between English and Scottish jurisdictions and adjacent to one of the main lines of communication between the two kingdoms, gave it increased significance in this period as a meeting-place for delegations from both sides. The greatest example of this occurred in 1424, when James I of Scotland, a prisoner in England since his capture at sea in 1406, was returned to his kingdom. At Durham on 28 March 1424, James had set his own seal to the treaty agreeing his ransom terms. From there, he travelled north along Dere Street into Scotland, and it was at Melrose on 5 April that he and his escort of English and Scottish nobles arrived. There, he was met by a large gathering of the Scottish nobility, led by James's cousin, Murdac, duke of Albany, the governor of the kingdom in James's absence. On their meeting, Albany surrendered his seal of office to the King, who used it to seal a ratification of the ransom treaty. The abbey provided a very public and formal setting for what must have been a highly charged meeting between the cousins.

Melrose was one of the few places on the Scottish side of the border that could have accommodated the large assembly of nobles, officials, and their servants, that had gathered to greet their returning King, and the retinue from England that escorted him north. Kelso Abbey probably had sufficient space, but it lay in the shadow of English-held Roxburgh and may not have been considered a safe location at which to gather so many of the Scottish leadership. Melrose, however, may also have been able to provide what was considered the most suitable accommodation for such a splendid assembly, for in May 1422, Abbot David de Bennyn received a papal letter which stated that he had 'rebuilt the monastery' of Melrose, which had been burned by the English. It is clear from the architecture of the church that rebuilding work there was perhaps never completed after the burning of 1385, but it is possible that the Pope was referring to the reconstruction of the monastic complex.

James I was back at Melrose on 12 October 1424 for a meeting with his nephew, Archibald, fifth earl of Douglas. The King's arrival at the abbey, in the heart of a region where the Douglases had held almost unchallenged authority for nearly 80 years, was a clear statement of James's intention to claw back royal power from his nobles. Although this was mainly a political meeting, with the King keen to assert his authority over an earl whose power and influence was significantly weaker than his father's had been, its outward purpose was probably the election of a new abbot. This was business of direct interest to Earl Archibald. In August 1419, his father the fourth earl of Douglas, described as 'special protector and defender of the monastery of Melrose...lying within his domain', had supplicated on behalf of the convent that the Pope would allow future elections and confirmations by the monks in chapter, following the rules of their order, to prevail over provisions. The earl had, presumably, expected to exercise considerable influence over the elections to such a powerful position, and King James was now concerned to ensure that it was he who decided the outcome. On the face of it, it would seem that the Douglas interest prevailed, for the successful candidate, John Fogo, was the earl's confessor. But by 1426 he was performing the same service for the King and was evidently in royal service. Fogo, a Melrose monk and master of theology, had risen to prominence as early as 1417, when he played a key role in the diplomacy that ended Scotland's adherence to Pope Benedict XIII and submission to Pope Martin V. He was clearly considered to be a man of diplomatic ability, and by 9 June 1425, Fogo was serving in a Scottish embassy to Rome.

In early June 1431, James I arrested the earl of Douglas at Linlithgow and imprisoned him in Lochleven Castle. The King moved swiftly to calm the disquiet of Douglas's tenants and supporters, heading straight into the territorial heartlands of Douglas influence. Between 20 and 27 June, James I and Queen Joan were at Melrose, where Abbot John Fogo provided a bridge between the King and the Douglas following. No doubt Fogo gave the King ample advice on how to deal with Douglas men in the region and helped to calm the anger and suspicion of the earl's supporters.

Fogo quickly emerged as a leading figure in the political life of the kingdom and was prominent in parliamentary debates. At Perth in 1433, he argued forcefully that James I should not be bound by his treaty with the French against making a separate and binding peace with the English. His views, however, landed him in deep water when the theological grounds that he gave to support them were questioned by the inquisitor, Master Laurence of Lindores. Fogo, according to the contemporary chronicler Abbot Walter Bower of Inchcolm, 'was solemnly warned and cited by the inquisitor to recant his harmful sayings and writings, or to defend them in due form. He made his appearance at St Andrews on a certain day and gave in to the inquisitor. Thenceforth, the said Kings (both of France and Scotland), their fears allayed by a calm state of mutual regard, were agreed on continuing their accustomed alliance.'

Despite James's default on payment of his ransom and other hostile postures towards England, the peace that had been agreed as part of the 1424 treaty held into the 1430s. In 1436, however, James broke the treaty and led a major, but ultimately fruitless, expedition to besiege Roxburgh Castle. All that resulted was a fresh destabilising of the border, compounded by political instability in Scotland after the King's assassination at Perth the following year. It was presumably with this uncertainty in mind that Fogo's successor, Abbot Richard Lundy, supplicated Pope Eugenius IV on 17 August 1443 for special ecclesiastical powers for him and his successors to exercise in times of conflict. His supplication stated that the abbey lay far from its diocesan centre at Glasgow, but very close to 'a certain fortress' (Roxburgh) where English forces would muster in times of war, or Scots and English would clash in battle, which would prevent the bishop from free access to the abbey. Failure on the bishop's part to be able to visit Melrose would, it was claimed, severely compromise its functioning, for there was a risk that the abbey could require re-consecration or purification as a result of bloodshed within its walls. Eugenius granted them that if ever the abbey church, chapels and any other consecrated places depending on it were violated by effusion of blood or strife or by burial of excommunicates, Lundy and his successors could purify them. He granted them the right to exhume and throw out the bodies of excommunicates, to have holy water blessed by a priest of their choosing, and the right to bless their novices with the tonsure, and also to bless all paraphernalia used in divine worship. It was a significant raft of concessions and ones that reveal clearly many of the practical concerns of ensuring the continued spiritual function of a community sited in what was a dangerously exposed location.

Lundy's fears for the immediate future were, fortunately, ill founded: England was not in a position in the 1440s to re-open significant warfare with the Scots at a time when they were losing the conflict against France. Tensions, however, remained high, and Lundy's successor, Andrew Hunter, was to be employed regularly in the service of King James II in diplomatic missions to England. From September 1449 through to August 1451, Hunter served as one of the principal Scottish commissioners negotiating for the peace with England, empowered to enter into binding agreements. Like John Fogo before him, Hunter was also confessor to the King of Scots, a position which gave him personal influence with the monarch, and from 1450 he also served in a more significant administrative role as royal treasurer. Hunter was a man of not only spiritual talents. Of necessity, his duties in royal service took the abbot away from his abbey for long periods, both on the missions to England and also on justice eyres and other functions of his role as treasurer. Nevertheless, he devoted much time to the continued recovery of his monastery from the conflicts of the previous century and a half, and presided over a significant redevelopment of the abbey's estates and further episodes of building at the monastery itself. Andrew Hunter's coat-of-arms features prominently on the fifteenth-century tower built at the estate centre at Mauchline (**100** and **17**) and occurs in various places around the church at Melrose.

Hunter proved to be the last of the great medieval abbots at Melrose, for he was followed by a succession of men who bribed, sued or coerced their way into office. Despite the 1419 concession regarding elections to the abbacy, the non-Cistercian Robert Blackadder secured the reservation of the abbacy at Rome whilst Hunter was still alive. Early in 1471, the Pope confirmed his provision, but also permitted him to hold office without having to wear a monk's habit or to take his profession as a Cistercian. His position was immediately challenged by Richard Lamb, a Melrose monk, who had the backing of both the convent and the bishop of Glasgow. Lamb pursued litigation at the papal court and secured papal provision himself in 1474, even handing over some of the 'common services', or fees, demanded by the papacy from successful appointees to major benefices. Blackadder, however, had still not given up, and it took the inducement of a substantial pension to persuade him to resign his rights in 1476. Lamb, however, did not enjoy his success for long, for by 1483 he was being described as old and having been suffering from leprosy from some time. In view of his incapacity, a coadjutor or assistant was appointed to aid him in the exercise of his office. The appointee, who was also designated as Lamb's successor, was another non-Cistercian, John Brown or Carnecorss, a Dominican friar. Unlike Blackadder, though, he did become a monk and duly succeeded Lamb. The other monks, however, may have regarded him as an intruder and, although he resigned his abbacy in 1486, it was clearly not an action made willingly. Down into the 1490s, Brown was still pursuing litigation at Rome seeking the recovery of the abbacy. Four aspirants emerged for the abbacy in 1486, with two of them, David Brown and Bernard Bell, fighting a long and debilitating succession of suits in the papal courts, all of which ate steadily into the wealth of the monastery. Before June 1488, Brown had been exiled by King James III, who favoured Bell, and who also benefited from the backing of James IV for a number of years. Bell, however, was induced to resign his claims in 1503, receiving a substantial pension from the abbey's estates in compensation, to make way for a new rival litigant, William Turnbull. It was a squalid and debilitating episode and one which saw a drastic decline in the quality of spiritual life at the abbey.

James IV and Melrose

For nearly 40 years after 1471, the abbacy of Melrose was squabbled over like a choice bone thrown to hungry dogs. The headline-grabbing detail of that long dispute, however, should not obscure the fact that the routine of the monastery continued whilst the rivals fought it out in the courts. There is no question but that the spiritual life of the community and monastic discipline waned in the absence of an active, strong guiding hand at the helm, but it would be wrong to suggest that monastic life ground to a halt. Nevertheless, there were those ready to take advantage of the abbey's lack of an undisputed spiritual head, including the King, James IV, who made free of the hospitality of the monastery in extended stays there from 1496 onwards.

The abbey formed a mustering point for Scottish forces in the course of James's two northern English campaigns of 1496 and 1497 in support of Perkin Warbeck, a pretender to the English throne. Even although James's enthusiasm for Warbeck waned rapidly, the King was keen to make war against England on his own account, for Berwick still lay in enemy hands. He was at Melrose over the Christmas and New Year period of 1496-7, a sign of how seriously the military preparations for war with England were being taken, since he habitually spent those seasons at Linlithgow and Stirling. The choice of Melrose was not dictated solely by the comfort of the lodgings available to the King, but was also influenced by the fact that past Scottish policy had seen the destruction of all the major castles in the eastern and middle sectors of the border that could have housed the King and his retinue for extended periods. Melrose was a major establishment that could provide accommodation for the King and the royal household. His Yuletide stay in 1496 was no cheerless military-camp experience. The King's accounts show that he made offerings on the altars in the church at Christmas mass, gave cash gifts to his heralds, rewarded entertainers and, as was his wont, lost heavily at cards. In early June 1497, the King returned to Melrose with a large army and his highly prized artillery train. On 12 June, this force set out on a raid into Northumberland, but accomplished nothing of significance. James lost interest in the project and effectively withdrew from the war. Fortunately for him, Henry VII was in no position to prosecute the war on his own part, with the result that the conflict fizzled out having accomplished nothing but a further souring of Anglo-Scottish relations.

James IV did not return to Melrose until 1502, this time to receive the English ambassador, Lord Dacre, at the start of the long negotiations for a 'perpetual' peace with England to replace the succession of truces interspersed with brief phases of conflict that had become established after 1357. In March the following year, when diplomacy was far advanced for this treaty and for the King's marriage to Margaret Tudor, daughter of Henry VII of England, James ordered that a requiem mass or 'dirge' be offered by the monks of Melrose for the soul of his prospective bride's recently dead mother. The abbey was also expected to offer more material aid towards the King's marriage, being taxed £300 towards the costs of the ceremonies and festivities that surrounded the event in the summer of 1503.

James IV's interest in the dispute over the abbacy had waxed and waned throughout this period. It was rekindled in 1506 when he re-opened the question of the disputed succession at the papal court. Although he claimed to be operating in the interest of David Brown, who was still pursuing his litigation at Rome, and to put right a wrong committed by his father, he was now actively promoting the interests of a candidate of his own choosing, Robert Betoun, abbot of Glenluce. In a letter of 1 October 1506 to Pope Julius II, the King urged the Pope to appoint Betoun as a man who would 'administer for a tightening of monastic order and the succour of a decadent place'. On the same day James wrote to the cardinal of St Mark, detailing the case for Betoun's appointment. He spoke glowingly of the abbey's original condition and how, by its situation on the borders and its generous landed endowment, it could once 'minister supply to military defenders and promote by counsel and material aid the common good'. That, though, was in the past and, using lurid language, he described how its lands had been alienated to laymen, how its remaining revenues were almost incapable of supporting the proper number of monks, and how it was able to offer neither hospitality to visitors nor spiritual support to its patrons. It was, he said, 'all in neglect, buildings once magnificent falling, or already fallen, in ruins, what his ancestors had established as a bulwark for the general safety now a secure refuge for rebels and exiles'.

In the interim, Betoun was postulated for the abbacy of Coupar Angus, but James was determined to get his man into Melrose. A deal was struck whereby William Turnbull, who had possession of Melrose, would exchange abbeys with Betoun, and on 1 April James wrote to the Pope to ask that this arrangement be ratified. James added that since the income of Melrose had been significantly reduced by the award to Bernard Bell of a pension based on the revenues of Mauchline, Betoun should be allowed to retain the abbacy of Glenluce for at least a further year. The King clearly had firm ideas as to what Betoun's role would be, for on the same day he wrote to the abbot of Cîteaux urging that the traditional commission of the abbots of Melrose as visitors for all Cistercian houses in Scotland should be renewed, and hinting that if the abbot did not agree then he would seek papal authority for the appointment. Betoun, James suggested, was to oversee a reform of monastic discipline within the Scottish Cistercian houses. How the King might have aided this programme of reform remains unknown, for in September 1513 he perished with the cream of his nobility at Flodden, and royal policy disintegrated in the ensuing long minority of his son.

Visitation, reform and resistance

How effective Betoun was in fostering a spiritual regeneration at Melrose is very unclear. Certainly, there is no record of any programme of reform and, overall, the standards of monastic life as well as the number of monks appear to have declined over the period of his abbacy. There were, moreover, worrying signs that the struggle to secure the abbacy that had so debilitated the community between 1471 and 1506 was to repeat itself in the years ahead. In December 1524, Henry VIII of England wrote to the Pope on behalf of his nephew James V, or rather in his name on behalf of his sister Queen Margaret Tudor and her second husband Archibald, earl of Angus, nominating John Maxwell, abbot of Dundrennan, as Betoun's successor. As Betoun's health deteriorated in December 1523, however, he had requested the appointment of Andrew Durie, a monk of Melrose and nephew of the Archbishop of St Andrews, as his coadjutor and it was expected that Durie would succeed to the abbacy on Betoun's death. The Archbishop, however, was aligned with the political enemies of the earl of Angus, who controlled the young King James V, and Angus had no wish for so rich a prize in the middle of what he regarded as 'his' sphere of influence to fall into the hands of his opponents. Nevertheless, it was Durie who was the quicker off the mark following Betoun's death. He secured papal letters providing him to the abbacy sometime in November 1524, whilst it was only on 2 December that Henry VIII wrote to Pope Clement VII to request the provision of Maxwell, with the reservation of a pension from Melrose's revenues for James's mother and Henry's sister, Margaret Tudor. News of Durie's provision had reached Scotland by 4 December, when a letter in James's name was sent to Cardinal Wolsey, Henry VIII's Chancellor, asking for his aid in securing a revocation of the award to Durie and provision instead of Maxwell. Rumours that the Pope had refused to provide Durie circulated widely but, while Douglas continued to support Maxwell and, in the King's name, denounced his rival in Parliament as late as 17 November 1526, on 17 December James issued an order under his privy seal instructing that Durie be given possession of the lands and revenues of the abbey.

The initial royal hostility towards Durie was largely a matter of Douglas opposition to a rival, and, following the overthrow of the earl's regime, that hostility disappeared. By the 1530s, the abbot had emerged as an important and favoured crown servant, very much in the mould of Andrew Hunter (although not holding such high political office). His dedication to his monastery, however, was never of major concern to him and, from the beginning, it appears to have been the abbey's revenues that interested him.

Burdened with the debts accumulated in his litigation to procure the abbacy and from the payment of the 'common services' demanded on his successful provision, he presided over an era in which the asset-stripping of the community by its superior became normal practice. By 1530, his regime at Melrose was exposed to stern criticism.

King James V had made a show of appealing for strong action to be taken to reform the Church and to curb the continued decline of spiritual standards amongst the monastic orders. As a consequence, Walter Malynne, abbot of Glenluce, was given a commission as visitor for Scotland by the Cistercian chapter-general. Although Malynne's own entry into the order had been somewhat irregular, he proved to be a very zealous visitor. His requirements, however, were too zealous and complaints against him from the visited monasteries forced the King to write in January 1531 to request that the abbot of Cîteaux send a special visitor from outwith Scotland. The result was the award of the commission to the French abbot of Chaalis, who acted with even greater firmness and severity, ordering disciplinary action against some of the Scottish brethren. This result was even more unpalatable and the King now asked for a restoration of Malynne's commission. Much to James's displeasure, in 1533 the chapter-general gave its backing to the abbot of Chaalis and had also ordered Durie to attend to answer charges of negligence in the dispensation of his duties. The King's attachment to Durie is shown by his intervention at Cîteaux to block the summons. The chapter-general still took steps to set internal reform of the Scottish Cistercian houses in motion and granted a five-year commission as visitors to two Scottish abbots, Walter Malynne of Glenluce and Donald Campbell of Coupar Angus.

Surprisingly, the new visitors gave their full backing to the actions taken and proposed by the abbot of Chaalis. Central to their demands was a return to the strict principle of a common existence and lifestyle in the abbeys: no more private quarters and gardens, personal portions and individual clothing allowances. Instead, they wanted all the monks' daily necessities in food and clothing to be shared equally and dispensed centrally to common standards by the officials of the abbeys. At Melrose in 1534 they ordered an immediate end under threat of excommunication of the arrangements whereby the monks received personal pensions, private portions and kept private gardens in the monastic precinct. Such decisions provoked a storm of protest from several Cistercian houses, but led by the monks of Melrose who may have had most to lose individually. Eventually, a compromise was reached in 1535, whereby the most outrageous of the abuses of the system were purged, but individual portions were retained. At Melrose, the monks were allowed to keep their gardens, but only if the produce went to the common use of the abbey and was not sold for personal profit. One important concession, however, was that the monks could not build up personal 'savings' by keeping any money left over each year from their personal portions. There are indications that the monks of Melrose ignored most of the compromise arrangements and were fined, but whether the fine was paid or not is unknown.

Secure in the King's favour, Durie escaped censure. That favour strengthened towards the end of the 1530s, and James based himself in the abbey in November 1539 whilst on a hunting trip to the borders. From there he sent 'wyld mete' to Queen Marie de Guise at Falkland in Fife. Durie also sent personal presents to the King, for example, in May 1540 having one of his servants deliver a salmon to James in Edinburgh. There have been suggestions that James aimed to dispose of Durie and eventually forced him to resign, but his actions throughout the 1530s indicate otherwise. Nevertheless, James had plans for Melrose that did not include the abbot. As early as August 1535, when the visitation row was past, the King had procured the commendatorship of Melrose for his eldest bastard son, James Stewart, who, since the previous May, had also been commendator of Kelso. He was five years old. Durie, however, remained in office as abbot, until in July 1541 he was nominated by the King to the bishopric of Whithorn and of the Chapel Royal, and provided to that benefice by the Pope on 22 August 1542. Even then, he received the reservation of a pension of 1,000 merks for life from the revenues of his old abbey, which he drew until his death in 1558. If there was any royal arm-twisting involved, then Durie certainly came out of it bruised only by the weight of the pay-off!

A month after Durie's nomination to Whithorn, James Stewart was provided in commend to Melrose. The 11-year-old was clearly not going to provide any leadership to his abbey for some time, lay or spiritual, and his charge was instead to be administered in his name by crown-appointed officials. The result was an accelerating programme of alienation of the monastic properties, encroachment onto monastic lands by lay landowners, and a rapid decline in both the numbers of monks and the standards of discipline and monastic life in the abbey. This situation was exacerbated by the death of James V in early December 1542, the accession of his infant daughter, Mary, which heralded the start of yet another long minority, and the outbreak of war with England, which would find Melrose exposed once again to pillage and fire.

Monastic twilight

War with England had broken out late in 1542 and reached an early climax with the disastrous defeat of the Scottish army at Solway Moss on 24 November. Only the lateness of the season and the death of James within a fortnight of his army's defeat prevented significant English response, and in 1543, Henry VIII preferred to use raiding to increase pressure on the Scots and use his Scottish prisoners to give him leverage to arrange a marriage between the infant Queen Mary and his son, the future Edward VI. The Scots first agreed to the proposed marriage, going so far as to accept the Treaty of Greenwich offered by Henry VIII, then, after intense behind-the-scenes lobbying by Cardinal David Beaton, Archbishop of St Andrews, the deal was repudiated. Infuriated, Henry unleashed his armies across the border in the savage episode known later as the 'Rough Wooing'. Towards the end of 1544, an English army crossed into Scotland and plundered its way up Tweeddale, and, following instructions that had been drawn up after careful discussion by Henry's councillors, sacked Melrose town and abbey, and desecrated the tombs in the abbey church, including those of the first and second earls of Douglas. The following February, a second raid was intercepted at Ancrum Moor between Melrose and Jedburgh, and the raiders, laden with plunder, were outmanoeuvred and defeated by a Scottish force commanded by Arran and the Douglas earls' descendant, Archibald, earl of Angus. The slain English commanders, Sir Ralph Eure and Sir Brian Laiton, were buried in the abbey that they had ordered to be pillaged the previous autumn. The Scottish victory provoked massive English retaliation, and an army commanded by the earl of Hertford returned later in the year to ravage the border region. As detachments from the force burned their way north and west, they sacked the stricken abbey still more thoroughly than their comrades had done the previous year. It was a blow from which Melrose never recovered.

James Stewart's rule as commendator was a major factor in ensuring the steady deterioration of the quality of monastic life at Melrose. Of course, until the early 1550s, the management of the monastery was administered in his name by a succession of 'yconomici' or stewards, whose primary objectives were to extract the maximum financial return with the minimum of investment. They continued with Durie's unofficial policy of preventing new recruitment to maintain the number of monks, which had declined steadily from the high figure of 35 in the early 1500s to under 20 by the 1550s. The motive here was, again, financial, for fewer monks meant a larger surplus on the income of the monastery. It was a policy maintained by Stewart when he assumed the running of his own affairs, and one which brought him into sharp conflict with the remaining monks. Friction was perhaps heightened by the commendator's periods of residence at the monastery, which usually coincided with occasions on which he sought the monks' agreement for further alienation of property at feu. There is no indication that he showed the slightest interest in the spiritual life of the community that was under his nominal leadership, the effective head of the monastic community being the prior. Relations between the two men were clearly strained most of the time. The records reveal to us a picture of the ageing monk fighting a long and seemingly futile rearguard action to preserve what he could of his monastery's spiritual and propertied inheritance from the depredations of a young and unprincipled nobleman.

Although a uniformly bleak picture is offered traditionally of the state of monastic life at Melrose between its sack and burning in 1544-5 and the Reformation in 1560, it is clear that the convent did try to repair the damage and continue the building operations under way since the 1380s. On 19 June 1556, the sub-prior, Thomas Mercer, and the convent of Melrose refused to ratify a charter drawn up by the commendator in favour of Gilbert Balfour, burgess of Edinburgh, giving him the feu of the former abbot's lodgings in Edinburgh. The feu-charter stated like many previous feus that the alienation of the property was being done to raise funds for the repair of the monastery and the maintenance of the community. The monks attempted to oblige Stewart to make real provision for the promised repairs, requiring, amongst other points, that their 'commoun office houses', that is the refectory, kitchen, bakehouse, brewhouse and malthouse, be repaired and properly equipped, since without these common buildings the basics of communal monastic life could not be adhered to. They also complained of the commendator's refusal to allow them to recruit new brethren to keep the number of monks up to the level required for basic monastic services, a refusal presumably driven by the commendator's wish to cream off as much of the revenues as possible. A willing novice, George Weir, was named. Mercer concluded with a plea that 500 merks of some 1,200 received should be assigned to one of their number who could oversee urgent repairs to the dormitory and church, as 'without the kirk be repairit this instant sommer God service will ceise this winter'.

Reference to the ruinous state of the dormitory again hints at the near collapse of communal monastic life in the abbey (86). It appears that the infirmary hall had been divided up by the middle of the 1550s to provide separate chambers for the remaining monks. This may have been a device to allow the brethren a means to avoid the spirit of the Cisterican rule which prohibited the eating of meat except by the inmates of the infirmary or those involved in heavy outside labour, but all references to individuals with 'cubiculi' in the infirmary date from after the burning of the abbey in the 1540s. The implication is that the dormitory was uninhabitable. Indeed, it is likely that most of the east range of the cloister was in a ruinous condition. There is no reference to any affairs being transacted in the chapterhouse, the usual venue for the settling of the common business of the convent such as issuing charters or agreeing feus, although there are occasional early sixteenth-century references to transactions being settled in the parlour. Instead, between 1556 and 1559, all such business was concluded in the abbey church, usually within one of the chapels in the transepts or south aisle of the nave, although one legal instrument was drawn up in the 'wax cellar' that opens off the north transept. The commendator, who was present, reacted furiously to their stance and 'displeasandlie and with furiosite wald nocht reid the said articles bot raif thame and cast thame doun at his [feet]'.

Mercer and the senior monks of the convent had a second confrontation with James Stewart on 21 August 1557, again over the issue of a feu-charter and non-delivery of promised funds (**6**). Stewart wished to feu the lands of Over Catrine in Kylesmuir to the tenant, Adam Aird. Mercer, however, reminded the commendator that despite his agreement in 1556 that 500 merks of the income from Kylesmuir plus 300 merks from Hassendean would be given to them for repairs to be undertaken on the abbey, no money had been advanced to them. As a consequence, the monks refused to agree to the feu or to allow their common seal to be used (**5**). After this answer, the commendator 'as apperit in his wult and exterieur mowing of his body grew crawbit', and threatened that if they did not agree to the grant he would prevent payment of the pensions due to them from the abbey's income for their support. Recognising that Stewart could and would make real his threat, the monks caved in but, shortly after the meeting with the commendator, drew up a legal instrument setting out the circumstances which lay behind their agreement.

Despite the failure of Mercer's effort to coerce the commendator into positive action in 1556 and 1557, as late as 13 November 1557 new work was planned on the south door of the church. One of the monks, Thomas Hallewell, made a formal offer of cash from his own resources to pay the master of works as soon as operations commenced, provided it began within a year of the date of the agreement. But that rider carries a note of pessimism or even cynicism over the likelihood that building would ever start, the events of the previous 20 years having forced a harsh realism on the prior and monks. There is, indeed, no sign that the work ever began and

6 *One of the charters of Commendator James Stewart by which he feued lands to raise funds,* *supposedly for the repair of the abbey, 1555/6.* Historic Scotland

only four months later the sub-prior reported a further plundering of the abbey, this time at the hands of men who were nominally in the service of the monks. On 2 April 1558, the new sub-prior, John Watson, and other members of the convent witnessed Walter Balfour, parson of Linton, Michael Chisholm, 'alleged' Baillie-depute of the regality of Melrose, and their accomplices, tearing the lead from the roof of the cloister. Some 11 stones of lead, they claimed, were taken by the plunderers, whose strength was too great for the monks to resist. Watson and his fellow monks publicly cited Balfour, Chisholm and the others in the great cloister at the abbey and tried to secure legal remedy, but as the country teetered on the brink of all-out civil war in the late 1550s, their efforts were in vain. Nevertheless, sometime around December 1559, the Justice Clerk promised to deliver money for the repair of the abbey buildings and '…presentlie salbe deliverit to you xx merkis togidder with ane pot and ane pan for neidfull thingis to your kechen and hall…'.

The stripping of lead from the roof by Michael Chisholm tellingly reveals how little regard was given to the rights and authority of the abbey, even by its supposed servants. On 9 April 1558, when the prior, Ralph Hudson, 10 of his monks and the parishioners were gathered for Easter Eve's service in the 'gret kirk' of Melrose, the convent attempted to serve a precept on a number of their tenants. One of the tenants, Matthew Chisholm, ripped the precept from the monks' hands, for which he was solemnly cursed by the convent before the assembled people. Rather than bringing about Matthew's humble submission, the cursing brought him the support of Walter Chisholm of that Ilk 'allegeand him baillie deput'. Matthew remained in the church, disrupting the service, while Walter threatened that if anyone tried to serve the precept at the monks' behest he would 'stuw his luggis'. Threats of excommunication clearly carried no fear for these men, and the prior and convent had been exposed before the eyes of the whole parish as powerless to enforce their rights.

On 25 September 1557, in the midst of these crises, the commendator, James Stewart, had died. His removal, of course, brought no recovery in the position of the abbey. Even before Stewart's death, Louis de Guise, cardinal of Lorraine, the brother of the Queen-Mother Marie de Guise, was attempting to secure a pension from the abbeys of Kelso and Melrose, and was provided as commendator on 17 April 1559. That same day, however, one James Balfour was also provided in commend, and, as the French hold on Scotland crumbled through 1559, it was increasingly unlikely the cardinal would ever make good his claim. By the end of 1559, the Reforming party in Scotland was gaining the upper hand, with aid from Elizabeth I of

England. In March 1560, an English army joined the Protestant lords to besiege the French-held citadel at Leith and, when the Queen-Regent died in June, the triumph of Protestantism seemed certain. Two months later, a parliament dominated by the Protestants and their sympathisers assembled in Edinburgh, and passed a raft of legislation which overturned the old Church hierarchy in Scotland, declared the ties with Rome severed, and set out a religious future for Scotland in which monasticism had no place. For the remaining monks of Melrose it was an official notice of redundancy.

Sunset and afterglow

Unlike the Protestant Reformation in England, there was no formal dissolution of the monasteries in 1560. Some of the abbeys and friaries had been effectively destroyed by Protestant mobs in the turbulent days of 1558-60, including Scone Abbey and the friaries in Perth and Dundee, and Melrose's daughter-houses at Balmerino and Coupar Angus had been ransacked by Protestants from Dundee. Most Scottish monasteries, however, were left to wither away, remaining as nominally religious communities under the control of lay commendators who milked them for their revenues, while the remaining monks were permitted to receive their portions and live on in the decaying splendours of the abbeys, but were refused permission to recruit new members. When the last monks died, the monastery effectively died with them. Some monks and canons chose to join the Reformed Church and served as parish ministers of churches that had once been controlled by their old communities. At Melrose, a steadily declining number of monks lingered on into the 1580s.

The Reformation Parliament of 1560, for most abbeys, simply formalised a state of affairs that had prevailed for most of the sixteenth century. Wealthy houses like Melrose were simply assets to be controlled and managed by the crown, milked for their fruits, or used as items of patronage in the portfolio of rewards at the disposal of the crown. After James Stewart's death in 1557, the abbey had in fact been under royal administration, with the revenues being creamed off for the crown's use. Commendators were appointed at royal sufferance, often only receiving a portion of the fruits whilst the crown pocketed the remainder. James Balfour found himself in this position. He had been provided as commendator in April 1559 after what had been an eighteen-month vacancy during which the Queen-Regent had taken the fruits of the abbey. Two years later, a second commendator was intruded into the abbey by crown authority, although Balfour was not deprived of his appointment. On 5 March 1561, Thomas Randolph, the English agent in Edinburgh, reported to his masters that Queen Mary had given the commendatorship of Melrose to James Hepburn, earl of Bothwell. He wrote again on 24 September, to report that the abbey was being held against Bothwell and his men by an armed band, who were taking up the teinds (tithes) due from the abbey's estates. In November, Randolph reported that the earl of Arran had also claimed that the Queen had awarded him the revenues of Melrose and other monasteries. It is usually said that Bothwell was never able to make good his possession of the commendatorship, despite his issuing of several feu-charters at this time, for in March 1564 Balfour's position was ratified by Queen Mary. Nevertheless, in 1567 Bothwell was to act as though his 1561 commission still held effect.

Melrose was still a rich prize for any ambitious man to gain. In 1560, the income of the monastery stood notionally at around £5,000 Scots (roughly £1,000 sterling at that date), which placed it second to Coupar Angus, at £5,500, in the league table of Cistercian houses, but less than half the value of monasteries such as St Andrews, Arbroath and Dunfermline. Nevertheless, Melrose was still more valuable than the estates of most of the senior lay nobility. It is clear that there was a great deal of murky manoeuvring over control of the monastery in the years 1557 to 1564, the period in which a new political order was being built within the kingdom. Although John Balfour held the commendatorship, Lord James Stewart, later to be earl of Moray, another of James V's bastards, appears to have had a property interest in the abbey arising from his position as heir apparent to his late half-brother, the commendator James Stewart. In 1564, when Michael Balfour was confirmed as commendator, reference was made to the legal deprivation of Lord James's interest. It is possible that Stewart's interest in Melrose had been surrendered in return for the award to him of the politically more important and financially lucrative earldom of Moray. For Bothwell in 1561, the attraction of the abbey was as much the location of its lands as the revenue obtained from them. The earl had aspirations to build up a power-base in the central border region – he already controlled Liddesdale – and possession of Melrose would have provided him with lordship over a substantial network spread from the East Lothian/Berwickshire border to Dumfriesshire. For all these men, Melrose's lands and wealth offered a route to power.

After his confirmation as commendator in 1564, Michael Balfour appears to have enjoyed undisputed occupation of the abbey. As Mary's grip on power slipped away in the early summer of 1567, Bothwell headed into the borders and was at Melrose on 8 June and attempting to rally support there for the Queen's cause. Whilst there, Bothwell, possibly acting on the 1561 award of the commendatorship to him, had compelled the monks to recognise him as feuar of the abbey lands, and he had proceeded to issue feu-charters to his own supporters. After the collapse of the Queen's position in 1567, the monks clearly feared that they would be accused of willing partic-ipation in Bothwell's actions, and there was a risk that they could be portrayed as plotting to overturn the Protestant establishment through their underwriting of Mary's cause in this way. On 18 September 1569, four of the remaining monks testified how they had been compelled through fear to assign the feu on the monastery's lands to the earl. They described how he had threatened to deprive them of their livings, drive them out of the abbey, take from them the keys of their chambers, and brand their cheeks with red-hot keys. Bothwell did not remain for long at Melrose, for he had brought his men back to Lothian and was with Mary at Carberry Hill to the east of Edinburgh on 15 June. The victorious confederate lords led by Moray were sure enough of the security of Melrose in their interest, that in a bond arranging for Edinburgh Castle to be placed at their disposal by its keeper, Sir James Balfour, formerly a committed supporter of the Queen, hostages taken as security for the deal were to be housed at Dalkeith and Crichton castles and Melrose, which 'wilbe very handsum dwellingis for them.'

The shifting patterns of power in the period after the rising which overthrew Mary produced further changes at Melrose. In May 1569, James Douglas, second son of William Douglas of Lochleven, later fifth earl of Morton, was appointed to the commendatorship, with his father as adminis-trator and usufructor until James came of age. It was also arranged that on 24 September 1569, Michael Balfour's agents were to hand over to William Douglas, as administrator for James, or to Alexander Colville, commendator of Culross and steward of Melrose, the keys and charter 'kist' of the abbey, containing all its 'charteris, evidentis, rentallis, registeris and utheris writingis'. The baillie of the abbey, Sir Walter Scott of Branxholm, was instructed to put the new arrangements in to operation and not to interfere or obstruct Douglas's administration. However, between January and April 1569, Scott had been actively involved in stripping the abbey of salvageable materials, which were actions that were directly contrary to his duties as baillie. There were clearly going to be problems between Douglas and Scott, and in 1572 the Baillie was in ward in Doune Castle, evidently partly as a result of his actions regarding the abbey. On 7 July, Scott was released temporarily under caution from Doune, to return by 1 August, subject to his agreement that he would not 'meddle with William Dowglas of Lochleven in the intromission with the abbacy of Melrose'. Douglas possession was secured once James's grandfather, the fourth earl of Morton, became regent for the child, James VI, and survived even the earl's execution. In 1606, the commendator resigned the abbacy to his nephew, William, sixth earl of Morton, and in 1608 he surrendered the abbey and all its remaining properties to the King. Although any real existence as a religious institution was over, these acts marked the endgame in the long history of Melrose, for the abbey was now formally suppressed and, in June 1609, recreated as a secular lordship for John Ramsay, first Viscount Haddington.

Throughout this period a steadily diminishing number of monks survived at the abbey, until 1586 when only one remained. John Watson, described as 'only Convent' of Melrose, had his private house in the former precinct, living on in the ruins of the community where he had started his career as a monk. Surviving until 1609, he seems to have had neither interest nor intent in keeping alive any pretence of a monastic lifestyle, nor did he show any sign of adherence to the old faith. He lived a thoroughly secular life and, for the last few years, served as Baillie depute of the regality of Melrose. It is fitting however, that his death and the formal winding up of the abbey coincided, marking the end of an organism that had lived for nearly 500 years.

The ghost of the abbey lived on as the secular lordship of Melrose under the earls of Haddington. The Ramsays resigned their titles in 1618 to Thomas Hamilton, Lord Binning, who in 1619 was created earl of Melrose by James VI, then elevated to earl of Haddington in 1621. Melrose remained with the Hamiltons until the end of the seventeenth century, when it was sold to Anne Scott, duchess of Buccleuch, with whose descendants possession of much of the old abbey properties remains. In 1919, the then duke handed over the abbey ruins to the care of the State.

2
THE ARCHITECTURE OF THE ABBEY

The abbey and its precinct

The precinct

Based on a combination of physical and documentary evidence, the precinct of the Cistercian abbey founded in 1136/7 is thought to have covered an irregular area of around 16ha, with its northern boundary some 180m south of the river Tweed (**7**). The principal gateway into the precinct was on the south side, towards what later became the market place of the settlement that grew up here, and there is a reference in 1422 to a chapel above that gateway. There are known to have been lesser entrances on the east and west sides of the precinct, and there was probably one on the north as well. The abbey church was placed almost precisely at the centre of this precinct, reminding us that, since the earlier Cistercians had avoided contact with the outside world as far as possible, there was usually no reason to make provision for public access to the church by placing it close to the precinct perimeter. At Melrose, however, the abbey church appears to have been used for parochial worship from an early date, meaning that there was always a need for some public access across a part of the precinct, and this may later have created some difficulties.

Supplies of fresh water and drainage were a major factor in the location of any monastery, and at Melrose, while there was a stream within the precinct that was later known as the Malthouse Burn, and wells were also to be sunk, the main supply was drawn from the Tweed. The open lade through which this supply was carried came from a cauld across the river about 550m west-north-west of the abbey church, and it eventually returned to the Tweed about 1.5km east-north-east of the church. From this lade the main drain ran between the principal buildings, with smaller channels or runs of lead piping for the supply of fresh water branching off at a number of points. Some of

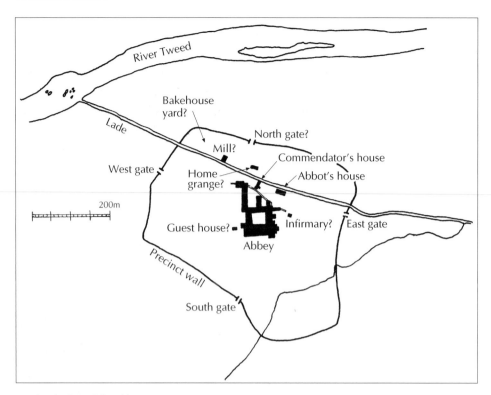

7 *Sketch plan of the abbey precinct.* Fawcett

the lengths of lead piping found during excavations are now displayed in the site museum in the commendator's house. For much of its length the drain was roughly constructed of rubble and was covered by lintels, except that where it passed below some of the buildings it was arched over for greater strength. The most finished section of the drain was the part below the monastic latrine, east of the monks' dormitory, where it was particularly important that waste was not allowed to collect (**8**). It was presumably the location of the main water supply on the north side of the church which led to the decision that the cloister should be placed against that flank of the church (**81**). Wherever possible at monasteries following the Rule of St Benedict, the cloister and its surrounding ranges of buildings were placed on the south side, where their light was not blocked by the church, since that was almost invariably the largest building on the site. There is only one other known case of a northern cloister at a Scottish Cistercian house, at Melrose's daughter-house of Balmerino, but the reason in that case is less clear. At Melrose the lines followed by the lade and the main drain were largely conditioned by the natural contours of the site, and in this the pre-glacial course of the Tweed may itself have been a factor, with the possibility that one or both of the lade and drain perpetuated earlier river courses.

Few buildings beyond the main nucleus around the cloister have been archaeologically investigated at Melrose, but we know from Cistercian precincts elsewhere that an order which placed particular stress on both separation from the world and self-sufficiency would have needed far more buildings than those of which there are now remains. There are a number of clues to the location of some that have been lost, however; we know from other monastic sites that it was common for the functions of some buildings to be perpetuated in later ones that succeeded them on the same site. On this basis it may be that the abbey's corn mill, for example, which required a specialised form of water supply, was on the same site as a later mill to the

8 *The drain below the site of the monks' latrine.* Historic Scotland

north-west of the abbey, the main structure of which is dated by inscription to 1773. Similarly, it must be at least a possibility that the buildings of Priory Farm, immediately to the north of the abbey, are on the site of a medieval agricultural complex, possibly even that of a home grange. One building which has unexpectedly thick walls that might point to the adaptation of a medieval building is Abbey House, to the west of the modern abbey boundary wall, and in that location it is one possibility that it was a monastic guest house. Even though the early Cistercians did not encourage visitors, all monasteries had a duty of hospitality.

A fragment of particular interest is to the east of the abbey church, within the walls of what used to be the outbuildings of a post-medieval brewery, in a location where it is attractive to suspect that it could have formed part of the monks' infirmary. The possibility of the infirmary having been in this area of the precinct may be supported by the siting of Cloister House, which used to be the manse of the parish minister, immediately to its west. In 1587, the lease of a residence and garden which was confirmed to John Knox, the minister at the time, appears to have been for a house in this area. Eighteenth-century descriptions referred to the existence close by the manse of the foundations of a large chapel and of pillars that suggest a major aisled building that would fit well with what we know of infirmary chapels and halls elsewhere. Assuming that the manse has remained on the same site since the late sixteenth century, all of this could be consistent with the infirmary having been nearby.

Further pointers to the location of outlying monastic buildings come from place name evidence, such as Bakehouse Yard and Bakehouse Green in the north-west corner of the precinct, which were being leased out in the 1580s; as late as 1743 there are references to a great oven having survived. Elsewhere within the precinct, it is likely that considerable areas were given over to gardens worked by the monks themselves. In 1534 they were accused of selling the produce of these gardens, apparently for their own benefit, and we are reminded that by the later Middle Ages the ideal of communal co-existence was being less rigidly pursued (pp.56–8).

A particular difficulty in understanding what is to be seen of the precinct at Melrose stems from the fact that after the Reformation much of it came to be progressively occupied by houses and other buildings, some of which we know must have developed around the core of monastic structures. In fact, this process of encroachment may have started even before the Reformation, since there are complaints of the precinct being violated by predatory lay interests for some years before 1560. This was especially the case after the abbey had come under the control of commendators, or secular administrators, rather than monastic abbots from 1541. The leading concern of most of the commendators, or at least the concern that required most documentation, was the income that could be generated from the abbey's estates and property, rather than the spiritual welfare of the community (p.58). An almost inevitable consequence of this was a need for more accommodation for those working on behalf of the commendator, and the monastic community may have felt it was being progressively marginalised, with the prime sacred functions of the abbey being lost sight of.

After the Reformation this process of accelerating secularisation was, of course, unstoppable, and around some of the larger post-Reformation houses erected within the precinct extensive gardens were eventually formed, especially in the eighteenth and nineteenth centuries. This must have entailed the demolition of many monastic structures, while the high boundary walls that enclosed those gardens became, and still are in some cases, a notable, and admittedly rather attractive, feature of this part of the burgh (**9**). At the same time, new roads had to be created to give access across the site, with Abbey Street, running north-south through the precinct to the west of the church, being the most significant, and Cloisters Road extending eastwards from it

9 *The site of the cloister before the start of excavations in the early 1920s, showing the gardens and boundary walls that overlay the site.* Historic Scotland

on the north side of the cloister site. But there were also less elegant developments within the precinct, including the brewery to the east of the church that has already been mentioned as being, a little surprisingly, immediately adjacent to the manse of the parish minister. It cannot be ruled out that this brewery was itself on the site of a medieval predecessor, since in 1556 there are references to a brewhouse and malthouse within the precinct, and beer had always been an important element in the monastic diet in an age when most water supplies were rather less than pure.

Archaeological investigation of the site

The area once occupied by the main core of abbey buildings was eventually taken into state care from the seventh duke of Buccleuch in 1919. Further areas of land within the monastic precinct were later added as the opportunity arose, with a field to the north of the abbey being acquired as late as 1958. Clearance excavations began immediately after the abbey was taken into care, under the supervision of the Office of Works' Inspector of Ancient Monuments, James Richardson, and the Office's Architect, John Wilson Paterson.

From the few records we have of the excavations, we know they were in progress from 1919, because we have lists of finds which start that year; and official minutes suggest that the first efforts were around parts of the cloister and that work on the church started very soon afterwards. Exchanges of minutes and drawings show that the chapter house was being investigated in 1920-1, and by 1923 the eastern parts of an earlier church, within the walls of its late medieval successor, had been traced. In 1924 work had moved on to both the western parts of the earlier church and the west claustral range (**10**). Following the acquisition of land immediately to the north of the cloister, beyond Cloisters Road and within the grounds of the house then known as The Priory, investigations were under way from 1932 on the outlying parts of the lay-brothers' range, and on the outer parts of the refectory and the east range. At the same time it came to be appreciated that The Priory itself had at its core a medieval building that was identified as the residence of the post-Reformation commendators of the abbey. It was decided that the original structure should be extricated from the later building and restored, with the decision being eventually taken that it should be adapted to serve as a site museum (**92** and **93**). But the process of adaptation of this building was interrupted by the war, and the museum was only eventually opened in 1946. Work moved back to the west end of the nave following demolition of the Abbey Hotel to its south-west in 1948. Further archaeological works have been carried out on a number of other occasions, including investigations within the chapter house in 1996.

10 *Excavations in the west range in 1924, before the demolition of the Abbey Hotel.*
Historic Scotland

In retrospect, it is perhaps unfortunate that the main campaigns of excavation, those which exposed the footings and foundations of the earlier church and of the monastic buildings, were carried out in the period between the two World Wars, when techniques that were being developed for prehistoric archaeology were still not generally applied to the 'clearance' excavations of medieval sites. The main goals of the largely unsupervised squads who were carrying out the work were to recover the plan of the buildings and to extract any finds that might have survived. This approach was not conducive to a sophisticated level of understanding of the structural evidence, and the problem was in some ways compounded in the subsequent process of consolidation of the excavated walls. The necessity of giving permanently displayable shape to frail and sometimes extremely fragmentary structural remains almost inevitably meant that subtle evidence for inter-relationships between the constituent parts was sometimes compromised or even lost, while elements for which there was at best incomplete evidence might have to take on an unjustifiable certainty of form. There were probably also significant changes in the character of parts of the masonry fabric.

No detailed report on the excavations was published, and the best discussions of the evidence are those which were eventually printed in the official guide-book, and in the more detailed account in the Roxburghshire inventory of the Royal Commission on the Ancient and Historical Monuments of Scotland. Although the account in the inventory provides an invaluable description of the church and monastic buildings, in view of the nature of the investigations it is not always possible to feel quite as certain about the precise inter-relationships and dating of what had been found as might be suggested there. Since so much reliance now has to be placed on that account, however, some of what will be said below also has to be regarded as potentially open to question.

The earlier stone-built church

The provision of a first church

It was Cistercian custom that the founder, or possibly in some cases the mother-house, should provide temporary first buildings for a new community, so that stable monastic life could be instituted immediately on the monks' entry to the site. These first buildings would have included a church, a refectory, a dormitory, an infirmary and a gatehouse, and would very frequently have been made of timber, as is known to have been the case from evidence found through excavation at Sawley Abbey in Lancashire, for example. It is possible that Melrose similarly had timber first buildings, since it is certainly to be expected that such an experienced patron of monastic life as David I would have made all the preliminary provision that could be required. It should also be remembered that David must have been personally acquainted with the most recent developments relating to the Cistercians and their requirements in northern England as a result of his close connections with St Ailred, and because of the interest in the order of his own step-son, Waltheof. Ailred had been a favoured member of David's household for about a decade before entering Melrose's mother-house of Rievaulx in Yorkshire in 1134, where he was to become abbot in 1147. Waltheof entered the religious life in about 1130, and became second abbot of Melrose in 1148, eventually being widely regarded as a saint.

The potential complexity of the early structural history of Cistercian sites has had a particularly illuminating light cast on it by modern archaeological investigations at Fountains Abbey in Yorkshire which, like Rievaulx, was a daughter-house of St Bernard's own abbey of Clairvaux in Burgundy. At Fountains it seems that a timber church was begun in around 1133, with a small stone church being started in about 1136, which was in turn enlarged and extended after a major fire in 1146. On this evidence, the earliest parts of the existing church at Fountains, the transepts, can hardly have been built before the mid 1150s, with the nave we now see being started in earnest some time after then. The complexity of Fountains' early architectural history may be at least partly a result of its troubled early history as an institution. Nevertheless, it was probably not unusual for there to be a relatively rapid succession of early buildings at Cistercian sites, as the numbers of those drawn to the hope of salvation through this most demanding form of religious life so rapidly increased.

Evidence for only one earlier church has been found at Melrose through excavation, within the walls of its late medieval successor (**11**). As mentioned above, the foundations of the eastern arm of that earlier church had been traced by March 1923, when a plan of them was drawn up, and record photographs show that the excavation of the west end of the earlier church must have followed the demolition of some modern buildings in that area in 1924. Further excavation of the south-west corner of the nave followed the demolition of the Abbey Hotel in 1949. In all of this no signs of any building pre-dating that earlier church appear to have been noted, though the workmen who were carrying out the digging may have stopped once they located one set of earlier walls, and the archaeological evidence for any first temporary structures within the areas investigated therefore may not have

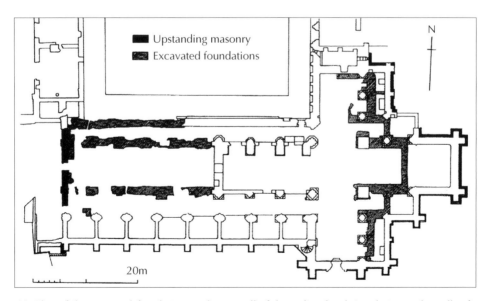

11 *Plan of the excavated foundations and west wall of the earlier church in relation to the walls of the later church.* Sylvia Stevenson/Historic Scotland

been reached. However, it is perhaps more likely that any temporary first structures would have been located away from the intended site of the permanent buildings, so that those temporary buildings could continue in use while the stone structures were being raised. Although at Fountains the first timber church was partly on the site of the south transept of the later building, at Rievaulx the first church is thought to have been in the area later occupied by the cloister, and any temporary structure may have been in a similar location at Melrose.

The plan

The excavated earlier church at Melrose has been found to have had a total length of about 65m, while the transepts had a width of some 37.2m, which was only a little less than the width across the transepts of the late medieval church. The nave had a width of about 17m over the central space and its narrow flanking aisles. As was usual in major foundations, the church was laid out to a basically cross-shaped plan, albeit to a form of that plan that is particularly associated with the Cistercians.

At the east end was the presbytery for the high altar, which was flanked by transepts with chapels on the east side of each for additional altars (**12**). The central space of the nave would have been almost wholly occupied by two choirs, one at the east end for the choir monks, and one towards the west end for the *conversi* or lay-brethren, with the two separated by a screened-off retrochoir. Public access to Cistercian churches was limited in the earlier years of the order's existence, so at first there was presumably no need for space for the laity within the nave.

The eastern parts of this cross-shaped plan were laid out on a variant of what is sometimes referred to as the 'Bernardine' plan, in reference to St Bernard of Clairvaux. It was during the time when he was exercising a dominant influence over the order that this plan came to be widely adopted at Cistercian churches, and especially at those of the affiliation of Clairvaux itself. It was only in the 1130s that Clairvaux itself was rebuilt to this plan, however, and so Melrose must be regarded as an early example of the type. The leading characteristic of the Bernardine plan is the way in which the short rectangular presbytery projected only a little further than the chapels along the eastern side of the immediately flanking transepts. In the variant found at Melrose there was an echelon, or stepped, arrangement, with the chapels flanking the presbytery extending a little further eastwards than the two outer chapels on each side, which were themselves apparently rather shallow. It would be dangerous to place excessive reliance on the results of the excavation in trying to interpret the plan too precisely, but it is possible

12 *Cut-open sketch showing the possible internal arrangements of the earlier church.*
David Simon/
Historic Scotland

that there were entrances to the presbytery from the adjacent chapels on each side, since the walls at this point appear to have stopped short at their western end. Related echelon variants on the 'Bernardine' plan are now known to have existed at Rievaulx Abbey as it was rebuilt by Ailred after 1147, and at the church at Fountains Abbey that was started in around 1154. Yet Melrose had almost certainly been started earlier than either of those. However, it now appears that the first stone church at Fountains started around 1136 had a smaller version of the echelon plan, and it is also thought likely that this may have been true of an earlier stone church at Rievaulx.

Since such an echelon variant on the Bernardine plan is highly uncommon, but is found within a short space of time at Melrose, Rievaulx and Fountains, it points to a particularly close architectural relationship between these three abbey churches. This may simply be because the builders of Rievaulx and Fountains were acquainted with each other's activities, being so close to each other geographically, and because these ideas were also shared with Rievaulx's daughter-house at Melrose. But it is attractive to suspect that there was a more personal link, and one candidate for this could be the slightly shadowy figure of the monk Geoffrey d'Ainai. It seems that Geoffrey had been sent from Clairvaux to Fountains in 1133 by St Bernard, to advise the new community there. While it is likely he was most directly involved in expounding the way of life and in advising on the temporary first buildings, it is not impossible that he was also consulted on the form of the first masonry structures at a time when they may have been under active consideration. It is also thought that Geoffrey was involved in building the new church at Clairvaux shortly before Melrose was started.

In speculating on the possibility of Geoffrey's presence behind all of these buildings, it would probably be wrong to assume that this was because of any draconian wish to impose architectural uniformity across all of the order's churches. Indeed, Clairvaux's own buildings before the mid 1130s were laid out on a very irregular pattern, and sending out advisers such as Geoffrey was perhaps no more than a response to a wish to ensure adoption of the approved forms of religious observance within buildings planned and built to an appropriate degree of simplicity for the requirements of the Cistercians. The architectural similarities that resulted from this were perhaps largely a by-product of form following function. Nevertheless, for some decades we do find buildings being erected for the order across Europe which owed much to Burgundy in their planning and general forms, while relying on the local architectural vocabulary of the area in which they were located for many of their details. This suggests that the masons who built Rievaulx, Fountains and Melrose, and who had themselves presumably originated in north Yorkshire, were receiving guidance provided by someone from the Burgundian head-quarters of the order, and an individual such as Geoffrey is one possibility. In the case of the early churches of Rievaulx and Melrose, the architectural inter-relationships appear to be particularly close in spirit, and it is likely that some of the same masons were involved at both of them, a reminder of the strength of family bonds between the communities of the order.

The likely appearance of the early church

So far as the architectural massing and spatial arrangements at Melrose were concerned, we may start by saying that it does not seem that there can have been a fully formed square crossing of four arches supported on responds or half-piers at the heart of the building, that is, at the junction of nave, transepts and presbytery. Such a crossing might be expected at the heart of most great twelfth-century churches, though in fact there was no great need for one at Melrose. This was partly because the Cistercians were tending to avoid the increasingly subtle articulation of the constituent parts of buildings that was being cultivated across Europe. But it was also because crossings were generally provided as a support for bell towers, and at Melrose it is almost certain that the initial Cistercian distaste for the hubris demonstrated by bell towers would still have been respected at the time when this early church was under construction. Indeed, statutory prohibition of towers was to be formalised in 1157, when work on Melrose must have been very much in progress. The internal space of the presbytery, at the far-east end of the building, appears to have been very slightly narrower than the main body of the church, evidently because of the greater thickness of its walls. The reason for this more massive construction is likely to have been the need to provide support for a stone vault over it; from what we know of early Cistercian churches elsewhere it may be suspected this vault would have been of barrel form and of pointed profile, as at other early churches of the order.

On the basis of the apparent absence of responds to define a crossing, the nave probably simply continued past the arches opening into the transepts, extending up to the entrance to the presbytery, which may itself have been defined architecturally by nothing more than the arched profile of the open end of the vault. The presbytery is likely to have risen to a slightly lesser height than the main body of the church, and it may also be suspected that the two arms of the transept were treated as lower and essentially subordinate lateral wings to the nave. Although the evidence found through excavation was ambiguous, it is likely that the main space of the two transepts was narrower than the nave, with three arches on the east side of each opening into the chapels. These chapels were presumably separated by solid walls, although possibly with arches from the inner chapels into the presbytery. Something of the possible relationship between the four arms can be understood from what is to be seen at the church of Fontenay, in the Cistercian order's homeland of Burgundy, which was started in 1139, shortly after Melrose. At Fontenay, however, as was usual in Burgundy, all of the spaces are vaulted, and while it cannot be ruled out that Melrose was vaulted throughout, it is more likely that only the presbytery, the transept chapels and the nave aisles would have been vaulted. The likelihood of vaulting being limited to those parts at Melrose is supported by the fact that this was probably also the case in the slightly later churches at Rievaulx and Fountains. So far as the transept chapels are concerned, if each of them were indeed covered by a vault, which was presumably of pointed barrel form, it is attractive to suspect that there was a saw-tooth pattern of external gables (**13**), as can still be seen in a partly surviving state at Fountains.

Even if the transepts were slightly lower than the nave, the arches opening into them from the main space would nevertheless have been wider and higher than those of the arcades that opened into the nave aisles. It may be that all of these structural arches were pointed, as has been suggested for the barrel vaults. In Burgundy, pointed arches became common rather earlier than in many other parts of Europe, and their use was often reflected in the order's churches elsewhere, as in the nave arcades of Fountains Abbey. At Melrose the nave arcades were probably supported on simple piers of square section, as was the case at Rievaulx; there the upper parts of the piers towards

13 *Reconstruction sketch of the possible appearance of the earlier church.* David Simon/Historic Scotland

the nave were broadly chamfered, and this could also have been the case at Melrose. There may have been low walls running between the piers in the areas used as the choirs of the monks and lay-brethren, against which their stalls would have been set.

The aisles into which the nave arcades opened were relatively narrow, evidently less than half the width of the central space of the nave. If, as has been suggested for the transept chapels, they also were covered with stone vaulting, it is again likely to have taken the form of a series of transverse pointed barrel vaults rising above arches which divided the aisle into bays. This arrangement may be seen in the nave of Fountains Abbey and is known to have existed at Rievaulx. As has been suggested for the transept chapels, and on analogy with Rievaulx, it is at least a possibility that there was a small gable over each bay of the aisles, though a horizontal wall-head is equally possible. Assuming that the main space of the nave was not vaulted, there is likely to have been an upper level of clearstorey windows above the nave arcades, as at Fountains, and as must have existed at Rievaulx.

Everything that has been suggested here about the early church is, of course, based purely on the excavated plan and on comparisons with what we know of Cistercian houses elsewhere, and it must be stressed that much of what has been said can be no more than speculation. The only element of the early church that is still partly visible above ground is the lower walling of the west front, which must have been one of the last parts to be completed (**14**). It now rises to a maximum height of about 80cm; its survival strongly suggests, incidentally, that the rebuilding of the late medieval nave can never have been completed as far as that. It is rubble-built, with a pair of pilaster buttresses of roughly squared ashlar on its west face, on the line of the nave arcades, and all of the masonry was presumably originally rendered over with a lime coating both internally and externally. It has no plinth course, and the central doorway was without any form of moulding, being simply rebated on the inner side for the hanging of the door. This is architecture of the very plainest kind, in which largely unarticulated and almost completely unadorned wall planes would have been dominant. It is fully consistent with the primary ideals of extreme austerity espoused by the Cistercian order, in which the unelaborated architectural harmonies of their buildings were intended to offer an appropriately unassertive background to their almost silent contemplative lives. However, we do know from more complete early Cistercian churches elsewhere that the resultant buildings could be extraordinarily beautiful in their stripped-down simplicity.

On the basis of what is known of the planning and architectural simplicity of this church, there is every reason to conclude that it must have been started

14 *The surviving fragment of the west front of the earlier church.* Fawcett

around the time of the abbey's foundation in March 1136/7. It is therefore also likely to have been the building that the *Chronicle of Melrose* says was dedicated on 28 July 1146, though that dedication may have marked the completion of no more than sufficient for the presbytery and eastern parts of the nave to be usable by the choir monks. Taking account of the fact that such a large church must have required decades rather than years to complete, support for its having been started around 1136 can also be drawn from comparison with the details of the narthex porch, or Galilee, that was an addition against its west front, and which thus provides a pointer to the date before which the church must have been completed.

The addition of the narthex

From the tiny fragments of this narthex that have survived, which consist of no more than the lowest courses of part of its north-west corner and of a short stretch of the north wall, together with one arcade base, it must have had a width from north to south of about 12.65m, and a projection of about 8.1m from the west front (**15** and **81**). Although a western narthex was a common off-shoot of all but the very earliest Cistercian churches, and provided a place where processions could be formed before entering the church through its west doorway, this example was rather unusual in being narrower than the combined nave and aisles, while being of relatively deep projection. The walls rose from a chamfered plinth course and there was a clasping buttress at the north-western outer angle. Internally, the location of the one surviving base suggests that there would have been four small piers of quatrefoil plan, which presumably supported four arcades of two arches running from east to west, or, perhaps less likely, a transverse arcade of five arches. These piers were insufficiently substantial to have supported stone vaulting and a wooden ceiling or open timber roof is a more likely covering for the space. The surviving base has a water-holding hollow between two rolls, the lower roll being of slightly compressed section with a high fillet around the lip of the hollow, which points to a date in the later years of the twelfth century.

On the evidence we have it must be said that, although the narthex certainly could not be regarded as in any way architecturally extravagant, it does represent a recognisable shift of attitude from the almost total rejection of architectural enrichment that there seems to have been in the early church itself. This is in line with what we can see at other Cistercian churches of the later decades of the twelfth century, as at Dundrennan Abbey, where extremes of simplicity were being superseded by what might be described as a degree of restrained elegance. Partial parallels may perhaps also be observed

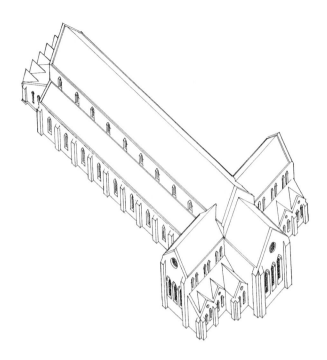

15 *Reconstruction sketch of the possible appearance of the earlier church after the addition of the narthex.* David Simon/Historic Scotland

with the approximately contemporary Lady Chapel added on to the west end of the great Benedictine cathedral priory church of Durham, which is often referred to as a Galilee. That chapel is like Melrose's narthex in being a little narrower than the combined width of the nave and its aisles, in being subdivided by four arcades running from east to west, and in having piers of quatrefoil plan, albeit that pier plan was the result of secondary modifications and the lobes of the quatrefoil are set out on different axes. But the Durham Lady Chapel is much deeper than that at Melrose, having arcades of four bays and, even though it has an imposing doorway in its south wall, it was probably never intended as a major processional entrance. The relatively deep projection of the Melrose narthex, when compared with those at other Cistercian houses, might suggest that it was intended for additional uses, as well as the formation of the monks' processions; one possibility that suggests itself is the worship of the local layfolk.

If we accept a late twelfth-century date for the narthex, and assume that there must have been at least a short pause between the completion of the nave and the addition of the narthex, this provides further support for the conclusion that a building of such a large scale as the church represented by the excavated foundations could not have been started many years later than 1136/7. On this basis it is inherently unlikely that there had been any buildings on the site of the excavated church before its construction was started. However, as already said, since any temporary oratory and domestic accommodation that was provided for the colony of monks brought up from Rievaulx would have had to continue in use while its permanent successor was under construction, they may have been located elsewhere on the site.

The later medieval church (I)

The existing abbey church at Melrose is one of the most delightful buildings to have come down to us from the later Middle Ages (**26**), and for many it is enough simply to enjoy its beauty. But for those who wish to appreciate the reasons why buildings were made to look as they were, to understand the range of sources from which the master masons and patrons drew at least some of their inspiration, and to study the evidence for the stages by which such structures took shape, Melrose is especially rewarding.

What is seen is the result of a protracted building operation which was started soon after an attack in 1385 by the armies of the English King, Richard II, and which eventually ground to an unfinished halt some years before the Reformation of the Scottish Church that took place in the years around 1560. Building works planned and executed to a very high level of quality were therefore in progress for the whole of the period that we think of as the later Middle Ages. Before saying more about what Melrose can tell us about the architecture produced in that period, however, we should remind ourselves that the 175 years in question followed almost two centuries during which lowland Scotland's closest architectural relationships had been with England, from the time of the great revival of the Church in the early twelfth century, to the outbreak of the wars necessitated by Scotland's resistance of England's predatory attentions in the 1290s. There had then followed the best part of a century when circumstances meant that little major church building had been carried out. At the risk of making what can only be a gross over-simplification, it may be said that by 1385 England, the country that had been for many years Scotland's closest partner in architectural creativity, had come to be regarded as the nation's bitterest enemy. It is fascinating to investigate the impact this change had on architecture of all kinds. At Melrose, which was one of the first major church buildings to be started as renewed architectural activity became possible, it can be seen, perhaps more clearly than anywhere else, how those responsible for erecting a great church responded to what was at that stage an unprecedented situation.

In the course of the first phases of rebuilding, when the basic plan and the scale of the new church were established, it seems that it must have been English masons who were in charge of the operation, and a great deal was accomplished at that time. But not many years after work had been started, it is known from inscriptions in the south transept that there was a mason from France at work (**50** and **51**), and his contribution can be detected in a number of details. France, however, was not to be the only continental neighbour to provide fresh infusions of ideas, because the proceedings of a court hearing showed that Melrose's choir stalls had been ordered from the Low Countries, which were by then Scotland's chief trading partner.

It is only after those earlier phases of work that the emergence of an essentially new approach to design can be observed, albeit at a time when there are indicators that the project was running into financial difficulties. In this new approach a synthesis of elements drawn from a wide range of sources is found, which possibly reflected among much else some of the architectural solutions that had earlier been current within Scotland itself, and that may have been regarded in some way as representing the nation's earlier achievements. What is seen in these middle and later stages of work is the development of an architectural vocabulary and syntax that, while drawing on a variety of sources, is arguably more completely distinctive to Scotland than that of any other period of our history. While this same approach is to be seen at many other buildings, at few others is the quality of work so consistently high, and nowhere else is the process by which this synthesis was achieved quite so well illustrated.

Another of the fascinations of Melrose is that, if relatively minor modifications in the detailing are considered together, it is possible to reach some understanding of the sequence of phases through which the construction process progressed. It is clear that in the earlier phases, at least, which were focused around the most sacred area of the setting of the high altar, many of these modifications took place in rapid succession. They do not necessarily point to changes of designing masons, so much as decisions to introduce minor items of fine tuning. In the later phases, however, there must certainly have been changes of master masons, and it is possible to understand something of how these new masons set about introducing their own ideas while trying to ensure that there was no disruption of the overall appearance of architectural homogeneity. For those who wish to have a closer understanding of the building, all of these modifications are very rewarding to investigate, and by describing one way in which this evidence can be analysed, it is hoped that others might be encouraged to look at it more closely.

One thing that does appear to emerge from the evidence is that the masons were probably not presented with an unencumbered site at the start of the operation. It has generally been assumed that it was the extent of structural devastation caused by the attack of 1385 that necessitated rebuilding and that is indeed likely to have been the case. But what the evidence suggests is that the first generation of masons after 1385 had to raise their new church around an existing building which had retained virtually the whole of its footprint, however much damage there may have been within the limits of that footprint. If this interpretation of the evidence is correct, the earlier church was probably only demolished section by section, as work on its replacement progressed. It is therefore likely that the twelfth-century church had not been left totally ruinous in 1385, and that substantial portions of it remained in use through successive partial demolitions. Beyond that, the survival of fragments of the west wall and narthex of the original church suggest that at least part of the original church never was fully demolished, with the further implication that the west end of the old nave may have been retained in use up to, and perhaps even beyond, the Reformation. Indeed, it is possible that it was those parts which continued to serve as the parish church of the local community until, in the early seventeenth century, a new church was formed within what had been the monastic choir of the later medieval church.

It may seem illogical to suggest that such trouble should be taken to retain parts of a building that was to be replaced, until demolition became unavoidable in the face of advancing reconstruction. But it is likely that this was a very common process. Religious communities could permit no break in their offerings of prayer and worship, and for this usable buildings were essential. Something of how this might be dealt with can be understood from Gervase of Canterbury's account of the rebuilding of his beloved cathedral after the choir there was burned out in 1185, and at Canterbury as much as possible of the old building was retained in the structure that replaced it. But one of the most striking illustrations of what might be entailed in the process of progressive rebuilding is to be seen at Beauvais Cathedral in France, where parts of the tenth- and eleventh-century nave still survive because the rebuilding that was commenced at the east end in about 1225 came to a stop in the 1550s and was never restarted (16). Melrose in the 1550s may have presented a similar picture, with the twelfth-century western bays extending back from the unfinished new church that had been started in the last years of the fourteenth century. On a smaller scale, a comparable process may have taken place at a number of collegiate churches, including those of Biggar, Crichton and Seton, where rebuilding

16 *Beauvais Cathedral, showing the relationship between the partly demolished earlier church and the unfinished later church.* Fawcett

probably never progressed beyond splendid new choirs and transeptal chapels, leaving the old churches continuing to serve as naves for the congregations of layfolk.

The dating evidence for the later church
To understand a building as fully as possible, it is important to take account of many types of evidence. In the next chapter attention will be concentrated

on the architectural evidence. But it is also essential to be aware of any indicators for the dating of the work, and the most important of these will now be briefly summarised.

1 The turning point in the history of the abbey church was the destruction inflicted by Richard II who, after staying within the abbey walls, on or about 10 August 1385, ordered its destruction, possibly on the pretext of the abbey's being excommunicate because of Scotland's support for the Anti-pope, Clement VII.

2 In restitution, in 1389 Richard II granted a reduction in customs on wool sent by the abbey to Berwick-on-Tweed, suggesting that reconstruction was either then planned or in progress. However, the English King's patronage was to be of only short duration.

3 A more specific reference which shows that rebuilding was by then in progress is found in 1398, when payments were made towards the 'new werke' of the 'kirke of Melrose'.

4 In the south transept is an inscription relating to the activities of a Paris-born mason named as John Morow (or Morvo), which lists Melrose among the buildings at which he had carried out work (**50** and **51**). These others included St Andrews, Glasgow, Paisley, Lincluden (Nyddysdayll) and Whithorn (Galway). Since he must have already started work at those other churches to be able to include them on his list at Melrose, their likely dating provides some clues to the period by which he had become involved at Melrose. At St Andrews Cathedral there was major rebuilding after a fire in 1378, with operations continuing well into the fifteenth century; at Paisley Abbey some work appears to have been in progress in around 1389, followed by a hiatus in activity under the abbacy of Thomas Morow (1418-44); at Glasgow Cathedral construction of one of the western towers may have been in progress under John Cameron, who became bishop in 1426 after having been previously provost of Lincluden Collegiate Church; at Lincluden itself work may have started as early as 1389, but was said to be still unfinished in 1406, and construction almost certainly continued for many years afterwards on the evidence of heraldry; at Whithorn Cathedral in 1424 the same patrons who were involved at Lincluden, the fourth earl of Douglas and his countess, were endowing a chapel. Accepting that Morow may have

been working on several projects simultaneously, all of this suggests a date for his work at Melrose no earlier than the last decades of the fourteenth century, but more probably into the first quarter of the fifteenth century.

5   In 1422 Abbot David de Bennyn was said, in a letter from the Pope, to have rebuilt the abbey after it had been burnt by the English. However, the architectural evidence shows that this claim was greatly over-stated, and that much remained to be done after his abbacy.

6   In 1441 the abbey had to go to law over choir stalls that had been ordered some years earlier from the Bruges carpenter, Cornelius Aeltre. This indicates that work on the monastic choir in the eastern bays of the nave had been sufficiently advanced some years before 1441 for it to be thought appropriate to order the stalls.

7   The arms of Abbot Andrew Hunter (1444-65) were carved at a number of points, demonstrating that those parts were completed during his abbacy (**17**). His arms are still to be seen on the high vault of the south transept and on the buttress between the fifth and sixth chapels from the east along the south side of the nave. It is also said that his arms used to be on the intermediate buttress between the two ranks of flyers above the wall separating the first and second chapels on the south side of the nave. Despite this evidence of building activity, it was during Hunter's time as abbot, in 1450, that the abbey began to plead a level of poverty that made it difficult for it to maintain itself properly, as a result of the impact of the wars and the consequent reduction in rents. Such claims were usually greatly exaggerated in the hope of gaining as much practical sympathy as possible, though it must be assumed there was at least an underlying basis of truth.

8   James IV made gifts of drinksilver to masons in 1502 and 1504; this confirms that building was then in progress, even if it provides no evidence on which parts.

9   The piscina in the sixth chapel on the south side of the nave has the initials VT, which it has been suggested could refer to Abbot William Turnbull (1503-7).

17 *The arms of Abbot Hunter on one of the buttress tabernacles of the south nave chapels.*
Historic Scotland

10   The buttress between the eighth and ninth chapels on the south side of the nave has a plaque with the royal arms, the initials IQ (for Jacobus Quartus) and the date 1505.

11   In 1544, the abbey was burnt by English forces under Sir Ralph Eure.

12   In 1545, there was a further, probably more devastating attack by the English forces of the Earl of Hertford.

13   In 1555-6 the commendator, James Stewart, was said to be feuing lands to raise funds towards repairs and rebuilding, though he was then to be accused of misappropriating those funds.

The later medieval church (II)

In this section the architectural evidence, including the moulded details of the stonework (**18** to **22**), will be considered more closely in an attempt to come to terms with the likely sequence by which the constituent parts of the later medieval church were built. Some of the possible sources of the ideas which conditioned the design will also be briefly touched upon so that a picture can be built up of the wider architectural climate within which the abbey church was created.

In order to set out the information in a way that can be more easily understood, the building operation has been divided into eight main phases on the basis of changes of detailing that were introduced. At the start of each of the sections relating to these phases, a simplified sketch is given to illustrate the likely appearance of the building by the end of that stage. But it must be stressed that such phasing is by its nature an artificial construct, and it would be possible to offer fewer or more phases with almost equal justification. In the earlier decades of construction in particular, it is unlikely there was any great gap of time between several of the phases, and some of the phases may

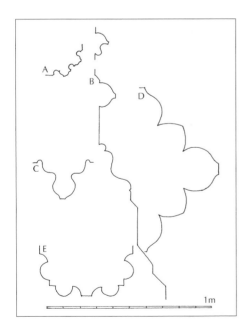

18 Left *Moulding sections: (A) presbytery tomb recess; (B) base course; (C) wall shafts; (D) responds of arches into nave chapels; (E) cloister wall arcading respond.* Fawcett

19 Right *Moulding sections: (A) presbytery arcade pier; (B) presbytery arcade arch.* Fawcett

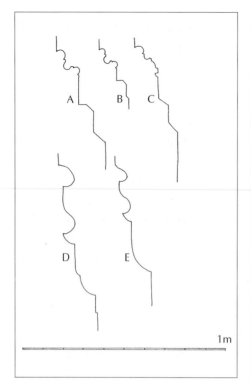

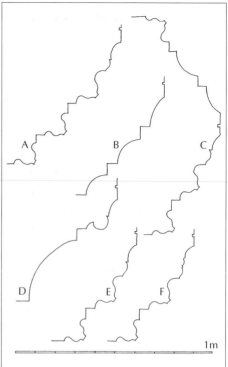

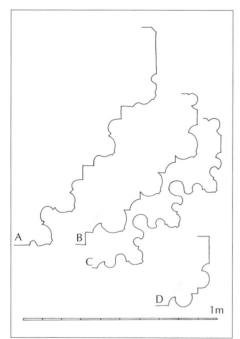

20 Above left *Moulding sections of bases:*
(A) presbytery arcade responds; (B) wall shafts
at junction of presbytery and transept chapel
walls; (C) presbytery arcade pier; (D) arches
into earlier south nave chapels; (E) arches into
later south nave chapels. Fawcett

21 Above right *Mouldings of window reveals:*
(A) south side of presbytery; (B) north transept
chapels; (C) south presbytery and transept
chapels; (D) first and second south nave
chapels; (E) later south nave chapels;
(F) fifth south nave chapel. Fawcett

22 Left *Mouldings of doorways: (A) south*
transept doorway; (B) jambs of north-east nave
doorway; (C) arch of north-east nave doorway;
(D) sacristy doorway. Fawcett

have been the work of the same master masons. By contrast, in the later years, when the pace of the work was faltering, there was possibly less continuity between the phases.

Phase 1. *The footings and lower walls around the presbytery, the presbytery chapels, and parts of the east walls of the transept chapels are built* (**23**).

There is little doubt that a leading aim of both the master masons and the religious community throughout the whole time that the new abbey church at Melrose was under construction was the maintenance of a sense of architectural homogeneity. This means that, even though we shall see there were to be many changes of detail in the course of the work, great efforts were made to ensure that these did not disturb the overall unity of form. It is perhaps in the base courses that we see this first (**18b** and **26**). Running around the building at the point where it rises clear of the ground, this had to be the first part of each wall to be built, and in work of high quality the proportions and detailing of this feature were an important contributor to the

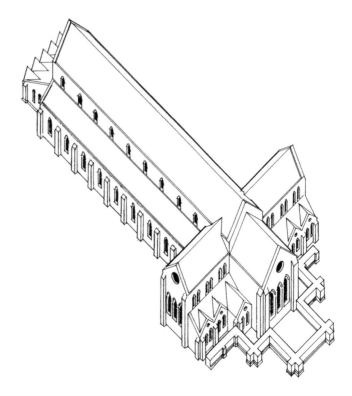

23 *Reconstruction sketch of the later church at the first phase.* David Simon/Historic Scotland

appearance of the structure being well founded and of having all of the forces that were running through the building kept in balance with each other. In many cases the base course can also be of great value in helping us to understand if a building was the result of a number of distinct campaigns of construction, since we often find that there are different base courses under each part when their construction was separated by any significant gap of time.

But at Melrose the same base course was employed throughout the whole late medieval campaign. Although now partly covered in places by raised ground levels, where it is still fully visible it can be seen to have had three levels of chamfered-back lower stages topped off by an ogee curve and a roll, and with a filleted roll and a small upper chamfer forming the uppermost string-course-like element. What we know of the building sequence indicates that this cannot have been laid out around the whole building in a single operation, and in the case of the outer chapel aisles it is likely that it had to be moved outwards from the original south wall of the aisle to its later location. Nevertheless, it was clearly considered essential that there should be no break in its continuity, except where it was pierced by the south transept doorway, and it runs around all of those faces of the church that were externally visible and brought to completion.

We therefore have to look to other details to understand how much was built in the first phase and both externally and internally one of the first clues to be considered is the predominant colour of the finely grained sandstone of which the walls were constructed. Except for the chapel on the north side of the presbytery, the walls of which were destroyed after the Reformation but which were partly rebuilt as rubble cores in the early twentieth century, the first phase of work was chiefly constructed of precisely cut buff or yellow sandstone. This type of stone extends around the presbytery, the south presbytery chapel, the middle chapel on the east side of each transept and the lower east wall of the outer south transept chapel, after which there is a change to red sandstone.

Internally, one clue to the extent of the first phase of work is the way in which the earliest parts of the eastern responds that were provided for the future presbytery arcades, and also the lesser responds at the junction of the presbytery and transept chapels, differ from what was built in the later phases. In constructing the eastern arcade responds, the basic design of the arcade piers themselves must have been already worked out, since those responds are essentially half of the main part of the piers. They have large rounded shafts in the cardinal directions and smaller keeled (pointed) shafts in the diagonal directions (25). In this it is possible that we find some continuing loyalty to earlier Cistercian approaches to design, because piers composed of bundles of shafts like this had been very common in the order's churches from the later decades of the twelfth century. We shall have to consider this further when looking at the piers themselves, however. The responds at the angles of the presbytery and transept chapels performed a lesser function than the arcade responds. Set at right angles to each other on the faces of the wall towards the two chapels, there are two triplets made up of a combination of a central filleted shaft (a fillet is a raised strip) flanked by two half-shafts (**18c**). In addition, the angle of wall between the two triplets is cut into so as to create a sunk keeled shaft. But what is important for our understanding of the building sequence is that the bases of these two sets of responds, while certainly differing from each other, are even more different from the bases that were to be designed for elsewhere in the building (**20a** and **b**). They are of a type known as 'water-holding', which is most commonly found in the late twelfth and thirteenth centuries, in which there is a deep hollow between two widely projecting rolls. An earlier example of this type of base in the narthex of the earlier church has already been discussed. As with the form of the arcade responds, it might be argued that the designers were showing reverence for earlier and possibly Cistercian types in the design of the bases. However, there are in fact a number of other buildings around this period in which we find bases of related type, one of which, the choir of St Giles' church in Edinburgh, was also being reconstructed after the English onslaught of 1385. The choice of this type of base was perhaps therefore simply a reflection of current fashions.

The fact that these first bases are different from those that came later is additionally significant when we look at a further pointer to the extent of the work carried out in the very first phase. It seems that there was a particularly telling change of design after only a few of the lowest courses of the presbytery and flanking presbytery and transept chapels had been built, and thus only a short time after these respond bases had been set in place. This change, which will be discussed more fully in the next section, involved a decision to add wall shafts to rise up across the wall faces or in the angles where the walls meet in order to provide visual support for the vaulting. Remarkably, these shafts simply start at the point where the decision was taken to add them, apparently with no attempt to insert the missing lower sections (**25**). However, at the western end of the aisle-less section of the presbytery, the slight hollows on each side of the shafts can be seen to have been extended downwards, so it is possible that some effort may have been made to ease the transition between the plain wall of the lower level and the shafts above them.

The easternmost parts of the new church were almost entirely outside the footprint of the earlier church and could be built with relatively little interference with that church, other than some paring back of the external angles of the presbytery chapels (**11**). This supports the idea that there was a strong wish to retain as much as possible of that earlier church for as long as could be achieved; it also suggests that, as might be expected, it was the liturgically most important parts of the new church that were being first laid out. But one of the implications of starting with the part that required the most complex elements of the ground plan was that the basic layout of the new church had to be established from the beginning. In this case there seems little doubt that a decision was taken to reflect the modified echelon 'Bernardine' plan of the original church in the new building; this is to be seen in its rectangular presbytery, in the stepped-forward chapels immediately flanking the presbytery, and in the two further chapels on the east side of each transept.

There had always been strong loyalty to such plans in Scotland, and even the final foundation for the Cistercian order at Sweetheart, in about 1270, adopted it at a time when elsewhere in Europe it was generally being replaced by plan types which allowed space for greater numbers of altars. Nevertheless, although the basic outline of the earlier church at Melrose was to be reflected in its successor, the internal treatment of spaces was to be very different. Instead of the solid walls that there would have been between the presbytery and flanking chapels in the earlier church, in the later church there were to be two bays of arcades opening into the flanking chapels to the west of the aisle-less eastern section of the presbytery. In this there was perhaps a marriage of the 'Bernardine' plan with another plan type that had been found in Scotland as early as around 1138, in the eastern parts of Jedburgh Abbey. This type, which was later to be employed at varying scales at such as St Andrews Cathedral after 1160 and Elgin Cathedral after 1270, might have an aisled section of anything from two to five bays long, terminating in a shorter aisle-less eastern section.

Phase 2. *The aisle-less part of the presbytery is built up to full height* (**24**).

It is doubtful if there was any pause between the first and second building phases, and the distinction has simply been made here because of the modifications in design which were introduced after the lowest courses of the presbytery and flanking chapels had been built. The great achievement of this second phase was the construction of the walls of the easternmost aisle-less part of the presbytery; there may also have been some further work on the presbytery chapels, though this is less certain. Of the modifications introduced in this phase, the decision to add wall shafts that has already been

24 *Reconstruction sketch of the church at the second phase.* David Simon/Historic Scotland

mentioned is the most obvious, since this was to have implications for the way the vaulting was to relate to the walls. In the eastern corners of the presbytery these wall shafts take the form of single keeled shafts, while at the west end of the aisle-less section, next to the arcade responds, they are triplets of shafts, and as already said, they simply start at an arbitrary point, with no provision for support by bases or corbels (**25**). In other respects, it is at this stage of the building operation that it becomes particularly clear how every effort was being made to ensure that the architecture was of the finest quality, and there is a particularly carefully handled balance between the expanses of the superbly squared ashlar of the walling and those elements that are more lavishly decorated (**26**).

The principal features of this part of the presbytery are three vast windows. Those in the north and south flanks rise through the equivalent height of the two storeys that were soon to be built in the aisled parts of the building, while that in the east wall is even taller, rising into the gable and thus making clear that there was always the intention that the vault over the presbytery should be of fully arched profile. The reveals (window arch mouldings) of all these windows are of three orders both internally and externally; beyond the usual absorbed half-mullion for the glazing, each order has a filleted roll running

25 *Lower walls of the south side of the presbytery and the south presbytery chapel, showing how the wall shafts start at a point well above ground level.* Fawcett

continuously around jambs and arch (**21a**). While tracery was probably inserted in the east and south windows virtually immediately, that in the north window is of a very different type (**27g** and **57**), and it is a possibility that it was left open to allow access into the new presbytery at a time when the retention of the eastern parts of the early church would have made access difficult otherwise. It is even possible that the arch and hood-moulding of this north window were only completed at a later stage. This is because, while the east and south window hood-mouldings have similar corbels, in the form of carefully detailed human busts which are relatively unusual in portraying both head and shoulders, the north window hood-moulding is without corbels. Further discussion of this window will be postponed to the section dealing with phase six.

The tracery of the east and south windows is strongly rectilinear in character (**27a** and **c**). Scotland has very few examples of tracery of this grid-like and most characteristically English late-medieval type of tracery, the principal other examples being at Corstorphine and Carnwath churches, which may date from around 1405 and 1424 respectively, and which are likely to be significantly later than the first of the examples at Melrose. The preponderance of such tracery throughout the earlier phases of work at Melrose provides the clearest demonstration of the strength of English influence over this part of the work, suggesting that it was an English master mason who was responsible for the design. The four-light south window, with its pair of sub-arches and concentrations of small vertical lights, is of a relatively common type in England, and it would be difficult to suggest where the masons who designed it may have come from. But the five-light east window is altogether more individual in

26 *The presbytery from the south-east.* Historic Scotland

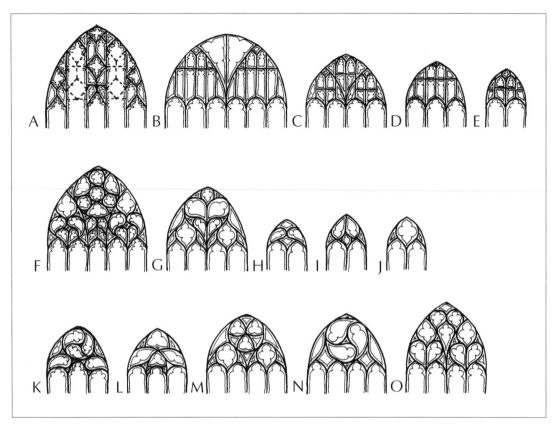

27 *Diagrammatic sketches of the principal window tracery types:* (A) *east face of presbytery;* (B) *north presbytery clearstorey;* (C) *south flank of presbytery;* (D) *transept clearstoreys;* (E) *south presbytery chapel and transept chapels;* (F) *south wall of south transept;* (G) *north flank of presbytery;* (H) *north transept chapels;* (I) *south face of outer south transept chapel;* (J) *north nave aisle;* (K) *west face of south transept;* (L) *first south nave chapel;* (M) *second south nave chapel;* (N) *third, fourth, sixth and seventh south nave chapels;* (O) *fifth south nave chapel.* Fawcett

character, and might be most appositely described as 'prismatic' in its extreme angularity. The four mullions rise vertically unbroken to the arch, while the heads of three of the five lights are triangular and the heads of the other two appear to have taken the form of short horizontal transoms. But the most striking feature of the window was a series of diamond shapes decorated with cusped cusping interspersed through the tracery field. Tracery of such extreme angularity has its closest affinities in the eastern counties of England. At St Nicholas in King's Lynn (Norfolk) there is tracery of even greater angularity in the church that had been rebuilt by 1419, though there are rather closer parallels in a window of around 1400 that was retained in the west front of Beverley St Mary (Yorkshire) when it was rebuilt in around 1520.

Eastern English parallels are also to be seen in the design of the east front as a whole (**26**). The two corners are framed by pairs of buttresses set at right angles to each other, which extend upwards through three principal stages. The middle stage of each, which rises above an intake weathered back in three chamfers, with a grotesque figure at the centre of the bottom chamfer, has a sunken tabernacle (image niche) with a crouching figure corbel and a handsomely-detailed polygonal canopy that terminates with a flat band of miniature crenellation or foliate cresting. The upper stage of the buttresses, and also the pinnacle which rises through the junction of the pairs of buttresses, have shallow blind tracery across their faces. The greatest enrichment is to the gable above the east window, which is decorated with a series of shallow tabernacles with triangular cusped heads, the outermost on each side being deeper and having a nodding canopy head. Running across the upper part of the gable is an ogee super-arch that was originally capped by a finial. The moulded cornice of the gable is decorated with square-flower caving, and above this there was an open parapet silhouetted against the skyline which had circular quatrefoils set within steps. The tabernacles of the gable housed a series of images, of which one saint and four worshipping angels survive below a pair of finely carved figures set beneath a central canopy within the super-arch (**28**). The iconography of this pair of figures is uncertain. They are both crowned, and it is one possibility that the scene represents the coronation of the Virgin following her Assumption into heaven, and in view of the dedication of the abbey church to the Virgin this would certainly be an obvious theme to represent at this point. Against this, the costume of both figures looks rather masculine, and it is therefore an alternative possibility that it represents two of the persons of the Trinity, the older bearded figure being the Father and the younger beardless figure the Son; in that case there may originally have been a dove above them to represent the Holy Spirit. But there can be no certainty about either identification and, as an argument against the figures representing the Trinity, it would be rather unusual at this date for Christ to be portrayed as beardless.

The design of this gable, with its enriched buttresses and its lavishly detailed tabernacled gable, has parallels with an eastern English approach to design that had first emerged some decades earlier, and that is now best illustrated by the east gable of Howden Collegiate Church (Yorkshire) as started in the 1320s. Parallels for the tabernacles of the gable could also be drawn with the east gable of the Lady Chapel at Ely Cathedral, which was probably completed in around the 1350s. If we look for other comparisons, the flat-headed polygonal tabernacle canopies of the buttresses, with gablets framing an arch to each face, bear similarities with some of the internal tabernacles

28 *Statuary at the apex of the east gable, possibly representing either two persons of the Trinity or the Coronation of the Virgin.* Historic Scotland

flanking the east window of York Minster built before 1373, or with the canopies above the gallery of kings along the west front of Lincoln Cathedral of the later fourteenth century. There might also be some analogies between the slightly metallic flattened treatment of the drapery which clothes the figures in the eastern gable at Melrose and that of the kings at Lincoln, though this is not a comparison that that should be pressed too far.

In drawing these parallels there is no intention of suggesting that the designer of the first parts of Melrose had necessarily received his training, or had even worked, at any one of those buildings. Nevertheless, considered together the weight of evidence does seem to indicate that what we see at Melrose is best understood within the context of an approach to the design of large-scale buildings that had begun to take form from perhaps no later than the early 1320s in the area of eastern England that runs from the eastern parts of Yorkshire down through Lincolnshire and Cambridgeshire and into the eastern parts of Norfolk. If we have to be more specific, the closest links are perhaps those with eastern Yorkshire, and we shall see that further links will be found with that area when looking at some of the details in subsequent phases of work. On balance, therefore, an origin in eastern Yorkshire might be most convincingly argued for the master mason responsible for designing these first phases of work. In saying this, it might be remembered that the master mason of the earlier church had probably come from the abbey's mother-house at Rievaulx in North Yorkshire. However, under the circumstances, it is unlikely that the origins of these two masons in Yorkshire was anything more than coincidental, since the detail of the later work appears to owe little to specifically Cistercian prototypes elsewhere.

Internally the main features surviving from this phase of work are liturgical furnishings, which will be discussed in a later section (see p.164) (**73**). But a pair of details that must be mentioned here, since they were probably carved and installed in this phase of works, are the capitals of the responds to the presbytery arcades. As will be seen, changes in cap types are a particularly useful pointer to the phasing of the work. These respond caps have sprigs of foliage in one or two tiers below a deep abacus, and are very different from the caps that were to be used in the next phase (**30**). The closest parallels are in fact with a cap and respond in the south transept arcade, and it may be that those transept caps were originally cut for the aisled section of the presbytery, but set aside when a slightly modified design for the piers was adopted.

Phase 3. *The east end of the earlier church is largely demolished; the shell of the presbytery chapels is built up to full height, along with the two bays of the presbytery arcade and clearstorey; work is continued in the south transept and the eastern parts of the north transept; the first bay of the arcade towards the transept on each side is built, together with the lower parts of the other transept arcade piers* (**29**).

There was little further new building that could be set in hand without demolition of what remained of the presbytery, transepts and eastern parts of the nave of the earlier church, and this is probably what was done next. Once these were out of the way the evidence suggests that construction of the aisled two western bays of the new presbytery and of the two chapels that immediately flanked them on each side was rapidly pressed ahead. Work then appears to have extended into laying out the lower walls of the outer chapel of the north transept, and of sections of the north and south transept lower walls up to a building break east of the sacristy doorway in the former, and an intake east of the south transept doorway. (The reason for the intake is uncertain, though it may have stemmed from inaccuracies in the initial setting out of the wall.) The bases and lower courses of all the piers and responds in the two transept arcades may have been laid out at an early stage of this phase, though it was only the innermost pier in each transept that was then completed in order to carry the arches opening into the presbytery

29 *Reconstruction sketch of the later church at the third phase.* David Simon/Historic Scotland

chapels. In the outer chapel of the north transept and the south face of the south transept we see a change of masonry colour from predominantly yellow to pink.

The design of the two aisled bays of the presbytery was to be of enormous importance for the rest of the building operation since, whatever scope there might be for further changes of detailing, much of the basic internal disposition of the church as a whole had to be fixed at this stage. Only one side of one bay survives, but it can be assumed that the rest of the presbytery followed the same design (**30**). As was becoming increasingly common in major late medieval churches, the decision was taken to have a two-storeyed elevation, with an arcade opening into the flanking chapels or aisles at the lower level, and an upper tier of clearstorey windows directing light into the central space. It should be said here that there was a later revival of three-storeyed designs in Scotland, in which there was a dark gallery stage at mid-height corresponding to the sloping aisle roof, and the nave of Dunkeld Cathedral, as started in 1406, was perhaps the first of these. However, within Europe as a whole two-storeyed elevations had become more common, and at Melrose the attractions of two storeys may have been increased by the likelihood that the earlier church had only had two

The internal elevations were carefully articulated into bays by wall shafts running up the full height of the piers and walls, while the storeys were horizontally divided from each other by a string course set between the apices of the arcade and the sills of the clearstorey. The arcade storey rose through considerably more than half the height of the interior, while the clearstorey extended up into the wall arch of the vaulting. Slightly unexpectedly, and presumably because of the relationship between the arcade respond and the walls shafts as set out in the second phase of works, the clearstorey is not strictly vertically aligned with the arcade arch in the surviving bay. At clearstorey level there is a passage within the wall thickness which stopped on the east side of the surviving bay, and the window is set behind this passage on the outer plane of the wall. An apparent wish to avoid having expanses of blank internal walling corresponding to the area where the roof over the aisle or chapel abutted the outer face of the wall, led to the floor of the wall passage being set well below the sill level of the window. This meant that the blank wall corresponding to the roof was set largely out of site at the back of the passage and it was further masked by a traceried balustrade of square quatrefoils running along the inner side of the passage. Rather more unusually, a skeletal matrix of a mullion and two sub-arches, corresponding to the main divisions of the window, was constructed within the arch on the inner skin of the wall.

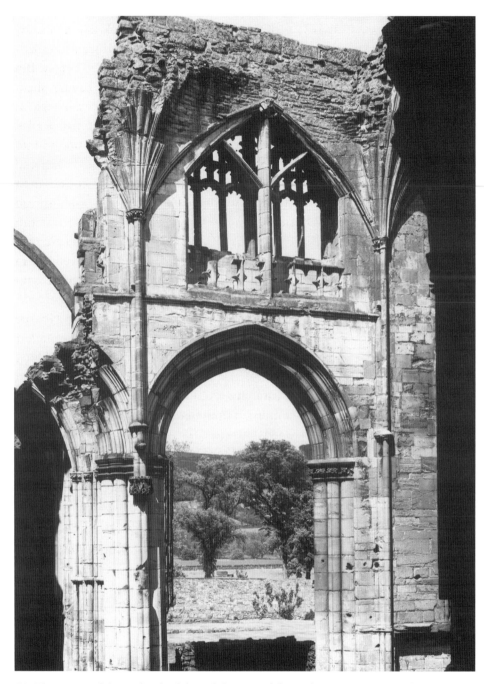

30 *The interior of the north side of the aisled section of the presbytery.* Historic Scotland

If we now look at the details of this design a little more closely, as already said, the basic form of the octofoil clustered-shaft piers had been foreshadowed in the responds built along with the aisle-less part of the presbytery. But the presbytery piers themselves are further complicated by having shafts towards the central space which extend upwards across the wall face to support the vaulting (**19a**), and they also have corbels and flat-headed canopies for statues. Piers of this basic octofoil type had been imported into Cistercian churches in England from eastern France around the 1150s, and were probably first used in Scotland, in a non-Cistercian context, at St Andrews Cathedral in the 1160s; afterwards they continued in wide-spread use throughout the later twelfth and early thirteenth centuries, in both Cistercian and non-Cistercian churches. It should be mentioned here that variants on this pier type were later to enjoy a wide-spread renewed use in Scotland in the fifteenth and sixteenth centuries, and it may have been from Melrose that the idea was taken.

However, we must ask where the idea came from for these piers at Melrose itself. As with the plan, one factor could have been a wish to respect earlier Cistercian traditions. As we have seen in the first phases of the rebuilding, however, there is much to support the idea that the mason who had designed the new presbytery of Melrose had come from northern England. Since that is the case, it should be said that piers composed of bundles of shafts had once more come into fashion in northern England from the early fourteenth century, as is to be seen in the rebuilt parts of the chancel of Carlisle Cathedral. Perhaps more importantly, a modified version of them is also to be found in the eastern bays which served as a Lady Chapel at York Minster, and which were started around the 1360s. These latter piers have an added significance for Melrose, since they incorporate wall shafts which run up the full height of the interior from the base of the piers to the vault springing, and they also have corbels and canopies for images. That is certainly not to suggest that the York piers explain everything that we see in the Melrose piers; the way in which the individual shafts of the York piers are separated by deeply rounded hollows is particularly unlike what is seen at Melrose. Nevertheless, they may help us to understand something of the likely background of the designer of the presbytery.

The detailing of the shafts which run up the piers and wall at Melrose is particularly intriguing. They rise as paired shafts from the sub-base of the arcade piers, without any base of their own, and above the canopy head they pass unbroken past the capital, after which they are brought forward and acquire an additional corbelled-out filleted shaft in order to become a triplet. Nothing quite like this arrangement has survived elsewhere in Scotland,

31 *The capital type introduced in the presbytery.* Historic Scotland

though it would be good to know more about some of the piers in the nave of St Andrews Cathedral as rebuilt after the fire of 1378, since the surviving bases there show that they were elongated towards the central space as if intended to incorporate additional shafts. It should be noted here that the one surviving presbytery pier at Melrose introduces a new type of base that was to be used with relatively little change throughout the rest of the building (**20c**). Above a square socle and a two-stage chamfered sub-base, the main element of the individual bases has an ogee-curved profile below a hollow and a roll.

However, if the arcade bases remained more or less constant from this point onwards, there was still considerable scope for changes in the design of the capitals. In the one surviving presbytery arcade pier the cap is very different from those of the arcade responds in having two rather plastically carved bands of horizontal mouldings below a deep abacus, with small square flower and pellet carving in the hollows between the mouldings (**31**). The only other examples of this type of cap were to be in the two piers of the transept arcades immediately adjacent to the sites of the east crossing piers, further demonstrating that work was progressing on the chapels flanking the presbytery at the same time as work on the presbytery itself. However, as spaces of lesser liturgical importance than the presbytery, the transept piers were not to have corbels and canopies for images, and there is a slightly simpler two-stage transition from double to triple shafts above the level of the capitals (**43**).

As was the case with the bases, although not with the capitals, the form of the arcade arch type in the presbytery was to be repeated through the rest of the church with only minor changes. On the axis of the arch is a heavy filleted roll flanked by smaller rolls and angled fillets, and there are two further orders behind with smaller filleted rolls as their main feature (**19b**).

The presbytery clearstorey has a six-light window subdivided by sub-arches into two three-light groupings, the heads of which are filled with rectilinear tracery of standard patterns (**32 and 27b**). This window is virtually round-arched, and is a very early example of the revived use of such arches, with other examples being found a little later in the building campaign. By contrast, the internal clearstorey arch is almost triangular (**30**). As with the design of the piers, the internal treatment of this bay of the clearstorey further supports the idea of a Yorkshire origin for its mason, in the way that a balustraded parapet has been constructed along the sill of the inner arch. This was a feature that had earlier been introduced in the choirs of Selby Abbey and Howden Collegiate Church, both of which had been designed around the turn of the first and second quarters of the fourteenth century. Yet neither of those offers a precedent for the skeletal inner tracery. It may be that in designing this inner screen the master mason was looking back to later thirteenth-century experiments with double-skin tracery construction, as in the clearstorey of the Angel Choir of Lincoln Cathedral, or the north window of the eastern transept of Durham Cathedral. But it cannot be ruled out that the Lady Chapel at York Minster was again of some influence, since that also had a double-skin construction at clearstorey level, although there the window was on the inner skin, with the more skeletal traceried treatment on the exterior.

The likelihood that, whatever minor changes of detail there were, the same designer was responsible for both the aisle-less section and the aisled section of the presbytery is indicated by the use of similar 'portrait bust' corbels to the window hood-mouldings in both parts. That same type of hood-moulding corbel is also used for the windows of the salient sections of the two presbytery chapels (though only one reveal of the north chapel east window survives), showing that they were built as part of a continuing campaign. Further support for this continuity is shown in the design of the

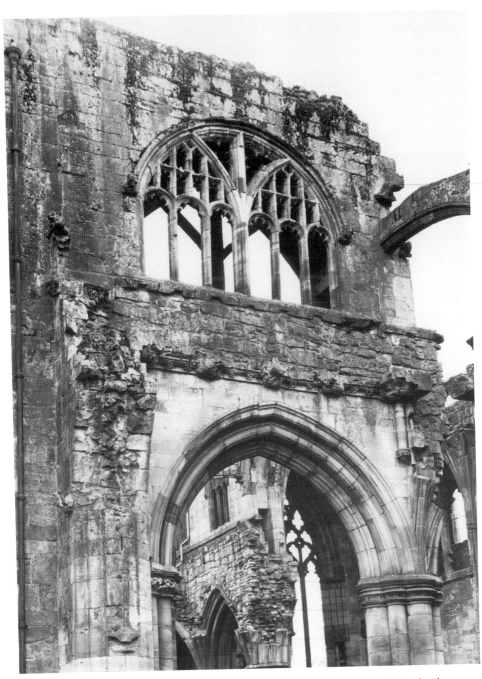

32 *The exterior of the north side of the aisled section of the presbytery.* Historic Scotland

tracery of the windows in the east and south faces of the south presbytery chapel, which is essentially a two-light reduction of the six-light north presbytery clearstorey window, albeit with a horizontal transom struck through the vertical tracery lights at mid-height, as had already been provided in the earlier windows of any great size (**27e**).

But there were to be some differences of detailing between the various parts as seen, for example, in the treatment of the buttress tabernacles. At the angles of the south presbytery chapel, while the tabernacles themselves were sunk into the body of the buttresses, they were capped by tall spirelets rather than by the flat-headed canopy heads of the eastern part of the presbytery (**26**). In referring to the presbytery chapel buttresses it may be mentioned that it was here that flyers to counter the thrusts of the high vaults first had to be constructed, and these were subsequently to be constructed throughout the aisled parts of the building. Other changes were introduced in the window arches, and there must be a suspicion that the stones of these arches were sometimes cut in advance of requirements and held in store until they were installed. The reason for suggesting this is that, while a reduced variant on the type of arch used in the presbytery is to be found in both the south presbytery chapel and in the windows of the two other chapels off the south transept, it was to be inserted into the walls in different ways (**21c**). In this arch type there are two orders of filleted rolls beyond the half mullion on one side, and broad hollow chamfers with a single filleted roll on the other. But there may have been some doubt about how they were to be installed, since the east window of the presbytery chapel has the hollow chamfers to the outside, whereas in the other windows they were on the inside. This smacks of confusion!

Work on the lower parts of the south transept middle chapel, and to a lesser extent of the outer chapel, is likely to have been in progress along with the presbytery chapel, and certainly the middle chapel has window tracery of the same type as the presbytery chapel, even if it may not have been installed until slightly later. At the same time, on the north side, the shell of the presbytery chapel may have been completed, together with the lower part of the middle transept chapel (**42**). For these a simpler window arch moulding was chosen, with hollow chamfers both internally and externally (**21b**). In these chapels, various methods of incorporating wall shafts into the design can be seen. Between the two transept chapels, where the lower walls had been at least partly built in the first phase, the wall shafts were simply made to start above the string course that ran below the windows (which was itself later cut back). But in the outer eastern corners, which were evidently set out later, it was possible to have them starting at ground level, though they now have later bases for reasons that are no longer clear. A shaft was also provided in the south-western corner of the outer chapel of the south transept (**39**), though its lower part has been cut away at a later stage, perhaps when it was eventually decided that there was to be no use for it. It is significant for our understanding of the sequence of building that no shaft was provided in the corresponding situation in the north-west corner of the north transept chapels, indicating that by the time that part was being built, it was appreciated that a shaft was no longer needed in this position.

Phase 4. *The presbytery and the eastern bay of the presbytery chapels are vaulted; the shell of the middle and outer south transept chapels is completed to full height, together with their arcades towards the transepts* (**33**).

Arguably the most inventive feature of the rebuilt church at Melrose was the vaulting over the presbytery (**34**) and the two presbytery chapels. No more than one complete bay of the presbytery vault and some of the wall ribs of the chapel vaults survive, but these are enough to show that great ingenuity was shown in their design, even if we end by feeling that they deserve more marks for effort than for achievement.

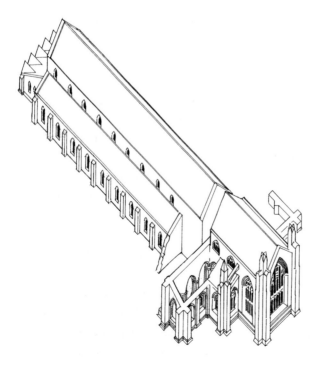

33 *Reconstruction sketch of the later church at the fourth phase.* David Simon/Historic Scotland

34 *The net vault over the unaisled eastern bay of the presbytery.* Historic Scotland

The presbytery vault was of a type usually described as a net vault, in which the vault rises well above lateral arched intersections around the window arches, resulting in a rather tunnel-like overall profile. Across the surfaces of this tunnel a closely-patterned network of ribs was spread (**35a**). We must assume that the pattern of ribs in the east bay was repeated in the two bays to its west, and the rib springings in the second bay suggest this was indeed the case, although there must have been some difficulties in continuing the pattern since the two western bays were shorter than the eastern bay. From each of the corners of the vault, three ribs extended across to the opposite wall, first to the mid point of the bay at the apex of the wall rib, next to the diagonally opposite corner of the bay, and then evidently to the opposite diagonal corner of the next bay. There were also transverse ribs between and at the centre of the bays and a horizontal ridge rib at the apex of the vault. One of the chief consequences of designing vaults in this way was that, rather than creating an impression of a series of individual units of

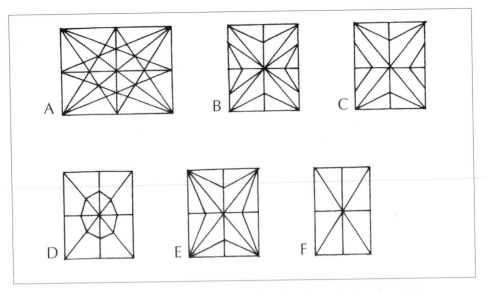

35 *Sketch plans of some of the vault types: (a) east bay of presbytery; (b) south presbytery chapel (?); (c) north presbytery chapel (?); (d) first south nave chapel; (e) transepts, nave, south nave aisle and later south nave chapels; (f) north nave aisle.* Fawcett

vaulting, one over each bay, the vault as a whole took on the appearance of a unified feature running unbroken down the length of the part that it covered. This resulted both from the continuous tunnel profile and from the way in which the ribs must have crossed into adjoining bays.

It has been suggested by one writer that the origins of such vaults should be looked for in the Anjou area of western France, where a series of vaults with a net-like pattern of ribs was built in around the 1220s. However, it is doubtful if it was those vaults that lay at the root of the later developments in Britain. Many of the sources of the particular type seen at Melrose are probably to be traced to the western counties of England, from around the second quarter of the fourteenth century onwards, though the Melrose vault must also be looked at against a background of other developments within Scotland itself. Earlier English examples of net vaults include those in the nave of Tewkesbury Abbey of the 1320s and in the choir of Gloucester Cathedral of the later 1330s. In both, we see how the lateral intersections over the windows are minimised and the ribs are extended across adjoining bays. However, the Melrose presbytery vault differed from those in a fundamental structural way, and that is the way that the vault and the roof were integrated with each other. It seems that the original roof had stone flags set directly on to the outer surface of the vault, whereas in the English examples the roof was a separate timber-framed structure resting on the wall-heads.

Apart from the structural differences, those West Country vaults at Tewkesbury and Gloucester can help us to understand some of the background to what we see at Melrose. But one reason why this approach was taken up so readily at Melrose may have been that masons in Scotland were already beginning to show an interest in tunnel vaults. At St Giles' church in Edinburgh, for example, the spaces over the eastern arm and transepts were covered with arched vaults, although in this case with a simpler cross-pattern of ribs reflecting four-part vaulting. These vaults, which survive over the choir aisles, probably post-date the English destruction of 1385, like the presbytery vault of Melrose. Related experiments in ribbed tunnel vaulting were also being made at the royal castle of Dundonald, where work was again in progress in the last quarter of the fourteenth century. Around this time there were also the beginnings of a revival of simpler types of tunnel vaulting, as at Bothwell Collegiate Church, where parallel transverse ribs were constructed for the vault over the choir that was started in the later 1390s, and where the vault and roof were integrated in the same way as at Melrose. Therefore, it is arguable that, although the design of the Melrose vault is likely to have been drawn up by an English mason, it was Scottish masons who interpreted and executed that design because of the way in which awareness was shown of what was happening at other Scottish buildings. It should also be mentioned that at Melrose the ribs, together with the bosses at their intersections, appear to be essentially a surface application, because in places where they have fallen away it appears that they were not embedded in the webbing of the vaulting. In this, as in the integration of vault and roof, the Melrose presbytery vault may have been one of the forerunners of a series of Scottish late medieval ribbed tunnel vaults, in which the ribs were treated as little more than an optional decorative extra, even if the complexities of Melrose were never repeated.

The vaults over the two chapels flanking the presbytery are particularly enigmatic, since so little survives of them. On the evidence of the wall ribs and the stumps of ribs that branched out from them, we can have no more than a partial idea of the general design, with no information about any lierne (subsidiary) ribs there might have been at the centre of the vaults. The south chapel vault had as its basis a standard four-part design, with arched diagonal ribs and horizontal ridge ribs (**35b**). There also appear to have been tierceron ribs on the east and west sides which presumably ran from the corners of the bay to an intermediate point on the east-west ridge rib. However, the lateral intersections of the vault, over the presbytery arcade arch and the south window, had pairs of ribs that emerged from an intermediate point between the corner springings and the north-south ridge rib. It is likely

36 *The wall rib of the north presbytery chapel vault.* Fawcett

that one of those ribs ran parallel to the diagonal ribs to meet the transverse ridge rib, while the other rib may have branched off to the rib junction at the centre of the vault.

The evidence for the vault over the eastern bay of the north presbytery chapel is even more puzzling. As in its southern counterpart, in addition to the usual cross pattern of ribs there appear to have been tierceron ribs on the east and west sides, and again there are intermediate rib springings on the north and south sides (**35c**). What is unique about this vault, however, is that the wall ribs show that it must have been flat (**36**). Flat vaults were not unknown, though they had to be of relatively small span and were usually supported by flying ribs, as may be seen in the vestibule to the Berkeley Chapel at Bristol Cathedral, of the early fourteenth century, or the pulpitum of Southwell Minster, of around 1330. But at Melrose there is no trace of flying ribs, and in any case the span would be too great for a flat stone vault. As a result, it is difficult not to conclude that the main part of the vault must have been of timber. Scotland certainly had timber barrel ceilings from at least the mid-thirteenth century, as for example over the choirs of Glasgow and Elgin Cathedrals, and soon after 1406 there may have been timber four-part vaults in the aisles of Dunkeld Cathedral. It is also very likely that there were flat ribbed timber ceilings from an early date, though the only surviving example over a church is that in the nave of Aberdeen Cathedral of around the 1520s. However, there are no clear precedents for a flat-ribbed timber ceiling that had stone ribs around its edges in this way, and it is hard to avoid the suspicion that the work was started with the intention of having a flat stone vault, but without having thought through the full structural implications of this. By the time the western bay of the north presbytery chapel was being vaulted, a rather less unorthodox approach was taken, though its surviving springing shows it was to have had a complex pattern of ribs, some of which intersected with each other.

At the same time that these vaults were under construction, work would have been continuing without break on the south transept chapels, with the completion of the window arches of the middle and outer chapels, together with the insertion of the tracery in the middle chapel, if that had not been done already. But the tracery of the outer chapel, which is different from that in the other chapels, was almost certainly not yet ready for installation (27i). For the hood-mouldings of the windows in the two external faces of the outer chapel, a new type of corbel was introduced, which has particularly attractively carved musician angels (37). There were also changes of detailing in the two levels of provision for images in the buttresses and pinnacles at the angles of the outer chapel. At the lower level, on the buttress itself, are projecting crouching figure corbels to support the images, below flat-headed canopies of triangular plan. At the upper level, where the buttresses become pinnacles, the tabernacles are recessed, each with a foliate corbel and a canopy head of uncertain form.

The arcades between the chapels and the main space of the south transept would probably also have received their final touches at this stage. The crossing pier, which is now gone, together with the surviving arcade pier immediately to its south, had almost certainly been built along with the aisled part of the presbytery, and it has already been said that the first arcade pier in the south transept had a cap like that of the presbytery arcade. But for the next pier and the respond built in with the south wall of the transept, there is a different capital type, in which the bell is surrounded by formalised sprigs of foliage below a deeply-moulded abacus, while the necking has pellet decoration (38). Apart from the pellet decoration to the necking, the caps which show the closest similarities to these are on the east responds of the presbytery arcades (30). In view of this, and taking account of the fact that these two caps are of yellow rather than pink stone, is it possible that

38 Above: *One of the later south transept arcade capitals.* Historic Scotland

37 Left *A window hood-moulding corbel of the outer south transept chapel.* Historic Scotland

they had originally been cut for the presbytery in the second phase of work, but then put to one side after it was decided the presbytery arcades should be of a different form?

At this stage it was evidently still expected that the vaults would be supported around the walls by shafts, as in the unaisled section of the presbytery. Apart from those along the east wall of the chapels, shafts had therefore been provided in the previous phases on each side of the south transept arcade respond (**39**). These were intended to support the south-west corner of the chapel vault and the south-east corner of the transept high vault. But while there were also vaulting shafts on the side of the arcade piers towards the main space to support the high vaults, no corresponding shafts were ever provided on the side of the piers towards the chapels, and this was to cause some difficulty when the time eventually came for the chapels to be vaulted. This will be discussed more fully below (see p.156).

Phase 5. *The shell of the south transept is completed. The shell of the north transept is completed on the east side at both chapel and clearstorey levels, on the north side up to wall-head level, and on the west side up to the lower stage; the eastern parts of the nave of the earlier church are demolished; the three bays of the monastic choir in the nave are built up to arcade level; the eastern parts of the south nave aisle are started; the first bay of the north nave aisle wall is built; the lower stage of the tower is built (**40**).*

This phase of work must have been one of the most productive in the entire building history of the abbey church, with much of the shell of the transepts and crossing being completed, and work being started on the three-bay monks' choir in the nave. As had been the case in the earlier phases, the same basic design was being followed as before, and it is changes of detailing which suggest that this should be identified as a separate phase. To allow work to proceed into the crossing and nave, at least four further bays of the earlier church nave must have been demolished.

The first operations in this phase would have included the completion of the north transept arcade, and in this we see two significant changes from what had been done in the south transept. So far as the northern respond of the arcade is concerned, it was decided not to have a wall shaft on its eastern side to support the chapel vaults, as a consequence of which the vault would have to spring directly from the abacus of the respond capital. Another significant change was the introduction of a new capital type, in which a convex band of closely spaced and minutely detailed foliage runs continuously around all parts of the cap, between a deep moulded abacus at the top and a

39 *The vault springing at the south-east corner of the outer south transept chapel; it can be seen that the wall shaft adjacent to the respond has not been used to support the vaulting, and the vault springing is crowded a little uncomfortably above the capital of the respond.* Fawcett

40 *Reconstruction sketch of the later church at the fifth phase.* David Simon/ Historic Scotland

simple roll necking at the junction with the pier (**41**). It is difficult to find precise parallels for the treatment of foliate capitals in quite this way, and it should probably be seen as essentially the individual creation of a particular mason. It is possible, however, that this way of treating foliage as a continuous convex band had some of its roots in an approach that had emerged around the second quarter of the fourteenth century in parts of northern and eastern England. Examples include the nave arcades of Patrington church in east Yorkshire, and the rebuilt choir arcades of Carlisle Cathedral. Suggesting such partial prototypes does not diminish the personal creativity of the mason who developed the Melrose type of cap, though it is always reassuring to find that ideas are not entirely without precedent.

The east and north walls of the north transept chapels were also largely completed at this time. Their window tracery was not yet inserted, though the arches may have been finished, with the three orders of continuous hollow chamfers that had been introduced in the third phase of work on this transept (**21b**), but with simpler foliage corbels to the hood-mouldings. Once the arcades and walls of the north transept chapels were complete, work could move on to the eastern clearstoreys above the arcades (**42** and **26**), and to the other walls of the main spaces of both transepts. This progression was relatively straightforward for the south transept, which was free-

41 *One of the later north transept arcade capitals.* Historic Scotland

standing, but was more complex for the north transept, which adjoined the east conventual range and cloister, and for each of which the rebuilding inevitably carried major implications (**86**). Nevertheless, it appears that work was started on the upper parts of the north transept before those of the south, because in what remains of the bay next to the crossing there are slight indications that a design closer in spirit to that of the presbytery was started (**43**). But that was soon abandoned, and in some ways the final design for the upper parts of the transepts can be understood as a reassessment of what had been designed for the presbytery, with a number of perceived awkwardnesses being ironed out.

From the start it was evidently felt that the net vault of the presbytery had not been a success, and the decision was taken to have more orthodox tierceron vaulting over both the main spaces and the chapels. Again, however, there are signs that it had initially been intended that aspects of the presbytery chapel design were to be extended round into the north transept chapels. This is seen in the way that the north transept middle chapel vault has the springing of a subsidiary rib emerging from the transverse rib that it shared with the western bay of the presbytery chapel (**44**). In the event this

42 *The north transept from the east.* Historic Scotland

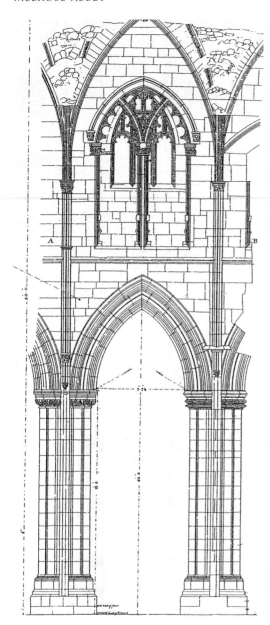

43 Left *Elevation of the middle bay of the east side of the north transept; it shows that the wall arch in the bay to the right has been modified.* Pinches, 1879

44 Opposite *The vault springing at the junction of the north presbytery chapel and the adjacent transept chapel.* Fawcett

more complex type of vaulting was abandoned, perhaps partly because installation of the vaulting was to be postponed for some years. Nevertheless, the choice of tierceron vaulting must have been taken at the time that upper walls of the transept were under construction, and this had implications for several aspects of the design. Internally it meant that the wall ribs around the clearstorey windows had to be more steeply arched than those associated with the net vault in the presbytery. It also meant that, since the vault was not of a

tunnel section that rose higher than the lateral intersections, the south transept window, which was set within the transverse wall rib, could not rise as high as the east presbytery window. Externally this meant that there had to be a greater height of masonry above the window in the south gable than above that of the presbytery.

So far as the eastern clearstorey of the two transepts were concerned, the double skin construction of the presbytery was continued into them, with a traceried balustrade and a skeletal tracery matrix to the inner skin. However, the windows, which were given rectilinear tracery patterns related to those in the presbytery clearstorey and the south presbytery and transept chapels, were made smaller, each one being in essence just a half of the six-light presbytery clearstorey window (**27d**, **42** and **43**). This was partly because the transept bays were narrower than those of the presbytery, though there also seems to have been a wish to give the windows a less crowded relationship with the wall. Another fresh nuance introduced at this level was a carefully contrived counterpoint between the window tracery and the inner skeletal matrix, with just two multi-cusped arches to the latter against the three lights of the former.

The great showpiece of this phase of works was the south transept façade, which looked across to the main gateway into the precinct and within which was the principal processional entrance into the church pending the construction of the new west front (**45**). The design of this front took its lead in nearly all essential respects from that of the east façade of the presbytery. The chief emphasis was on a great window, even though it was inevitably smaller than that in the east front since a doorway was required beneath it, and also because, as has been said, it could penetrate less deeply into the gable. But the front was similarly framed by angle buttresses surmounted by a pinnacle at each corner, and the gable was comparably enriched by stepped tabernacle work and capped by a traceried parapet, though the latter was penetrated by deep corbels which were perhaps intended to support statuary. Other similarities of detailing are seen in the treatment of the window arch, which has three orders of filleted rolls, albeit with diagonal bands of foliate caps between the jambs and arch springing. There are also two tiers of tabernacles with flat-topped canopies to the buttresses (**46**), and blind tracery decoration of the top levels of the buttresses and the pinnacles. But there are also differences, as seen in the way that all of the gable tabernacles, rather than just the end ones, have nodding canopies at their head. Differences are also evident in the way the buttresses are of four rather than three stages, and are slightly set back so that the angles of the transept project between them, with these angles having a sunk tabernacle at mid-height.

The biggest differences between south and east fronts, however, are in the form of the window tracery and in the requirement for a doorway. The window tracery must be seen as a secondary insertion, and will be discussed as part of the next stage (see p.144). It is also possible that the doorway in its present form was a later insertion, since the masonry of the wall is stepped back to its east and there is a vertical building break a short way to its west; further discussion of that will therefore also be postponed to the section covering the next stage of works.

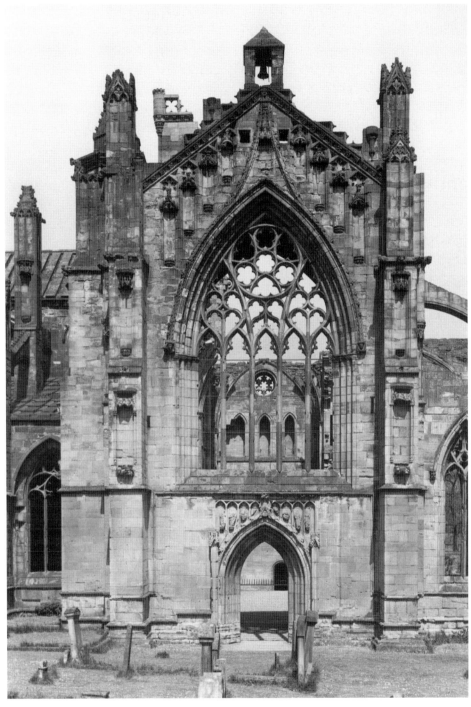

45 *The south front of the south transept.* Historic Scotland

46 *One of the tabernacles of the south transept.* Historic Scotland

The west wall of the south transept is perhaps its least completely resolved feature, and it is no longer certain how much had to be rebuilt when it was decided to add the outer row of chapels along the adjacent south nave aisle (**64**). As is now seen, internally there is simply a square-headed doorway to the stair turret at the lower level (**50**), and two windows at the upper level, one of three lights and the other of two, though if the arches of both were constructed in this phase of works the tracery must be a later insertion. Externally, the most attractive feature of this wall is the stair turret which projects off its west side, and which has polygonal upper levels with sunk rolls to the angles and two tiers of tabernacles. The sunk rolls are related to those at the angles of the lower storey of the tower, which must also have been built up to the intended apex level of the surrounding roofs around this time. The turret was designed to be finished with a parapet carried on a handsomely decorated cornice running around an octagonal cap house; that cap house is surmounted by a spirelet decorated with crockets at the angles and two horizontal bands, the upper one with foliate cresting. However, the turret is likely to have been extensively rebuilt when the outer nave chapels were added, and certainly the base of the newel to the stair itself is of a late type.

The interior of the north transept presented considerable problems for the master mason because of the need to accommodate it to the east claustral range and the east cloister walk (**47**). This also meant that it had to contain the night stair from the adjacent first-floor dormitory; the stone steps of that stair were carried on a segmental arch, of which the springing may be seen below the doorway in the north-west corner. Both the dormitory doorway and the entrance to the sacristy in the north wall were given round arches framed by relatively simple continuous mouldings, which relate closely to the blind arcading along the lower part of the west wall towards the cloister (**22d** and **18e**). Above the level of the dormitory doorway a horizontal rectangular panel was sunk into the north wall; it has a series of fourteen small bases running along its bottom edge which were presumably intended for diminutive images, and smaller bases between, which were perhaps intended to carry arcading around the figures. At the level corresponding to the eastern clearstorey, a continuation of the mural passage in that clearstorey extends across the north wall, which opens towards the interior through three widely spaced single arches with a traceried balustrade at their base, and above these is a circular traceried window.

The clearest indications that work was started on the three bays of the monks' choir at the east end of the nave in this phase of building are in the detailing of the arcades (**61**). However, the work is likely to have extended no further than the three bays of arcading, part of the lower walling of the south nave aisle together with the first buttress on that side, and the first bay of the north nave aisle. In setting out this part of the building it was accepted from the start that the north nave aisle should be retained at the same narrow width as its predecessor, presumably to avoid impinging on the area of the cloister (**81**). By contrast, fragments of what appears to be the lower walling of the south nave aisle within the arches opening into the first two chapels that were later added against it, show that the south aisle was always intended to be considerably wider.

The piers of the nave arcades in the area of the monastic choir were interconnected by low screen walls that functioned as a backing to the choir stalls, and the stubs of these walls can still be seen. In other respects the piers closely reflected the pier and respond of the middle and outer north transept chapels, with the same type of bases and foliate caps. But there is a subtle differentiation in the treatment of the sub-bases: whereas in most of the piers and responds the upper sub-base is of circular plan, in the central piers of the

47 *The interior of the north transept, looking north.* Historic Scotland

south nave arcade this element is of polygonal plan. Other slight changes are apparent in the arcade arches, where the leading filleted roll has become a little broader than was the case in the transept arches, giving more of a sense of a flat soffit (under surface) to the arch.

The case for only the easternmost bay of the north aisle outer wall having been built as part of this phase of works is best understood from the cloister, since that first bay has one arch of decorative arcading of the same type as was built along the west side of the north transept, and after that bay there is a change to a simpler type (**48**). There is also an intake in the masonry west of this bay, which again points to a significant change of mind on aspects of the design. The main reason for building this first bay at the earliest opportunity was presumably the need to buttress the west wall of the transept, though an

48 *The junction of the north transept and the north wall of the nave.* Historic Scotland

additional reason could have been that it had to contain the principal day-time entrance to the church from the cloister for the monks. As with the presbytery clearstorey window and the two doorways in the south transept this doorway was designed with a round arch (63). Nevertheless, as with the south transept doorway, the details of this doorway do not fit altogether comfortably within this phase of work, and it seems likely that it may not have been designed and installed within the wall until a little later (see p.151).

Phase 6. *The decision is taken to add an outer row of chapels on the south side of the nave and much of the base course for it is laid out; the easternmost south nave chapel is built and the second chapel started; tracery is inserted in a number of windows, including those in the south transept gable and the north side of the presbytery; the south transept doorway is possibly inserted; the bases of the south respond of the south transept arcade, of the south-east wall shaft of the south transept chapels, and of the north-east wall shaft of the north transept chapels are possibly modified* (49).

This was a phase that resulted in relatively little new building, and yet it was in many ways one of the most significant phases both for Melrose Abbey itself and for Scottish late medieval architecture as a whole. This is because it is associated with the Paris-born mason John Morow. The two inscriptions that record his contribution are in the south transept, and there can be little doubt that they are both insertions into the existing fabric. One, which gives his name and a slightly sententious aphorism on the relationship between a mason's compass on one hand and truth and duty on the other, is cut into the coursed masonry around the head of the doorway opening into the stair turret; this inscription also has a shield charged with compasses and fleurs-de-lis (50). The other inscription, which has now been replaced by a replica, is on a framed tablet, and it is the way this tablet ignores the coursing of the wall which shows that it too is an insertion (51). This tablet tells us that Morow had been born in Paris, and that he worked at St Andrews, Glasgow, Paisley, Nithsdale (Lincluden?) and Galloway (Whithorn?), as well as at Melrose.

Although it will be suggested that he was responsible for several things at Melrose, the work of Morow's team is probably most immediately identifiable in the tracery of a number of windows. Of greatest significance is the tracery in the first two of the added nave chapels, though the south window of the south transept and the north window of the aisle-less section of the presbytery are also of considerable interest. Beyond these, it is possible that he was responsible for the window tracery of the middle and outer north

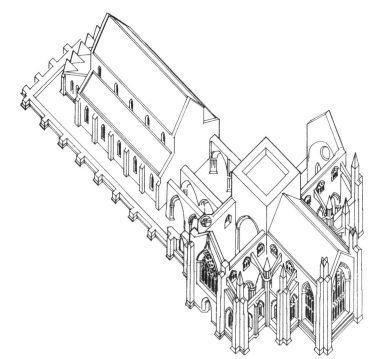

49 *Reconstruction sketch of the later church at the sixth phase.* David Simon/ Historic Scotland

50 *The inscription inserted around the head of the south transept stair doorway by John Morow.* Historic Scotland

51 *The inscribed tablet inserted in the south transept by John Morow.* Historic Scotland

transept chapels, that of the outer south transept chapel and the upper windows on the west side of the south transept. So far as the structure of the church is concerned, it is true that in most of what he did he was essentially putting the finishing touches to work that had been started by others; but his contribution was extremely important for the way it introduced a new approach to the design of what was always one of the most important features of any major building, the window tracery. His approach to tracery design will be considered a little more closely shortly.

Morow's one significant contribution to the plan of the rebuilt abbey church is likely to have been the decision to add an outer row of chapels along the south side of the nave (**52** and **81**). The Cistercians had always had some difficulty in providing sufficient space for altars at which all of the monks in priest's orders could celebrate mass, since the simple plan types that were still preferred at many houses did not readily lend themselves to large numbers of chapels. One solution adopted at several continental houses, from

Eberbach and Maulbronn in Germany to Fontfroide and Valmagne in France and Poblet in Spain, was to add a single row of chapels down the side of the nave away from the cloister. It seems almost certain that this idea was drawn for Melrose from the continent, since there were very few Cistercian precedents for the idea in Britain. It is true that the English Cistercian abbeys of Stanley and Coggeshall had chapels down part of the length of one side of the nave. It is also true that Chichester Cathedral in England and Elgin Cathedral in Scotland had a more or less symmetrical arrangement of chapel aisles down both sides of the nave. But none of those provide such specific parallels for the single chapel aisle at Melrose as the continental Cistercian houses mentioned, and the case for seeing continental inspiration behind the idea is therefore strong.

On completion, several of these chapels appear to have been taken over as the burial place of important families in the borders, where chantry masses would be celebrated for their welfare in life and the repose of their souls after death. Indeed, by the years after 1400, when construction of the chapels was

52 *The abbey church from the south-west.* Historic Scotland

probably initiated, that may have been as much what was intended for them as the provision of altars for the priest monks of the community. Crudely stated, they were perhaps at least partly a speculative venture aimed at generating income. On the architectural evidence, Morow must have designed and started building the first two chapels to the west of the transept, even if only the first can have been completed by him. The preliminary stages of the operation presumably involved dismantling the length of the lower outer wall of the south nave aisle that had been built at the same time as the arcades of the monastic choir, and rebuilding it on the proposed line of outer wall of the chapels. Since the tabernacle of the first buttress is of the same type as some of those on the south transept, that buttress presumably predates Morow's own contribution, and would have had to be dismantled and reconstructed along with the lower outer walling.

From this it can be seen that Morow was in many ways rather limited in his scope for innovation. Where we probably do see his hand most clearly is in the vaulting that covers the first chapel, and in the window tracery and window arch mouldings of the first two chapels. His influence is probably also seen in the design of the arches opening off the south aisle into the first chapel, which set the pattern for the rest of the nave chapels.

The vault over the chapel is basically of four-part form with diagonal and ridge ribs, albeit with traces of an additional ring of lierne ribs around the crown of the vault (**53** and **35d**); the possibility of a continental origin for its designer is suggested most obviously by the dropped cusping that can be seen to have been suspended from the ridge ribs. The European origins of the chapel's designer are most apparent, however, in the window tracery of the first chapel, in which there is a particularly elegantly contrived balance between gently flowing mouchettes (curved daggers) and spherical triangles (triangles with curved sides) (**54** and **271**). This tracery is framed by a window arch in which the chief element is a broad concave curve, which acts as a satisfyingly simple foil to the window itself (**21d**). The window of the second nave chapel has a circlet with the tell-tale spherical triangles at its head (**27m**), and since the arch of this window is the same as that of the first chapel it seems very likely that it had been designed by Morow, even if changes in the colour of the masonry around the window arch suggest he did not complete its installation.

The tracery of these windows is entirely unlike the almost grid-like variants on English rectilinear tracery that had been designed for the parts of Melrose completed so far. It could perhaps be argued that the reason for this was that it was the work of a mason who was looking back to English tracery designs of the first decades of the fourteenth century, in which richly

53 Above *The vault over the first south nave chapel.* Fawcett

54 Below *The partly restored window tracery of the first south nave chapel.* Historic Scotland

flowing curves had predominated. It is certainly true that some of the earlier English buildings that we have looked at, in trying to understand the architectural developments which lay behind the design of the first parts of Melrose, have elaborately curvilinear tracery. This is especially the case with the choirs of Selby Abbey, Howden Collegiate Church and Carlisle Cathedral. But the earlier years of the fifteenth century must have been reached by the time that the first of the nave chapels at Melrose were under construction, and by then such tracery had been almost universally replaced in England by the more severe forms of rectilinear tracery. It is hard to imagine a reason why any mason should have chosen to look to such exemplars by then. Within several countries of continental Europe, however, the curvilinear forms that had been abandoned in England were being taken up with fresh enthusiasm as a basis for exploring further possibilities. The rather restrained combinations of curved and spherical forms we see in the first nave chapel window at Melrose in particular, are quite closely paralleled at a number of continental churches from around the later fourteenth century, as in the chapels added to the nave of Amiens Cathedral by Cardinal de la Grange in about 1375, in the Halle-aux-Serges in Bruges of 1399, and in the choir of the church of Heiligenkreuz at Schwäbisch Gmünd which had been started after around 1351. Since we know that a French mason was working at Melrose at about this time, it would be almost perverse not to see his hand in these windows. His authorship is virtually confirmed by the fact that the same tracery design as in the first nave chapel at Melrose, and set within an arch with very closely related mouldings, is also to be seen at Lincluden Collegiate Church and Paisley Abbey, which are two of the buildings he listed that he had worked on.

The responds of the arches opening into these chapels off the south aisle take the form of a leading filleted roll flanked on each side by a keeled shaft and an engaged semi-filleted roll (**18d**), and they rise from bases in which the chief element is a deep and rather heavy ogee-section below a smaller ogee-section (**20d**). It may be mentioned, incidentally, that on the basis of the similarity between the details of this base and that of the southern respond of the arch opening to the south aisle from the transept, that arch must have been modified when the chapel aisle was added; slight modifications can also be detected in the mouldings of the arch itself on the side towards the transept, which were probably carried out around the same time. The foliage decoration on the capitals of the first chapel arch is of a type that is sometimes described a little dismissively as 'seaweed', but in this case it is very well detailed. If we are to look for a wider context for this type of foliage, it may be mentioned that drawings of related types are found in the collection of

55 *Corbel of a figure carrying an inscribed scroll from a tabernacle on the south transept.* Fawcett

the German mason, Hans Boeblinger, of around 1435, though comparable forms are to be found in European churches for some years before then.

Another feature that is found in this phase of work at Melrose is a type of corbel which has a large and strongly characterised crouching prophet or apostle figure carrying a scroll that was inscribed, or possibly in some cases painted, with his message (**55**). Crouching figure corbels had been used in earlier phases at Melrose, but these are different in their scale, in their robust sense of individual character, and in the scrolls they carry. They are found below the lower level of tabernacles on the south transept and also on the first buttress of the south nave chapels (**45** and **64**). All of these tabernacles themselves presumably pre-date Morow's involvement; however, inspection suggests that the corbels were insertions into the tabernacles. If that is the case, the main reason for attributing these corbels to Morow would be that this type is far more common in continental Europe than in Britain. Carefully individualised crouching figure corbels were a favoured motif of the Burgundian workshops of Claus Sluter in the years to either side of 1400, and in later years the idea spread widely. Amongst examples that might be mentioned are a number in the chapel of the house of Jacques Coeur in Bourges in central France, some in the Bourbon Chapel at Cluny Abbey in eastern France, and those on the tomb of Christ at Utrecht Cathedral in the

Netherlands. It is therefore attractive to assume that it was a foreign craftsman such as John Morow who introduced them to Scotland. There is corroboration for this in the fact that the only two other Scottish buildings at which corbels of this type are known are Glasgow Cathedral, where two displaced examples are thought to have come from one of the western towers, and the choir of Lincluden Collegiate Church. These are, it may be repeated, buildings on Morow's list of works.

The tabernacle corbels were almost certainly not Morow's only insertions in the transepts. The similarity between the bases inserted below one respond and a number of wall shafts, and those associated with the addition of the nave chapels, suggests that he could also have been responsible for those minor alterations. But the most important insertions made by him in the south transept could have been the south doorway and the window above it.

The doorway has four orders of filleted rolls rising from tall bases with deep ogee-section mouldings, but with no caps at the arch springing (**56** and **22a**). It is framed by buttresses capped with gablets and has a heavily crocketed hood-moulding with an ogee flip at the apex, within which are the royal arms. Instead of a finial at the apex of the hood-moulding there is a crouching figure of St John the Baptist carrying a scroll inscribed with a Latin text which can be translated 'Behold the Son of God', and this is set against a horizontal cornice with a foliage trail. Behind the doorway arch is an arcade of eight cusped arches containing carved images of Sts Andrew, Peter, Paul and Thomas and a pair of censing angels (**60**). There can be no certainty in attributing this doorway to Morow, but the crouching figure with a scroll at the apex of the arch is certainly very like the tabernacle corbels we have already considered, and several other features can be associated with his approach to design. The ogee-section bases, for example, show some similarity with the new type of base that was introduced for the nave chapels. But perhaps even more significant is the way that the doorway was framed by pinnacles and has an arcaded frieze set behind the arch and ogee hood-moulding. These features were not unique to Morow, but they do figure prominently in several works that are attributable to him. They are found at varying scales on the tomb, piscina and sedilia at Lincluden, for example, and they are to be seen at Melrose in the piscinae of the first two nave chapels and in a piscina inserted in the outer chapel of the south transept (see p.172) (**74**). On balance, it therefore seems there is a case for considering that the doorway could be Morow's. It is perhaps less likely that the images within the arcaded frieze are his, since some of them do not fit particularly well within their arches and they are therefore likely to be later insertions. Beyond that, the heavily falling blanket-like folds of the costumes show simi-

56 *The south transept doorway.* Historic Scotland

larities with the images of St Peter and St Paul in the north transept, which might indicate that they were only inserted in the arcading above the doorway around the time that work on the transepts was being completed.

When we move on to consider some of the windows in the presbytery and transepts that might be attributable to Morow, the picture is less clear than in the south nave chapels since the containing arches must have already been cut, and probably also installed, in earlier phases of work. Nevertheless, in the great south transept window, the combination of flowing forms and spherical triangles is consistent with the possibility that it was made for Morow, or at least that it was designed under his guidance (**27f** and **45**). The windows in the middle and outer chapel of the north transept and in the outer window of the south transept, however, are of types that were to become so relatively widespread that they could have been installed at almost any period in the later Middle Ages, and it would thus be difficult to attribute them so convincingly to Morow (**27h** and **i**).

The two windows that are perhaps most intriguing for the present discussion are those on the north side of the unaisled east bay of the presbytery and on the west side of the south transept above the outer nave chapels (**57**, **27g** and **k**). Both of these are altogether less restrained in their designs than the windows of either the first two nave chapels or the south transept gable, with combinations of forms that might be described as verging on flamboyant. It is certainly attractive to see these as having been designed by French masons, though they are rather unlike anything that we have seen as attributable to Morow himself. Is it therefore possible that Morow had compatriots working under him, and that one of those was given his head in two of the windows that still required to be filled? It is worth mentioning that the north presbytery window may have had at least one offspring in Scotland, in the even more complex tracery that was inserted in the west front of Brechin Cathedral at an unknown date. Perhaps one of Morow's masons had chosen to stay to continue working in Scotland after the departure or death of his master. But, for all that, Morow's overall personal contribution at Melrose was relatively limited in terms of quantity, its impact was to be disproportionately significant because of the way that it helped to make Scottish patrons and masons more completely aware of the wider architectural world that existed beyond the shores of either Scotland or England, and of the options that might be on offer. He was also able to show how forms that were at home in buildings of the grandest scale could be adapted for buildings of more modest pretensions, and for which less of a bottomless purse was available.

Phase 7. *The upper west wall of the north transept is completed; the transepts are vaulted; the parts of the north wall of the nave alongside the monastic choir are completed; the clearstorey over the monastic choir in the three eastern bays of the nave is built; the monastic choir and its flanking aisles are vaulted; the second south nave chapel is completed, the third, fourth and fifth nave chapels are built and the sixth chapel started; the tower is probably completed* (**58**).

57 *The window on the north side of the unaisled section of the presbytery.* Fawcett

Abbot Andrew Hunter (1444–65) was a great builder; apart from the works carried out under his administration at Melrose, he was also responsible for constructing the handsome tower house that presumably served as an abbatial residence on the abbey's cell at Mauchline (see p.238) (**100**). Mercifully for us, he was not reluctant to claim responsibility for his activities, and had his arms carved on the works he instigated at both Melrose and Mauchline (**17**). On the basis of the placement of his arms on the high vault of the south transept, on the fifth buttress from the east of the south nave chapels, and perhaps also originally on the first of the intermediate buttresses on the south side of the nave, there is no doubt that he must have been very active at Melrose. A difficulty in this is that we do not have dates for the previous building phase, which has been associated here with John Morow, other than that it is most likely to have been within the first quarter of the fifteenth century. However, it is implausible to assume that there would have been no building between the work designed by Morow and that carried out under Hunter's patronage, particularly since we know that the community was sufficiently anxious to have its choir completed to go to law over the unde-livered stalls in 1441. On balance it is therefore likely that, amongst the works to be considered in this phase, some had been started before Hunter's abbacy, but that he took forward the works he had inherited at the time of his election with considerable energy.

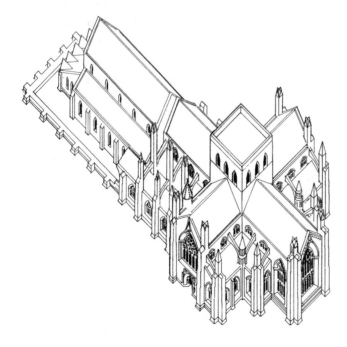

58 *Reconstruction sketch of the later church at the seventh phase.* David Simon/Historic Scotland

The operations which may be linked with this phase include the completion of the west wall of the north transept; the vaulting of parts of the two transepts and their chapels; the continuation of the north nave aisle wall and of the south nave aisle and south nave chapels; the vaulting of the nave aisles and of some of the south nave chapels; the construction of the clearstorey and vault of the three eastern bays of the nave; and the vaulting of the crossing and the addition of the upper storey of the tower.

Presumably the first major work to be set in hand would have been the completion of the upper west wall of the north transept so that the transepts could be brought into use (**47**). In the innermost bay on the west side of the transept a triangular-headed single window with a multi-cusped inner arch was placed above the arch into the north nave aisle, at the same level as the east clearstorey windows (**48**). In the two northern bays the lower part of the west wall was crossed by the night stair, the ghost of which is clearly evident in the rougher masonry. Above this a relatively simple approach was adopted in which there is a pair of single-light cusped arched openings in each bay, with the window on the outer plane and a corresponding arch on the inside of the wall passage, the latter with a traceried balustrade at its base. In the design of the inner arches to these windows the detailing that had been worked out for the arches on the inner face of the north wall was closely followed, and it may be wondered if those arches were only finished at this stage. Since the only factor that conditioned the height from which the windows along the west wall rose was the roof of the adjacent east cloister walk, the windows were pushed down below the level of the corresponding clearstorey on the east side of the transept. But they also stopped well short of the top of those clearstorey windows, which meant that a considerable expanse of blank masonry was left within the arches framed by the wall ribs of the vaulting.

Rising into those areas of blank masonry, and set between the paired windows of the two bays, are spired canopy heads over images assumed to represent St Peter and St Paul (**59**). Both of these statues are now replaced by replicas, and that of St Paul is so badly weathered that it is difficult to say a great deal about it. The statue of St Peter, holding the attribute of a book, is better preserved, however, and can be seen to have been carefully represented, with slightly dished facial features and curled hair, beard and moustache. The costume is made up of bulky blanket-like folds which fall heavily down to around the feet from the waist and left arm. If we compare this figure with the image of St Peter on the south doorway (**60**), we can see that there is some similarity in the heavily modelled drapery folds of both and they are certainly more like each other than either is to the figures within the

59 *Figure of St Peter on the west wall of the north transept.* Historic Scotland

60 *The statuary on the west side of the south transept doorway arch, with figures thought to represent Sts Peter and Paul; the slightly awkward relationship of these figures with the containing arches suggests they are later insertions.* Historic Scotland

east gable. It is therefore a possibility that the north transept west wall figures were the work of the same mason who inserted the smaller figures into the blind arches above the south transept doorway. The style of the north transept images fits comfortably within the broader artistic context of the time of Abbot Hunter. Partial parallels for the treatment of the drapery, although not of the facial types, can be seen in the work of the English royal master mason John Thirsk, for example, as in some of the statuary of Henry V's chantry in Westminster Abbey, which was completed in 1441. However, it is perhaps more likely that, rather then there being any direct connection between Melrose and Westminster, they were both individually indebted to works elsewhere. A possible candidate for the source of that inspiration might be the Netherlandish paintings that were exerting such wide-spread influence at this time, as perhaps best seen in the work of the Van Eyck brothers of the

1420s and '30s. Here we should also remember that, when the Melrose images were painted in a vibrant range of colours comparable with the works of the Netherlandish artists, the similarities in the way that the light must have played across the heavy folds of drapery would have been even clearer.

The general approach to design taken in the upper west wall of the north transept was continued into the eastern bays of the nave, where each bay of the clearstorey was given a pair of cusped lights to each bay, with a traceried balustrade at the base of the arches on the inner side of the wall passage (**61**). This arrangement was seriously disturbed when a pointed barrel vault was built over the parish church that was inserted into the eastern bays of the nave in the early seventeenth century. As a result of those later disturbances, each internal opening along the south clearstorey now has a segmental-arched head set well below the level of the external window head, while only the lowest parts of the original vault springings are still in evidence; on the north side most of the original design is lost to sight behind the massive arcade that was inserted to support the seventeenth-century vault (**94**). Nevertheless, there can be little doubt about the main elements of the design, or of the fact that we are looking at work of the mid-fifteenth century. It might be added that continuity of construction from the west side of the north transept to the nave clearstorey is supported by the way that corbels with foliage decoration were provided for the external hood-mouldings of each.

The completed eastern part of the nave was presumably deemed entirely satisfactory by its patron. And yet it is hard not to feel that an almost excessively safe path had been followed, particularly when we consider that the basic design shows little fundamental difference from what is to be seen, for example, in the north transept of Pluscarden Priory of the 1230s. It seems that, unlike some of their predecessors, Hunter and his mason were perhaps no longer seeking to blaze new trails of inventiveness.

The single-storeyed superstructure of the tower above the crossing of presbytery, transepts and nave is also likely to have been completed at this time (**62**). Its design continues many of the themes that had been established in the earlier phases of building the church: the spaced grouping of three single-light cusped windows shows similarities with the windows in the north transept west wall and the nave clearstorey; the shafts sunk into the angles recall the shafts in the angles of the south transept stair turret; the traceried parapet was comparable with those on the east and south gables and along the clearstorey passages; and the miniature bartizan-like turrets at the angles of the parapet may have had predecessors of a kind in the south transept parapet corbels. Things are never quite so simple, however. While the detailing clearly took much of its lead from what had already been done at

61 *The eastern bays of the nave, which contained the monks' choir; the vault and the clearstorey window heads are seventeenth-century modifications.* Fawcett

Melrose, it is possible that the basic arrangement of three spaced windows to the faces of the tower, which is not altogether what might be expected at this date, was partly inspired by the earlier thirteenth-century tower over the western crossing at Kelso, about 20km east of Melrose. It should be mentioned that, after Melrose's tower had been built, single-storey central towers with evenly spaced single windows became quite common in Scotland, as at Jedburgh Abbey, St Giles' church in Edinburgh, and St Mary's church in Haddington, amongst others.

So far as the north nave aisle is concerned, different approaches had to be adopted for the lower part of the wall within the south cloister walk and the part that rose above it (**48**). Within the walk the wall was treated very decoratively, as will be described when discussing the cloister (see p.177-8). As has already been said, the first bay of this wall had probably been built as part of phase five, though the processional doorway from the cloister to the monks' choir was perhaps only inserted at this phase, and there is a clear break in the masonry coursing to its west. Like the two doorways in the north transept,

151

62 Above *The west side of the tower; the medieval roof line is indicated by the triangular drip moulding; the existing off-centre roof covers the seventeenth-century vault.* Historic Scotland

63 Below *The north-east nave doorway.* Historic Scotland

64 *The eastern bays of the nave from the south.* Historic Scotland

it is round-headed, which confirms that the fashion for round arches in certain circumstances had become firmly established (**63**). But this doorway has three orders of mouldings to both the jambs and arch, with foliage decoration to the capitals and the hood-moulding. Above the level of the cloister roof, each bay of the aisle wall is lit by a two-light window with a quatre-foiled dagger at its head (**27j** and **48**). Rising above the wall head are rectangular buttresses with the lower parts of diagonally-set pinnacles emerging from the first two, and a foliage image corbel on the third, which suggests there was to be a tabernacle.

On the south side of the nave the external design of the clearstorey and chapels called for greater richness of effect (**64**), since they were on the more public side of the building and were next to the south transept doorway that was in use as the main entrance to the abbey church. The wish for a more opulent impact on this side was most prominently displayed in the chapel windows, which will be discussed shortly, but it was also to be seen in the high level of carved decoration. For many who visit Melrose the approach to decoration seen in this part of the church is best summed up in one detail: the bagpipe-playing pig on the south clearstorey cornice (**65**), a delightful example of the slightly improper tongue-in-cheek marginalia that are to be

65 *The pig gargoyle on the south nave clearstorey.* Historic Scotland

found in many medieval buildings and manuscripts. It should be understood that the pig was itself regarded as an unclean animal, symbolising gluttony, lust and sloth. There were further nuances in the bagpipes, which were made from pigs' bladders, and were seen as having scrotal connotations. The same theme is occasionally found on roof and vault bosses elsewhere, as at the church of Beverley St Mary. It is even more frequently found on misericords which, as a place to rest the bottom, were a natural target for ribald humour, and examples may be seen at Beverley Minster, Ripon Minster, Manchester Collegiate Church and St Mary's church at Richmond.

But the pig was never meant to be a prominent feature, and the south aisle was also the setting for sculpture with far more exalted aspirations. The decision to have an outer row of chapels meant that the flying buttresses which countered the outward thrusts of the nave high vault had to rise in two stages, with intermediate buttresses to separate those two stages above the wall between the aisle and the chapels. In the lower part of the pinnacles between the two tiers of flyers, tabernacles were provided, which were given very similar flat canopy heads to those in the adjacent south transept. Two of these have retained their images, though the originals, which are the highest quality sculptures to have survived at Melrose, have been removed to a sheltered environment and replaced by replicas. The image in the second buttress from the east represents St Andrew holding his cross, while the third buttress from the east houses an image of the Virgin and Child. The statue of St Andrew may not have been intended for its present location, since it is rather small, and has had to be supported by two levels of corbels (**66**); the lower corbel is decorated with a green-man head, and the one above it, which looks rather out of place in its present location, with foliage. There seems little doubt that the Virgin and Child were meant to be here, however, since they fit the tabernacle very well, and the high standing of the intended inhabitant is reflected in the additional enrichment of the tabernacle itself (**67**). There is highly finished miniature vaulting below the tall canopy head,

66 Left *Statue of St Andrew on the second intermediate buttress on the south side of the nave.* Historic Scotland

67 Right *Statue of the Virgin Mary on the third intermediate buttress on the south side of the nave.* Historic Scotland

and the flanks of the recess have bands of four smaller tabernacles on each side. Similar decorative treatment, incidentally, was also being applied to some of the piscinae in the chapels off the south aisle (**79**).

Even if they were not both initially intended to occupy adjacent positions, the style of carving of these two images suggests they could have been the work of the same mason. The faces are lost, but there are similarities in the way that an attractive contrast is created between the slightly compressed folds of the outer cloaks as they are drawn diagonally across the upper part of the body, and the more deeply undercut heavily falling vertical folds of the under garments before they break over the feet. There is admittedly something just a little formulaic in the suavely swaying contrapposto stance of the Virgin. But this in itself leaves small room for doubt that such a statue is an idealised expression of the wish to portray the Virgin as the Queen of Heaven, as seen in the large numbers of 'Beautiful Virgins' produced under the aegis of the International Gothic movement from around 1400 onwards. In the Melrose Virgin, affectionate motherhood is combined with regal condescension in a way that places it firmly within the European tradition.

When we move on to look at the vaulting over the transepts and nave, it is not clear at what stage the decision was taken that the highly innovative vaulting forms of the presbytery and presbytery chapels should be abandoned in favour of more orthodox types. As has been said, there was evidently at one stage an intention to continue the north presbytery chapel vaulting into the adjacent transept chapel (**44**). We have also seen that there were changes in the way that it was intended the vaults should be supported in the chapels of the two transepts, with the abandonment of the wall shaft that had been provided for this purpose in the south-west corner of the south transept by the time the corresponding corner of the north transept was built (**39**). A final decision on the form of vaulting in the chapels and high spaces of the transepts must have been reached by the time that their upper walls were under construction, however, since the vault springings, with provision for all necessary ribs, were built in with the walls. The chosen vaulting type indicated by these springings was the tierceron form, and this type was to be installed in almost all later parts (**35e**). Tierceron vaults have additional ribs rising from each springing at the corners of the vault to meet the longitu-dinal and transverse ridge ribs at a point between the boundaries of the bay and the central rib intersection. They may have been first developed in the nave of Lincoln Cathedral in around 1230, and by the mid-thirteenth century they are found over the crypt stairs at Glasgow Cathedral, while around the 1270s they were used on a larger scale in the aisles of Elgin Cathedral. They began to enjoy a revived use in late-fourteenth-century

Scotland, as in the main gate into the precinct of St Andrews Cathedral, and were to become one of the most favoured types for major churches by the mid-fifteenth century, as in the choirs of St Giles' church and Trinity College church in Edinburgh. Their use at Melrose in the mid-fifteenth century was therefore in no way extraordinary.

The only exceptions to the use of tierceron vaulting were the first chapel on the south side of the nave, where it has been suggested that John Morow was responsible for introducing a more complex type (**35d** and **53**), and the north nave aisle. In the latter case the extreme narrowness of the space made such a complex spread of ribs difficult, and four-part vaults were instead installed, with diagonal, longitudinal and transverse ribs (**35f**).

As we have seen, some tierceron ribs do appear to have been used, albeit in a rather unorthodox way, in the south presbytery chapel at Melrose itself, even if that could hardly be described specifically as a tierceron vault. But the earliest true tierceron vaults at Melrose were probably those over the chapels and high spaces of the transepts. From the surviving portions of the south transept vault, we can see that the high-level vaults over that part were well designed and very competently built, and that they rose fluently from the wall shafts. But the vaults in the transept chapels and south nave aisle evidently presented their designer with problems, because of the difficulty of accom-modating vault springings with so many ribs above the arcade caps and behind the arcade arches (**68**). In the transept chapels, parts of the arcade arches were cut back to gain sufficient space, but there was still some crowding of the vault springings on the abaci of the capitals. In the south nave aisle, flanking the monastic choir, the difficulties were even less satisfac-torily resolved, with the tierceron ribs being added at a point above the vault springing, and on this evidence it is possible that the original intention had been to have four-part vaults here, as in the north nave aisle (**69**).

So far as the row of chapels added along the flank of the south nave aisle is concerned, this phase of work probably embraced the completion of the second chapel to the design established by Morow. It then extended to the construction of the third, fourth and fifth chapels virtually in their entirety; part of the lower walling of the sixth chapel may also have been built, up to a vertical break below the centre of the window (**52**). Internally a change is seen in these chapels in the adoption of a smaller base type to the arches opening into them from the west side of the second chapel onwards (**20e**), though these smaller bases had already been used in the vaulting shafts of the first chapel. There are also slight changes in the arches themselves.

It is arguable that there were two phases to the continuing work on the chapels, since from the middle of the second to the middle of the fifth chapel

68 Left *Vault springing in the south transept chapels; it can be seen that the arcade arches had to be trimmed to provide space for it.* Fawcett

69 Opposite *Vault springing in the south nave aisle; the way in which the tierceron ribs emerge from above the vault springing may indicate that they were added after construction of the vault had been started.* Fawcett

there is a change of masonry from pink back to yellow, after which there is a further change back to pink. It is perhaps therefore only the final works here that are attributable to Hunter himself, with the earlier works pre-dating his abbacy. There are also changes in the provision for images on the buttresses: on the second, third and fourth buttresses from the east there were simply a foliate corbel and a polygonal canopy projecting from the face of the buttress, with no recess on the face of the buttress. On the fifth buttress, however, which is the one that bears Hunter's arms (**17**), there is the lower part of a tabernacle that is recessed into the buttress. But the most obvious changes were in the windows. In the second bay it has been suggested above that the window had been designed by John Morow, on the evidence of the mouldings of the arch and the spherical triangles in the tracery, even if it was only finished subsequently on the indiciations of the change of masonry colour. In the third and fourth bays a new type of tracery was introduced (**27n**), with three spiralling daggers set within a circlet, and the window arches in these bays were essentially a slightly modified reversion to an earlier type, with two orders of filleted rolls beyond the engaged half-mullion (**21e**). The window in the fifth bay, where there is a further change of stone colour,

was even more ambitious; it has three groupings of interlocking daggers, one each at the head of the two sub-arches and the third between the two sub-arches (**27o**). The arch mouldings of this window, which is a little more steeply pointed than its predecessors, were a marginally more complex version of those in the two previous bays (**21f**).

If these changes of detail and stone colour do point to two stages of work in this phase, with the earlier being an intermediate stage between Morow's contribution and the start of Hunter's patronage, we can nevertheless find support for the idea that both window designs are of around the mid-fifteenth century, by comparing them with windows elsewhere. The closest comparison for the type in the third and fourth bays is a window in the nave of St Michael's church at Linlithgow, which was almost certainly complete by 1489, and possibly some years earlier than that. So far as the window in the fifth bay is concerned, it has an almost identical twin in the south transept at Jedburgh Abbey, which is associated with arms thought to be of Bishop William Turnbull of Glasgow (1447-54). Of course, such comparisons can do no more than give a general idea of likely dating, particularly since in the later Middle Ages fashions were tending to change less rapidly than before. But they do at least offer some comforting support for the dating evidence that we have for Melrose itself.

Taking stock of everything we have seen in this phase of work, it seems that a different aesthetic approach was emerging, perhaps at least partly as a result of there being less of a sense of adventure and innovation than was evident in some of the previous phases. It is hard to avoid the impression from the single-light cusped windows of the north transept, nave clearstorey and tower, for example, that the mason was to some extent casting a sideways glance at an earlier architectural epoch within Scotland. Is it even a possibility that he was making some attempt to attune his work in the nave to the single windows that were probably still to be seen in the surviving fragment of the earlier church, perhaps with the growing recognition that it was likely to be there for many years to come?

By contrast, in the windows of the south nave chapels, impressive displays of window tracery were to be introduced, albeit with the possibility that the expense was being defrayed by the families who wished to use those chapels as chantries and burial places. But what is perhaps most important about those windows is that in their design there was clearly no longer any intention of taking a lead from contemporary English buildings. By the mid-fifteenth century the taste for the continental curvilinearity introduced into Scotland by John Morow, and probably by other like-minded masons elsewhere in Scotland, had completely won out over the patently English rectilinearity of the earlier phases. By the time the nave chapels were under construction it seems that Scottish masons were busily working out their own approaches to the design of such curvilinear forms. In this seventh phase, before and under the patronage of Abbot Hunter, what we therefore seem to see is a Scottish master mason working on a building whose essential design had been established about half a century earlier, and in which his predecessors had maintained architectural homogeniety while still responding to changing taste and fashion in the detailing. Faced with a choice between reverting to the use of first-phase details that were still in the height of fashion in England, or of developing an approach based partly on the ultimately European patterns introduced by Morow, and perhaps partly on buildings that were increasingly seen as part of Scotland's own architectural canon, it seems that it was the second path that he was following.

Phase 8. *The sixth south nave chapel is completed and the seventh and eighth chapels along the south side of the nave are built* (**70**).

There is a slightly desultory air to the final stages of work on the abbey church, almost as if there was little real hope that the work would ever be completed as first planned. By the end of Andrew Hunter's abbacy, in about

70 *Reconstruction sketch of the later church at the eighth phase.* David Simon/Historic Scotland

71 *The nave and north transept of the abbey church from the north-west, viewed across the west claustral range.* Historic Scotland

1465, construction of the walls and vaulting of the transepts and monastic choir was almost certainly finished. In addition, the first five of the south nave chapels had been completed, with work possibly extending as far as a building break visible below the window in the sixth chapel (**52**). We cannot be certain how much more was ever built after that. Clearly the walls of eight out of the ten south nave chapels were built since they are still to be seen (**71**), and the foundations were laid for the rest of the chapels and the new west front. But there are grounds for suspecting that no more chapels were built, and that little of the main body of the church west of the monks' choir was completed. The west wall of the eighth nave chapel is aligned with the west nave wall of the earlier church (**11**), and it would be difficult to argue that even the lower courses of that latter wall would have been retained if the late medieval nave had extended so far. It is true there is some suggestion that in 1742 there were three more bays of the nave. However, since they do not figure on the Slezer view of 1693 (**96**), there can have been no more than fragmentary remains of them, and by then it would perhaps have been difficult for most observers to distinguish between fragments that could have been part of either the earlier or the later church.

It might be suggested that it is difficult to understand why eight of the nave chapels should have been built and yet only three bays of the nave itself. However, if the western bays of the earlier church had been retained, as would be consistent with the retention of that church's west front, the five western chapels that were built would not have stood in isolation as they now do, and access into them could have been contrived from the earlier building. There can be no certainty on this, though, if more of the later church had been built, it is strange that it should have been completely lost when so much of the rest of the building has survived at least as a shell.

On this basis it is argued here that the only works which can be firmly associated with the century after Hunter's abbacy are the completion of the sixth south nave chapel and the building of the two following ones. As already said, the dating of this final phase of work is indicated by the inscription on the eighth buttress which gives the year 1505, and by the presumed initials of Abbot Turnbull (1503-7) on the piscina in the sixth chapel. This phase is partly differentiated from what went before in a number of ways. The walls are of mainly pink rather than yellow masonry, and from the fifth to the eighth buttress there is a change back to tabernacles which are recessed into the body of the buttress, though the canopies of all of these have been lost. These changes, however, had in fact been anticipated in the final stages of the phase that has been associated with Abbot Hunter. More subtle changes include the adoption of a slightly simplified base type to the arches of the two westernmost chapels, and a marked decline of quality in the window hood-moulding head corbels in the three western chapels (**72**).

So far as the windows of these final chapels are concerned, except in the eighth chapel, a design employed in the previous phase was repeated. Thus the sixth and seventh chapels have tracery with spiralling dagger forms within a circlet, which is essentially similar to the tracery in the third and fourth chapels (**27n**). The sixth chapel also has arch mouldings that are like those in the third and fourth chapels (**21e**); the mouldings of the seventh chapel are slightly different from those of the sixth, while being like those of the eighth chapel. On this evidence it could be postulated that two of the windows and one of their arches had been cut in the seventh phase but only installed when the chapels for which they were destined were eventually completed, meaning that even less work might be strictly attributable to this phase. Against that is the fact that they are cut from pink stone rather than the yellow stone of the earlier windows of this design. On balance, therefore, we

72 *One of the hood-moulding head corbels of the western bays of the south nave chapels.* Historic Scotland

should probably conclude that it had simply been decided to stick with established designs at this stage, for which the drawings were presumably still to hand in the lodge.

The liturgical fixtures and furnishings of the church

The presbytery

For those who wished to extirpate everything associated with the old forms of worship in the build up to, and the aftermath of, the Reformation, the liturgical fixtures and furnishings of churches were a particular target. The altars, as the main focus for the celebration of the mass, were usually the first items to be removed, along with anything else that could be taken away with relative ease, including choir stalls, statues and paintings. But by the later Middle Ages many of the principal furnishings of major churches were being designed as an integral part of the architectural fabric, and they were less easy to remove. It is because of this that at Melrose Abbey we still have many fine late medieval furnishings. The best of the liturgical furnishings would always have been in the presbytery, where the high altar was located a short way in from the east wall. Attention would have been focused on this altar by means of the finely carved and painted retable that is likely to have risen behind it and by the rich fabrics that would have hung around and in front of it, the latter being changed according to the colour required for the successive liturgical seasons and saints' days. But, of course, nothing survives of that.

Much does still survive in the presbytery at Melrose nevertheless, though we cannot be certain of the function of everything. This uncertainty is especially the case with two large rectangular recesses in the east wall, behind the site of the high altar. In this position one of them might conceivably have served as a Sacrament House, where the consecrated host was stored and made available for veneration. But it would have been very large for such a purpose and, in any case, if the host were reserved in a mural Sacrament House rather than being suspended in a pyx above the altar by the later fourteenth century, it might have been expected the Sacrament House would be located on the north side of the altar. On balance, it is perhaps a stronger possibility that these lockers were relic aumbries (wall lockers), since we know that by the later Middle Ages Melrose had built up a notable collection of relics that were a popular focus of pilgrimage. The reliquaries containing them might be safely stored in these lockers in close association with the high altar, being brought out on the appropriate festivals or as need arose. The lockers themselves would presumably have been lined with wood and fitted with securely lockable doors that may have been embellished with fine fabrics or paintings and metalwork. However, what were probably regarded as the most important relics at Melrose were those of St Waltheof, which were evidently in the chapter house, and we shall consider those below (see p.186–8) (**88**).

On each side of the presbytery was what appears to have been a tomb recess (**73** and **18a**), with delicate mouldings around the segmental arch that framed each of them. These may have been intended for the burials of abbots, though by the late fourteenth century it is equally possible that they were intended for great lay benefactors, whose munificence could be rewarded by burial at this most sacred location. Burials of the laity within Cistercian houses had originally been forbidden, but by the later Middle Ages the prohibition was more honoured in the breach than in the observance. The human remains of a major royal patron such as Robert I, whose heart was buried at Melrose after its return from Spain in 1330, would certainly have been prominently located, for example, even if that location is no longer known with certainty. The tomb recess on the north side of the presbytery may have served a second function as an Easter Sepulchre, where an image of Christ together with a consecrated host would be ritually entombed between Good Friday and

73 *The tomb recess and the credence and double piscina on the south side of the presbytery.*
Fawcett

Easter Sunday, in commemoration of Christ's own entombment. But it is also a possibility that a large rectangular recess to the west of the tomb could have served that function, unless it too was a relic locker.

Moving on from such relative uncertainty, the only surviving fixtures in the presbytery whose function can be more positively identified are a pair of small arched recesses towards the west end of the south wall, which display the finely embellished micro-architecture that was increasingly being applied to important liturgical furnishings by the later fourteenth century. Framing the sides of the arches are miniature buttresses, while the arches themselves were decorated with cusped–cusping within, and crockets and finials around the outer edge. The eastern of the two recesses would have been the credence, where the sacred vessels, the chalice and patten, together with the elements of bread and wine, were placed before being taken up to the altar. The western recess was a piscina, within which were two drained basins for washing the sacred vessels and the hands of the celebrant. Since it was believed that the elements became the body and blood of Christ through consecration at the mass, it was important that not even the water used for washing the things that had touched them should be desecrated, and it had to pass into the consecrated ground below the church. Usually one basin was enough for this, though double basins are also found quite frequently at major altars, one perhaps being intended for the vessels, and the other for the celebrant to wash his hands.

The transepts

The many side chapels throughout a great church were generally less richly furnished than the presbytery, though at Melrose several still retain high-quality fixtures. In two of the north transept chapels, and one of those off the south transept, we are reminded that the principal furnishing would have been an altar, since the lower stone courses of those altars remain in place against the east wall. In the two outer chapels of each transept the string course below the east window has been cut back, perhaps to accommodate altarpieces, while in the central chapel of the north transept are vertical chases that could have been to locate the supports at the back of an altarpiece. In the chapel on the south side of the presbytery is a relatively simple piscina with a pair of basins framed by a cusped ogee arch. Not all side chapels had piscinae; in some the priest presumably simply used a bowl that could be emptied elsewhere. In the chapel on the north side of the presbytery a piscina was inserted as an afterthought, and its drain is visible in the sub-base of the arcade respond. The handsome piscina in the outer chapel of the south transept also appears to be an insertion (**74**); similarities with a rather more ambitious example in the choir of Lincluden Collegiate Church suggest that it could have been installed when the mason John Morow became involved at Melrose. It has an ogee arch framed by miniature pinnacles, with a row of blind arches behind the arch and below a decorated cornice. It should be mentioned that all of the transept chapels have one or two aumbries, where the sacred vessels used at those altars may have been stored; as with the supposed relic aumbries in the presbytery, it can perhaps be assumed they would have had wooden linings and doors.

In the north-east transept chapel is an unusual shallow recess above a shaft capped by a foliate corbel, which looks on first sight like a piscina, except that it is to the north of the altar and does not have a drain; perhaps it was for a small image of the saint to whom the altar was dedicated. There was certainly the intention to have a statue in the outer south transept chapel, where a large foliage-decorated corbel was inserted to support it (**75**). But images of saints might not necessarily be within the chapels dedicated to them. In the north transept there are replicas of two fine statues at the higher level of the west wall, between the paired windows, where the originals presumably survived because they were inaccessible to iconoclasts. These statues appear to represent St Peter and St Paul (see p.147–9) (**59**), and it is thought that the two chapels on the

74 Left *The piscina inserted in the outer chapel of the south transept.* Historic Scotland

75 Below *The image corbel inserted in the outer south transept chapel, adjacent to the corbelled wall shaft.* Historic Scotland

76 *Holy water stoup at the foot of the night stair from the dormitory into the church.* Fawcett

opposite side of the transept, into which they are looking, had those dedications. The transept chapels would almost certainly have been enclosed by screens set within the arches that opened into them, the lower parts of the screens being more or less solid and the upper parts more open, with a doorway rising through both levels. The only evidence for any of those screens is slots that have been cut in the bases of the arcade pier and respond of the outer chapel of the south transept, and there are also slots in the sub-bases of the chapel to its north.

One other furnishing to be mentioned in the north transept is a stoup at the foot of the night stair for the holy water with which the monks ritually cleansed themselves on entering the church from the dormitory (**76**). This stoup was a basin set within a round-arched recess, above which was a hood-moulding with an ogee flip at its apex. Another stoup was placed outside the church, at the day-time entrance for the monks from the cloister. This took the form of a projecting foliage-decorated basin at the junction of the west wall of the transept and the north wall of the nave, next to the north-east nave doorway (**48**).

The monastic choir

The main furnishings in the monastic choir, within the three eastern bays of the structural nave, would have been the timber choir stalls of the monks, which were usually arranged in two ranks along each side. They were set against a low wall running between the arcade piers, the stubs of which are still to be seen (**61**), and they would have returned at right angles against the stone screen or pulpitum that closed off the west end of the choir. The stalls have, of course, gone, though we know that they were intended to be one of the great glories of the abbey church. They were ordered from the leading Bruges carpenter, Cornelius Aeltre, and it was specified that their design was to be based on the stalls at the Cistercian abbeys of Ter Duinen and Ter Doest, in what is now Belgium. The monks of Melrose eventually had to go to law about them in 1441 when they had failed to arrive, and the records of the court proceedings show that Aeltre was in financial difficulties, possibly because of fluctuating currency rates. The unfinished stalls were apparently being stored in the refectory of the Franciscan friary in Bruges, and Aeltre was so apprehensive about his reception when he eventually delivered and fitted them at Melrose that he had to seek assurances for his safety.

The processional western doorway into the choir, at the centre of the pulpitum, opens onto a short passage within the pulpitum that is covered by a small tierceron vault with a head of Christ on the central boss (**77**), and on the north side of the passage is a straight stair which used to lead up to the loft or platform on top of the screen (**78**). There may have been an altar on this loft, and possibly the organs that would have accompanied the monks' singing by the later Middle Ages. It was perhaps also intended to have altars against the west face of the pulpitum, and a large recess in the southern part of the screen could have been associated in some way with such an altar. Beyond the pulpitum, west of a space known as the retro-choir, it would have been intended to have a second screen, the rood screen. Above that screen would be located the great rood (crucifix) accompanied by the Virgin and St John the Evangelist, with the nave altar in front of the screen. But it is uncertain that anything of the late medieval church west of the monastic choir was ever brought to completion, though, as already said, it is possible that parts of the original church were retained in repair and continued in use for the worship of local layfolk. The stone pulpitum itself survived because it was solid enough to provide a firm base for the wall built above it in the early seventeenth century, at the west end of the parish church that was inserted within the monks' choir. The balustrades along the front and back of the loft have been destroyed, however, apart from the cornice of that on the west side, which is decorated with a foliage trail.

77 Above *The miniature tierceron vault in the pulpitum passage.* Historic Scotland

78 Below *The pulpitum at the western entrance to the monks' choir.* Historic Scotland

The nave chapels

Several of the chapels along the south flank of the nave appear to have been used as the chantry chapels and burial places of important families, and it is also clear from the large number of memorials within them that many continued in use as family burial places after the Reformation. As in all such chantry chapels, the principal focus would have been an altar against the east wall, and there is what may be the base of one in the second chapel from the east. In other cases the main clue to the location of the altar is nothing more than the cutting back of a string course, presumably so that a retable added behind the altar at a later stage might be set flush against the wall. As with the transept chapels, it is very likely that the nave chapels would have been closed off by screens of timber, stone or even metal, but nothing survives of these, and the best reminder of the chapels' original liturgical functions is the piscinae that they all contain, which provide a fascinating indicator of how fashions in church furnishings were becoming ever more ambitious.

In the easternmost chapel, which it has been suggested was largely the work of John Morow, above a bowl decorated with foliage is an arched recess flanked by pinnacles, and with a band of blind arcading below a cornice behind the arch. The basic design of this piscina is similar to that in the south transept chapel, and related designs were also to be adopted in the second and third chapels. After the first three nave chapels, the designs become even more complex and three-dimensional. Projecting canopies over the arched recesses have miniature vaulting below them, and there are sometimes smaller niches capped by diminutive canopies on each side of the main recess (**79**). In this we see how such furnishings were reflecting the same developments in design to be seen in larger-scale external tabernacle work (see pp. 155–6) (**67**).

Floor tiles

Evidence for an impressive series of tiled floors was found in the course of excavation, with the best being within the chapter house. Unfortunately, those that were left in place after being excavated are now so badly weathered that it is difficult to appreciate their original appearance, and we have to rely on the loose tiles that were removed to the site museum, and on the descriptions and analysis of the excavated pavements offered by James Richardson if we are to understand what was once there (**80**). More recently, the tiles have been carefully reassessed by Christopher Norton, giving us a more complete understanding of their place in the history of tile making and of how they related to tiled floors elsewhere.

The attitude of the Cistercians to tiled pavements can seem a little puzzling. St Bernard specifically attacked elaborate pavements in his *Apologia*

79 *Piscina in the eighth south nave chapel.* Historic Scotland

of 1124, and in the early thirteenth century a number of abbots were censured for allowing such pavements to be laid in their churches. Yet many of the best pavements known to have existed in Britain were at Cistercian houses, and the finest in Scotland were at Melrose and her daughter-house of Newbattle, with some of those at Melrose evidently copying higher-quality examples at the latter. Within the presbytery and chapels of the first church, green, yellow and brown glazed tiles laid out in geometrical patterns were found. These are unlikely to have dated from before the second quarter of the thirteenth century, and therefore point to a major redecoration of the eastern parts of the church around that time. Regrettably, nothing is now to be seen of these.

It has to be said that the quality of most of the Melrose tiles was not of the highest. They are rather thicker than might have been expected, the stamping

80 *James Richardson's drawings of some of the tiles found through excavation at the abbey.* Proceedings of the Society of Antiquaries of Scotland, 1928

of the inlaid patterns is very irregular, and there seems to have been some difficulty in obtaining clays of the most favoured colours. It is possible that tilers who were perhaps more used to producing roof tiles were being asked to copy complex designs for floor tiles from elsewhere, and were not fully equal to the task. There is a local tradition that a medieval tilery at a site close to Darnick, about 1.5km west of the abbey, was the place where Melrose's tiles were made. A number of glazed tiles have been found there, at a site known appropriately enough as Tilehouse.

The monastic buildings

The cloister

As has been pointed out above, the cloister at Melrose was atypical in being on the north side of the church (**81** and **71**), presumably mainly because the water supply came from that side. In its final form the cloister was a rectangle of about 42.7m from east to west by 37m from north to south, with alleys or walks around all four sides that would have been covered by roofs carried on open arcades. However, a short spur of foundation wall that was found not far from the west end of the face of the north range towards the cloister, suggests that the west side of the cloister was originally further east. This was presumably because there was at first an open lane between the cloister itself and the quarters of the lay-brethren in the west range, as is still to be seen at Byland Abbey. If that were the case, the original cloister would have been closer to square in plan, with a length from east to west of about 39.3m. The open garth within the covered walks would then have been about 30.75m by 28m.

Nothing now stands of the cloister arcades themselves, but in the site museum in the commendator's house are a number of capitals and bases from twin-shafted piers of the type that might be expected in a cloister (**82**). The caps are of either scalloped or water-leaf type, while the bases are of water-holding form with a relatively widely spreading lower roll, all of which points to a date around the last two decades of the twelfth century. A noteworthy feature of each of these piers is that one shaft is of octagonal section and the other round. This is a variant on what is seen in the reconstructed cloister fragment at Rievaulx Abbey, which must be of a similar date to that at Melrose, where each pier has a pair of either round or octagonal shafts. The two types presumably alternated from pier to pier at Rievaulx rather than being mixed in the same pier as at Melrose.

Projecting into the cloister from the north cloister walk are traces of a square pavilion, with a circular foundation inside it. Being close to the refectory entrance, this was clearly the *lavatorium* (washing place) pavilion,

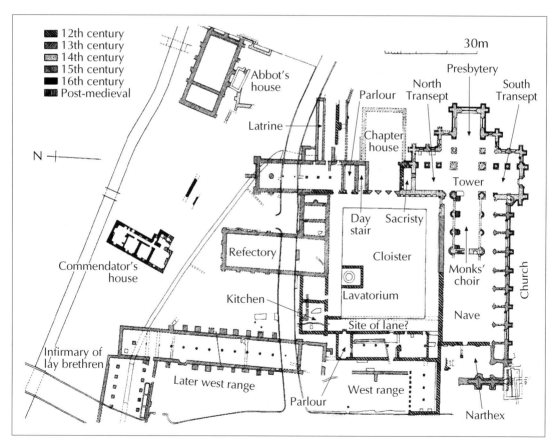

81 *Plan of the church and monastic buildings.* Sylvia Stevenson/Historic Scotland

82 *Double water-leaf capital in the site museum, possibly from the cloister.* Historic Scotland

where the monks washed their hands before eating. The circular foundation suggests that the *lavatorium* was in the form of a free-standing basin of the type still to be seen in a number of continental houses, such as Heiligenkreuz in Austria, and known to have existed at Louth Park in England and Mellifont in Ireland amongst other places. There might sometimes be an upper basin or cistern supported on a central pier, with taps or spouts feeding water into the main basin. The *lavatorium* pavilion was probably also the location for the weekly *mandatum*, the ritual foot washing that commemorated Christ's washing the feet of the disciples before the Last Supper, and which was an important part of the religious observance in the Cistercian order. In that case there could also have been a lower basin nearer ground level. It was said by the excavator that the water for the *lavatorium* had been brought through lead pipes from a well to the south, known as the Locket Well. Traces of a small drain aligned with the *lavatorium* were found within the refectory range and to its east, where it connected with the main drain.

There seems to have been some ambivalence of attitude towards the existing cloister when the church was rebuilt after 1385. On the one hand there was such anxiety to avoid impinging on the area of the cloister that the dimensions of the north nave aisle of the earlier church were repeated in the new building, resulting in an aisle that must have looked like a narrow corridor by contrast with the much wider new south aisle. Yet, at the same time, lavishly detailed decorative blind arcading was provided towards the cloister walks on the west side of the south transept, and against the eastern-most bay of the north aisle next to the processional doorway from the cloister (**83** and **48**). This suggests that the cloister walks themselves were being at least partly remodelled when the church was rebuilt. Rising above a bench with a broadly projecting lip, the decorative arcading against the south transept had arches set at roughly 1.85m intervals, each of which had continuous mouldings rising from bases of deep ogee profile. Around each arch head was an ogee-arched hood-moulding with crockets and a finial that rose into a cornice decorated with square-flower of various kinds, while between the arches were small-scale buttresses and pinnacles.

This arcading, with its elaborate miniature architecture, must have been costly to produce, and after the first bay of the nave it was superseded by

83 *The decorative arcading on the west side of the north transept, towards the east cloister walk; the sacristy is behind the narrower arch to the left.* Historic Scotland

177

84 *The more richly finished section of the decorative arcading on the north side of the nave towards the south cloister walk; this may have been the abbot's seat at the evening* Collatio. Historic Scotland

much shallower and more closely spaced blind arcading, consisting of a series of round-headed trifoliate arches with a revived version of dogtooth moulding in the hollows. The only exception to this simpler form is one arch in the fourth bay from the east, which has cusped-cusping within the arch and an ogee hood-moulding rising against a traceried frieze (**84**). This is likely to have been the abbot's seat for the evening *Collatio*, between the services of Vespers and Compline, which usually took the form of a reading from the works of John Cassian, who wrote at the turn of the fourth and fifth centuries.

There are good indications of the structural form of the cloister roof against the rebuilt parts of the church in the form of timber sockets, corbels and drip mouldings. Despite the lavishness of the decoration towards the cloister, there was no intention of covering the cloister walks with stone vaulting and, as with the avoidance of extending the later church out over the area of the cloister, this suggests that much of the old cloister arcading may have been retained. The upper ends of the rafters of the lean-to roof were secured into a horizontal wall plate carried on corbels, and the roof covering was protected at its junction with the wall by a drip moulding like a string course. There are sockets for half-collars at mid-height of the rafters, which were evidently braced by raking struts projecting up from the wall at an angle that probably reflected the angle of the rafters themselves. This would have resulted in a combination of structural timbers of semi-hexagonal cross-section, and the rafters, collars and struts may have been boarded to create a barrel ceiling of polygonal profile over the cloister walks.

The east claustral range

In common with the other ranges grouped around the open space of the cloister, the east range has been remodelled on a number of occasions (**85**). As first built, it may have projected little further north than its junction with the north range, but in its final form it extended for about 53.65m from the north transept of the abbey church, the main body of the range being about 10.35m wide. The dormitory would have occupied the whole of its first floor, and where it abutted the south transept of the church we have the only

85 *The lower walls of the east claustral range, between the north transept and Cloister Road (compare with **9**).* Historic Scotland

86 *The north wall of the north transept towards the east claustral range; the vault of the sacristy is at the lower level, with the south wall of the dormitory above.* Historic Scotland

surviving evidence for the upper level of any of the claustral ranges (**86**). On the ground floor of this range, immediately next to the north transept was the sacristy, beyond which was the chapter house, after which was a sequence of two small spaces, one of which would have housed the original day stair from the dormitory to the cloister, while the other would have been the parlour. The northern part of the range was internally subdivided to varying extents at ground-floor level, presumably to serve a variety of periodically changing functions. Projecting eastwards at a right angle from the mid-point of the range, and straddling the drain, was the rear-dorter or necessary house (latrine block). Each of these areas will now be considered individually.

THE SACRISTY AND THE SOUTHERN END OF THE DORMITORY

The sacristy, which is entered through a round-arched doorway from the north transept (**47**) and does not communicate with the rest of the east range, was remodelled when the church was rebuilt after 1385. The south, east and west walls were thickened in the process of remodelling, and this has resulted in an asymmetrical shape for the retained barrel vault that covers it. The external evidence for the thickening of the east wall is seen in the way that it has encroached upon part of the base course of a thirteenth-century buttress to the chapter house, and also upon a late fourteenth-century buttress on the line of the east chapel arcade of the south transept. This suggests that the range on the east side of the cloister was overall a little narrower when first built in the earlier twelfth century than it later became. It is true that the greater part of the east range appears to have achieved its present width by no later than the mid-thirteenth century, whereas the sacristy east wall can only have been thickened after 1385. But there is no reason why the sacristy should not have been retained at its old and slightly narrower width for a while, since from the mid-thirteenth century it was separated from the rest of the range by the projection of the chapter house. As we shall see, there are parallels in this with the north range, where the part of that range east of the refectory was also slightly widened through wall thickening at a later stage, while the part west of the projecting refectory was retained at its earlier width.

The sacristy was the room where the vestments, vessels and other items required for the services at the altars were stored, and where the priests celebrating mass at the altars vested themselves. At Melrose this space appears also to have been known as the 'wax cellar', presumably because candles were kept here. It became common in Cistercian houses for this space to be divided into two parts by a timber partition, with the eastern part being the sacristy itself, and the western portion serving as a library and entered from the cloister. If this was the case initially at Melrose, the partition and western doorway were suppressed in the later rebuilding. The north wall of the chamber, which is probably one of its older parts, has three round-arched aumbries, and the chamber is lit, albeit rather inadequately, by a narrow window in the east wall, and an angled window in the north-west corner. Its floor level is lower than that of the church, and four steps lead from one level to the other, the lower step being a reused gravestone which commemorated an individual named as Johanna de Ros.

Directly above the sacristy are the only surviving sections of the walls of the dormitory, which also incorporate buttresses projecting from the corners of the transept (**86**). This end of the dormitory must have been rebuilt along with the transept of the church after the attack of 1385, with the same high quality ashlar, but it is unknown if anything of the upper level north of this section was rebuilt at the same time. One jamb of a window can be seen in both east and west walls, the window in the east wall having been square-headed. In the south-east corner of the dormitory an elevated doorway opened on to a spiral stair which led up to the clearstorey mural passage of the north transept, to the wall-head walkways of both the transept and the dormitory, and to the dormitory roof. This stair was housed within a polygonal projection into the dormitory. High in the south-west corner a corbelled-out projection accommodated the short flight of steps that connected the differing floor levels of the mural passages in the west and north walls of the adjacent transept. The drip moulding of the dormitory roof shows that it was steeply pitched, but that it was hipped at its junction with the transept to allow space for a small rose window set within the arch of the transept vault. There are traces of what appears to be fire damage to the internal lower masonry of the dormitory, particularly on the west side and up the inner angle of the south side of the west window embrasure. This presumably resulted from the attack by the English forces of the earl of Hertford in 1545, and it may be doubted if the dormitory was ever fully repaired and brought back into use, since it is likely that most of the monks had private chambers elsewhere within the abbey by that date.

THE CHAPTER HOUSE

As the principal meeting room of the community, and the place where a chapter of the monastic rule was read each day, the chapter house was the second most important of the abbey's buildings, and it was in some ways regarded as the physical expression of the abbey's standing as a religious corporation. It is therefore not surprising that at Melrose the chapter house was rebuilt on more than one occasion to meet changing needs and architectural tastes. The main surviving evidence for its appearance at any stage is the lower parts of the west wall and of the western portion of the south wall. The information those walls offer has been supplemented by what was found through excavations in 1921 and 1996, together with the results of a geophysical survey carried out shortly before the second campaign of excavation. Considered together, none of this provides conclusive evidence for the form of the building at any point in its history, though it is thought there were four main phases of construction.

In the first phase, initiated around the time of the abbey's foundation in 1136, the chamber was probably entirely contained within the body of the range as it then existed. It is possible that it was wider from north to south than its successors, however, since there is what seems to be an early masonry face along the west wall behind its junction with the existing north wall, suggesting the first chamber could have extended by as much as 1.65m further north. The original chamber therefore appears to have been considerably longer on that axis than from east to west. Assuming that the chamber as first built was entirely contained within the body of the range, there would be parallels with the first chapter house at Rievaulx, as well as with a number of other early Cistercian chapter houses in England. It would presumably have had either one central pier, or perhaps more likely a pair of piers along the central north-south axis. Such piers would almost certainly have been required to carry the floor of the dormitory above, and may also have supported stone vaulting in such an important room.

By the second phase of the chapter house's structural history, its north-south width was the same as is now seen, though any reduction in width was more than compensated for by the way that it was extended eastwards beyond the body of the range, by possibly as much as four bays. The new eastern part beyond the range was evidently divided by arcades along each side to create a central space flanked by aisles, and all of this would presumably have been covered by stone vaulting. This phase is probably datable to shortly before 1240, when the *Chronicle of Melrose* records that the bones of the abbots who had been interred near the entrance were entombed more appropriately at the east end, suggesting the chamber had only recently been extended. This was evidently a time when major expansion of the buildings was underway. Abbot Matthew (1246-61) was credited with architectural activity by the *Chronicle of Melrose* following his deposition and this, considered with what we know about the chapter house, suggests that he had inherited and actively continued a major campaign of rebuilding at the abbey.

The surviving lower walls of the entrance front to the chapter house date from this second phase, and we can see that it had three handsomely detailed arches opening off the east cloister walk which together extended across the full width of the chamber as it then stood (**87**). It might have been expected that there would instead have been the more usual arrangement of a central doorway flanked by a pair of unglazed windows, as can still be seen to have been the case at Melrose's grand-daughter-house of Culross, or at the Premonstratensian abbey of Dryburgh, for example. Is it possible that the provision of three arches stemmed from a wish to provide easier access from the cloister to the tomb-shrine of St Waltheof for those who were not members of the community? In this there could be partial parallels with the arrangements made at Rievaulx when St Ailred greatly enlarged the chapter house in the mid-twelfth-century. The entrance front of Rievaulx's new chapter house was also given three arches, though in that case the chamber was so large that there was in addition space for intermediate openings, within one of which the shrine of St William was located.

At Melrose the jambs of the three entrance arches were of four orders, with free-standing shafts placed against the leading faces and within the re-entrant angles of masonry set out to a stepped profile; the salient angles of the stepped profile in the central arch were given additional emphasis by sunk rolls. There is no evidence of doors having been hung within the arches, indicating that they were open towards the cloister walk. Nothing is known to survive of the shaft caps, but the bases were of a fully developed water-holding form that fits well with a mid-thirteenth-century date of construction. The combination of a stepped-profile core and shafts had been a common treatment for the jambs of doorways from at least the mid-twelfth century. If we try to place it more precisely within the wider British Cistercian context, we can see that it was essentially the same formula as in the west doorway of Fountains Abbey of around the 1160s, although the details of the bases and caps were of earlier types in that case. Broadly similar treatments that are closer in time to Melrose, albeit with differences of detailing and scale, are to be seen in Scotland in the west doorway at Glenluce Abbey and the chapter house doorway at Culross Abbey.

So far as the main body of the second chapter house is concerned, as mentioned above (see p.181), there is a fragment of what appears to have been a mid- thirteenth-century base course for a buttress at its junction with the east wall of the sacristy. Within the chapter house, at a point corresponding with that buttress, is what looks like the sub-base of a rectangular respond or projection, with a chamfered upper edge, which has no counterparts elsewhere on that wall. One interpretation of this could be that it was

87 *The south jamb of the central doorway into the chapter house.* Fawcett

part of a cross arcade on the line of the east wall of the dormitory above. East of this point the side walls of the chapter house are known to have continued on the same line for at least a short distance, showing that the mid-thirteenth-century eastward extension of the chapter house must have been of the same north-south width as the part of the chamber that was within the range.

It was very common to extend chapter houses as the wealth and size of the communities they served increased. Frequently, this simply meant an eastward extension of the chamber itself, with no internal reflection of the fact that part was within the range and part outside, other than the way in which only the walls of those parts beyond the range had windows. However, a limiting factor in such cases was that the height of the chamber was restricted by the floor of the dormitory on the upper storey. One way of achieving a greater height for the new structure was to make the old chapter house into a vestibule, and to build beyond the range a completely new chamber that was unconstrained by the dormitory floor level. There are examples of this at the Cistercian houses of Balmerino and possibly Newbattle, a Benedictine example at Iona, and Augustinian examples at St Andrews and Holyrood (in the last case the chapter house itself is of polygonal plan). We cannot be certain that this was the solution adopted at Melrose, though the respond projecting from the south wall on the line of the east wall of the range is consistent with the possibility that it was. Not many years after the extension was completed the chamber was given a splendid new tiled pavement.

In the third phase of works on the chapter house, it was concluded by the excavators who investigated it in 1996 that there had probably been a further eastward extension of the chamber, by perhaps one bay, and it seems it may also have been laterally expanded to north and south. The most likely time for this would perhaps have been around the start of the great campaign of rebuilding that was initiated after the English attack of 1385. The way this lateral expansion appears to have been confined to the part of the chapter house beyond the range supports the suggestion made above that the portion within the range had been reduced to a vestibule, since otherwise there would have been an awkward change in alignment of the side walls about a third of the way down their length. Lateral expansion of chapter houses beyond the range is unusual, though a partial Scottish parallel has been found through excavation at the Augustinian Abbey of Jedburgh, and there were parallels in northern England at the Benedictine Abbey of St Mary in York and at the Augustinian priory of Lanercost, for example.

By the fourth phase of operations on the chapter house, it seems that, as with the final stages of work on the church itself, it had been accepted that ambition after 1385 had outstripped what was either achievable or necessary, and towards the end of the community's life the chapter house seems to have been cut back to a chamber within the body of the range. The date this was done is unknown; it might have followed the attack by the earl of Hertford in 1545, though by that stage the community was perhaps barely able to carry out new building, even when it was essentially contraction, and it seems that business was increasingly being carried out elsewhere (see p.61).

THE TOMB–SHRINE OF ST WALTHEOF

David I's stepson, Waltheof, who was abbot of Melrose between 1148 and 1159, came to be considered as a saint, though he was never formally canonised. At his death he was buried within the chapter house, the traditional place for abbots to find their last resting place, and close to its entrance. In this latter respect, Melrose may have been following the lead of its mother-house at Rievaulx, where William the first abbot, who was also regarded as a saint, was buried in a similar location. Being close to the entrance, Waltheof's tomb was accessible from both outside and within the chamber, and this may have been intended to make it easier for favoured layfolk to visit the tomb. His grave was re-opened in 1171 and a fresh slab then placed over it; it was further disturbed in 1206, when a new burial was being prepared next to it, and it was yet again opened in 1240.

88 *Fragments thought to be from the tomb-shrine of St Waltheof.* Historic Scotland

On this last occasion a shrine-like memorial may have been placed over his remains, in the hope that he would eventually be canonised; fragments assumed to be from such a tomb-shrine, and with details that point to a mid-thirteenth-century date, were found when the chapter house was excavated in 1921 (**88**). Its main feature would have been a tomb chest with sides decorated by quatrefoils, some of which were pierced through the stone slabs which formed the sides. These openings were presumably to allow closer access for pilgrims to the burial itself, as in the *foramina* type of shrine, a thirteenth-century example of which may be seen in the shrine of St Bertelin at Ilam in Staffordshire. The ways in which pilgrims might seek closer contact with the saint through such apertures – at some risk to life and limb – are graphically illustrated in medieval depictions of pilgrims visiting the shrine of St Edward the Confessor at Westminster. Along with portions of the tomb chest, fragments were also found of small triplet shafts, which suggests there was a superstructure over the chest (**89**). These shafts presumably carried arches, above which may have been a gabled roof of the type that perpetuated the idea of the elevated shrine. An example of such a gabled roof is to be seen over the tomb of Archbishop Walter de Grey (d.1255), at York Minster, where it is possible there were hopes of Grey eventually achieving

89 *Sketch reconstruction of the possible original appearance of the tomb shrine of St Waltheof.* David Simon/Historic Scotland

canonisation. However, the de Grey tomb is more architecturally ambitious than would have been considered appropriate for a Cistercian house, and certainly the fragments found at Melrose show greater decorative restraint. Nevertheless, even at Cistercian houses, shrine-tombs of this kind would almost invariably have been painted, and the fragments at Melrose still have slight traces of gilding.

THE TILED PAVEMENTS IN THE CHAPTER HOUSE

The finest tiled pavements of which we know anything at Melrose were all in the chapter house, where they must have been laid at some date after the reconstruction of around 1240, though perhaps not before the third quarter of that century. Various patterns were found. At the far-east end of the chamber was a design with square tiles decorated with inlaid fleurs-de-lis or star patterns, and set within a chevron arrangement of angled tiles. Further west were a number of other designs, including diagonally-set squares, some inlaid with a range of motifs. Close to the central axis of the chamber, interlocking hexagonal patterns were laid out with six rectangular 'spokes' of yellow against a green background, radiating from a hexagonal tile with a six-petalled flower within a circlet. One of the rarest tiles associated with the chapter house had the remains of the letters I and A, which Christopher Norton has suggested may have come from a tile tomb of one of the abbots, with the letters forming part of the inscription '*hic jacet*' meaning 'here lies'.

THE EAST RANGE BEYOND THE CHAPTER HOUSE (**85**)

In its final extended form the east range continued some 38.5m further north beyond the chapter house, with an offshoot projecting out at right angles for about 20m on the east side of the range. Since so little survives to any significant height, and there are no more than partial excavated footings north of Cloisters Road, it is difficult to be certain of either the building sequence or the uses of the internal spaces. As has already been said, it cannot be ruled out that when first built the range was slightly narrower than it later became. While there are certainly extents of cubical masonry of a type that might be of mid-twelfth-century date in the east as well as the west wall, and this might suggest that the range was always of the present width, that masonry in the east wall may have been re-used in its present context.

Immediately north of the chapter house are two relatively narrow spaces with doorways towards the cloister. If, as suggested above, the chapter house initially extended further north, the first of those spaces would initially have been even narrower than what is now there. That space may have contained the day stair to the dormitory, before it was moved to a more convenient situation in the remodelled north range, where it would not cut into the space of the dormitory. The original stair was evidently entered from the cloister through an open arch of the same width as the chamber itself. The rather wider space further north has the lower courses of stone benches down each side, showing that it was the parlour, where limited conversation was allowed to the brethren at certain times. Although there is no evidence of a second doorway on the east side of the range, as might be expected with such use, this may be because the wall does not survive to a sufficient height. A group of plain tiles set out on a chequer pattern in this chamber is thought to be a late medieval import from the Low Countries.

THE PART OF THE RANGE NORTH OF THE PARLOUR

This part was rebuilt as a single extended space, with what is likely to have been a row of six cylindrical piers along its north-south central axis. The form of the round bases of these piers, which have double rolls, together with evidence for a clasping buttress at the north-east corner of the range, point to a mid-thirteenth-century date for this part of the range in its present form. This suggests that it was rebuilt as a continuation of the programme of work already seen in the remodelling of the chapter house, and it may be tentatively attributed to the abbacy of Matthew. The piers probably supported four-part rib vaulting over the lower storey, of the type of which fragments are to be seen in the site museum. The northward extension of the range meant that the main drain ran under its north-eastern corner; this may have led to some concerns about structural risk, because a spur of buttress walling was found to have been built against the centre of the north gable of the range. Apart from the pier stumps, one of the few architectural features of the east range is the jamb of a doorway that once opened to the area beyond the adjacent north range. This jamb, with two orders of chamfers rising from a chamfered base course is now set back behind the thickened east wall of the remodelled north range.

One of the requirements of the ground floor of the east range was to house the novitiate, where those who had not yet taken final vows were initiated into the way of life to which they were about to commit themselves. There may also have been a day room for the choir monks. But the functions of these spaces would almost certainly have changed periodically, with areas being partitioned off in different ways as the need arose. While initially those partitions may have been of timber, traces were found of later inserted stone walls on the axis of the row of piers near the middle of the space, and projecting from the east wall towards the southern end.

Once the main drain had passed under the north-east corner of the range, where the channel was arched over for greater strength rather than lintelled, it ran along the east side of the range for a short distance before turning at right angles to flow below the rear-dorter or latrine block. The principal bank of latrines would have been at first-floor level, where they could be reached directly from the dormitory, and the drain at this point was particularly carefully constructed of fine ashlar masonry rather than rubble, with a chamfered course at the base, so that the waste would pass on as smoothly as possible (**8**). At ground floor-level there was a narrow corridor-like space along the south side of the compartment that enclosed the drain, and at Rievaulx it has been suggested that the space in this location housed the novitiate, though there is no evidence to suggest that this was the case at Melrose. Here the space was apparently made even narrower at some stage, and this resulted in the blocking and reconstruction of a doorway from the east range. Evidence was also found for a narrow corridor-like pentice against its south wall, which could have been constructed either entirely of masonry, or of timber on masonry footings. To the east of the latrine block this pentice may have become a free-standing gallery which deviated towards the south-east, possibly heading towards the building that it has been suggested was the infirmary. If that was the case, this gallery could have been the main connection between the quarters of the choir monks around the cloister and the infirmary to its east. At a later stage a small block of unknown function was added on the northern side of the latrine block at its junction with the east range, with doorways into it both from the range and from the exterior.

The north claustral range

The range of monastic buildings on the north side of the cloister is the least well preserved of any of the conventual buildings at Melrose. In its first, mid-twelfth-century form it was probably divided into three main spaces. At the centre was the refectory or dining hall, which is likely to have occupied over half of the total length of the range; it is not clear if the *lavatorium* pavilion which projects into the cloister was built to serve this first refectory or the larger one that succeeded it. East of the refectory would have been the cale-factory or warming room, where the choir monks were allowed their only social fireplace in the abbey; west of the refectory was the kitchen, where it could serve both the refectory of the choir monks to the east, and that of the lay-brethren to the west. The best preserved part of this first arrangement is the kitchen, the plan of which suggests that the range was initially built with thinner walls and thus with slightly less overall width from north to south than the eastern parts of the range that were later rebuilt. Some of the main functions of the kitchen are still identifiable from the drain in its floor, the servery hatch in its west wall, and what may be the base of an oven towards the west side; the fireplace was perhaps a free-standing structure, represented by footings towards the east end of the space.

THE REFECTORY

The main change to the range followed on from a decision to re-align the refectory so that it projected at 90 degrees from the cloister, as yet another part of the mid-thirteenth-century rebuilding that we have seen in the chapter house and the northern parts of the east range. Re-alignment of the refectory in this way was a common modification at Cistercian abbeys, and is seen particularly vividly at Rievaulx, where the magnificent shell of the new refectory that was completed by about 1200 is the second most prominent feature of the site after the early thirteenth-century choir of the church. Re-alignment had the advantage that the refectory could be made larger than if it were entirely contained within the range. It also left more space for other functions within the range, and this was important for an order that stressed the need for the enclosure of the monks within the cloister, except at certain times of the day when they were allowed to go into the wider precinct for physical labour, such as gardening.

It is assumed that one benefit of freeing up space within Melrose's north range was that the daystair from the dormitory could be relocated from the east range to the east end of the north range. This eastern end of the range was evidently rebuilt along with the refectory itself, and was given thicker walls, perhaps to support inserted vaulting. There are indications of fewer changes to the western end of the range, where the walls were left at their original thickness, though it appears that the north-east corner of the kitchen was cut off from the main space of the room for some reason.

Of the rebuilt refectory itself, little remains apart from partial footings, which survive best at the junction of the east and north walls. It extended for about 36.5m from north to south, and was about 13.5m wide. The part that projected beyond the north range was divided into five bays on the long axis, and three narrower bays on the short axis, on the evidence of the spacing of the buttresses found through excavation, and assuming that the part now covered by Cloisters Road was similar to the part to its north. The main room of the refectory block, the dining hall itself, is likely to have been elevated to first-floor level above a vaulted undercroft, with a staircase up to it inside the range, perhaps to the east of the kitchen in the area originally taken up by the west end of the refectory. Within a monastery eating was imbued with spiritual significance. The weekly washing of feet, which took place at the *lavatorium* near the refectory entrance, together with the analogies between the first-floor location of the refectory and the *cenaculum* (upper room) in Jerusalem, must both have been seen as bearing deeply symbolic parallels with the arrangements for the Last Supper which Christ took with his disciples before his Passion. Further emphasising the underlying spiritual nature of taking bodily sustenance, eating was accompanied by appropriate readings made from a pulpit built out from one of the long sides of the refectory hall.

So far as the architectural character of the refectory is concerned, the best clue we have is some fragments of windows said to have been found on its site, and now displayed in the site museum (**90**). The grouped pointed-arched openings were framed by moulded arches carried by shafts set into hollows, which created an appearance that still showed some concern for Cistercian precepts in the way that nothing was done to excess, but which nevertheless displayed carefully considered proportions and high-quality workmanship.

The west claustral range

The west range of the cloister and its associated structures represented the most complex group of buildings in the entire abbey (**91**). This was because,

90 *Fragments thought to be from the windows of the second refectory.* Fawcett

as the home of the *conversi* or lay-brethren, who carried out the greater part of the abbey's manual labour, this area not only had to accommodate the equivalent of all of the domestic functions provided for the choir monks in the east and north ranges and the infirmary, but it also had to afford space for a number of work areas. One of the most striking features of the earlier history of Cistercian monasticism is the very large numbers of men of all social strata who were driven by the fervent hope of salvation to join the order as lay-brethren, sometimes relatively late in their life. In the first heady days of the order they were seen as occupying no less important a place in the community than the choir monks, being Martha to the latter's Mary. The frequently gruelling work these unlettered lay-brethren undertook was regarded as being an equally effective path to God as the long hours of prayer and study of their literate brethren, the choir monks. In many houses the lay-brethren so far outnumbered the choir monks throughout the twelfth and thirteenth centuries, that very large-scale accommodation was required for them.

It was presumably to insulate the cloister of the choir monks from the bustle and noise of the areas occupied by the lay-brethren, that there was originally an open area known as a lane between the buildings of the latter and the rest of the cloister. It is not known when this lane was absorbed into the cloister, but it was perhaps in the fourteenth century, by which time most of the work once allocated to the lay-brethren was being carried out by paid servants.

The width of the west range is about 9.6m, which is similar to that of the western part of the north range, and one wonders if the east range may also at first have been of around the same width before the thirteenth-century

91 *The west claustral range up to Cloisters Road, from the south-west.* Historic Scotland

rebuilding. The range was contained within relatively thin and unbuttressed walls, and the piers of circular or octagonal form down the central axis of much of the range are likely to have been later insertions associated with the addition of stone vaulting. The range was eventually divided into at least five spaces of varying dimensions. That at the north end was linked with the kitchen by a hatch and was presumably the first refectory of the lay-brethren, though it was later built over when an extension to the range was built. A narrower room to its south, with doors on both the east and west sides, would have been a parlour. The uses of the other spaces can only be guessed at. The largest of the rooms, which may at first have run for about half of the length of the range before being divided into two unequal parts, must have served some mundane use in its final state from the presence of a long trough and drain. In the course of subdivision, a half-pier attached to a spur of wall was embodied within a cross wall.

Projecting about 18m westwards from the southern end of the range is a cross-range, which had a width of about 10.5m in its final state, though a stump of wall at its eastern end suggests an earlier cross-range on this site may have been narrower. The roof, or an upper floor if there was one, was carried down the central axis of the range by timber posts rising from three socket stones, but the range was open to the elements towards the north. On that side there was a cloister-like arcade carried on small piers, the bases of which survive, and which point to a late twelfth-century date for its construction. This arcade had piers of alternating round and octagonal form, terminating against the west wall with a respond in the form of a keeled shaft. At the eastern end of the arcade was a more complex pier, with an octagonal main part and a pair of smaller engaged shafts on its eastern side, one of which was octagonal and the other round. Such a combination of small round and octagonal shafts is very like what we have seen in the fragments thought to be from the cloister itself, and this pier was therefore presumably built around the same time as the cloister. Since the engaged shafts suggest an intention to have an arcade of paired octagonal and round shafts extending outwards from it, it may be that the pier has been either partly turned or that it was not originally designed for this position. Could an open arcade have been intended to run along the west side of the west range? If it was, however, it appears to have been replaced by an enclosed lean-to pentice, the foundations of which are still to be seen. The function of the cross-range itself is difficult to identify, though whatever was done within it was something that did not require full enclosure. One attractive possibility might be use as a mason's lodge, but there is nothing else to support that idea. Within the small courtyard in the angle between the cross-range and the west range itself a number of tiles stamped with small six-petal flowers and rosettes were found, which may be of fourteenth-century date. It is rather unexpected to find a tiled pavement within a roofless courtyard, and it is thus almost certain they were being put to secondary use in this position. On the west side of the courtyard, projecting below a modern boundary wall, are the footings of a substantial wall that presumably closed off the quarters of the lay-brethren from the rest of the precinct.

THE EXTENSION TO THE WEST RANGE AND THE INFIRMARY OF THE LAY-BRETHREN

The high levels of vocations for Cistercian lay-brethren throughout the twelfth and much of the thirteenth centuries meant that the buildings provided for them might have to be periodically enlarged. At Melrose the first west range was augmented by the addition of a new building which partly overlapped the northern end of the original range, and which eventually reached over 70m in length, possibly as a result of more than one thirteenth-century building campaign, since there is a slight change in the character of the masonry part way down its length.

Perhaps because of the presence of other structures on the site, this building was set at a slight angle to the earlier west range. It had an almost square chamber at the southern end, but the rest of the range was set out as a single space, in its final state having a row of thirteen cylindrical piers rising from chamfered bases along its central axis. From the excavated evidence these piers carried vaulting at ground-floor level, the ribs of which emerged from the piers without the intervention of capitals, a satisfyingly stripped-down approach to the integration of piers and ribs that is often associated with the undercrofts of ancillary structures. These piers and the vaulting they carried may have been later insertions but, whether original or inserted, there seem to have been fears that they were threatening the stability of the building at some stage, since a series of unusually massive buttresses was added along the flanks of the range. Although built as a structurally undivided space, it was presumably always intended that the interior would be partitioned to some extent, and traces have been found of at least four later cross walls. To heat one of the chambers a fireplace was added against the west wall, suggesting that part was the warming house of the lay-brethren.

Extending westwards from the range at its northern end, and with the lintelled-over main drain running down its central axis, are the foundations of a large building which evidently once extended under where Abbey Street now runs. It appears to have been a large hall with an aisle down both its north and its south sides, and with the piers of the two arcades carried on square sub-bases. The most likely function for a building of this form and in this position is an infirmary for those lay-brethren who were too old or too ill to carry out their duties. We can assume from what we know of infirmaries elsewhere that it had a taller central space flanked on each side by an aisle, and it gives us some idea of how the infirmary of the choir monks to the east of the cloister could have been laid out when first built. Related locations and plans of infirmaries for lay-brethren are to be seen at a number of English Cistercian abbeys, as at Waverley for example, though there on the south side of the complex since that was the position of the cloister. In some cases *conversi* infirmaries with similar plans were aligned from north to south rather than east to west, as at the abbeys of Fountains, Jervaulx and Roche. All of these English infirmaries for lay-brethren are of the twelfth or thirteenth centuries, and were built when recruitment was still running high. The excavator of Melrose considered an early fourteenth-century date possible for this example, though it is not clear on what evidence this conclusion was reached. On balance, construction no later than the thirteenth century must be considered more likely. This is because by the mid-fourteenth century there was a marked decline in the recruitment of lay-brethren throughout the order, and it seems most unlikely that such a large infirmary would still be required at so late a period.

With the decline in recruitment, alternative uses had to be found for the buildings of the lay-brethren if keeping them in repair was to be justified. Tantalising pointers to some of these uses were found in the traces of a tank and of what appears to have been the base of an oven or kiln of some form in the extended west range, while a series of pits constructed in the south aisle of the infirmary point to this part being used for the tanning of leather, a noxious industrial process that the monks certainly would not have wished to have carried out any closer to their own quarters.

The monks' infirmary

One of the most important buildings beyond the ranges around the cloister itself would have been the infirmary for the choir monks. As with the *conversi* infirmary, this was for members of the community who were too old or ill to take part in the demanding daily round of religious observance; it was also the place where supposedly health-giving blood-lettings were administered to all the monks on a rotational basis. It was usually located a short distance to the east of the cloister and, as has been said above, may have been close to the post-Reformation manse of the parish minister, where it was recorded in 1743 that there were the foundations of a chapel and a large aisled building (**7**). The latter was perhaps of a similar plan to the building thought to have been the infirmary of the lay-brethren to the north-west of the cloister.

The only potentially medieval fragment now to be seen in this area, however, is a barrel-vaulted substructure embodied within the outbuildings of what used to be a brewery. This appears to be of relatively late medieval date, and perhaps represents modifications to the infirmary from a period when a number of buildings were being adapted to create accommodation for some of the monks that could offer a higher degree of comfort and privacy than could be contrived within the old conventual buildings. We certainly know that some of the monks had chambers in the infirmary in the 1550s, when there was a meeting to discuss the perceived faults of the commendator. The infirmary was possibly connected to the east claustral range by a pentice, or covered gallery, and traces of what could be such a pentice have been found along the south side of the latrine (see pp.190–1).

The abbot's house

The earlier Cistercians insisted on a strict interpretation of the clause of the Benedictine rule which required the abbot to live in common with his monks. This meant that he was expected to sleep either within the main space of the dormitory, or in a small cubicle that was most usually off its end next to the church. An early deviation from this rule took place at Melrose's own mother-house of Rievaulx, however, where the poor state of St Ailred's health meant that he had to be provided with separate accommodation before his death in 1167 if he was not to disturb the life of the brethren too grievously. But, perhaps inevitably, as the administrative burdens of abbots became greater, as the requirement for offering hospitality to important visitors increased, and as the wish for expression of status became less resistable, increasing numbers of abbots decided they must have their own self-contained accommodation. At first this was usually set close to the dormitory, so that at least the letter of the rule was followed, and the expedient was sometimes adopted that the dormitory and abbatial residence inter-communicated through the latrine. Indeed, this arrangement may have continued to be the case throughout the Middle Ages at many abbeys, and it certainly appears that the imposing residence which Robert Reid built at Kinloss Abbey after 1528 had its origins in a residence connected to the latrine, for example.

At Melrose, however, even by the mid-thirteenth century there was a willingness to deviate from the letter of this part of the rule, and an abbatial residence was constructed to the north-east of the claustral ranges, on a site that must have been selected more for its amenity than for its proximity to the monks' quarters. The *Chronicle of Melrose* says that a great abbot's chamber on the bank of the river was one of the buildings raised by Abbot Matthew (1246-61), and this reference can be associated reasonably certainly with foundations located adjacent to the lade. These foundations had at their core a structure of elongated rectangular plan aligned from south-east to north-west, which was divided into two unequal parts and heavily buttressed. This makes it likely that what it contained were the two principal elements of the great majority of aristocratic dwellings, a hall and a chamber, with the hall being the more 'public' space and the chamber the more secluded inner living space and bedroom of its fortunate occupant. An abbatial residence of similar form and in a comparable situation is to be seen at the Cistercian abbey of Croxden in Staffordshire, though it is later than the Melrose example, dating from 1335-6, and this again reminds us that the abbot's move away from the cloister took place relatively early at Melrose.

The house had an entrance doorway towards the eastern end of the south wall, and the base of one jamb of a fine doorway embellished with a triplet of shafts is still there; the doorway probably had a porch added in front of it, since tiles were found in this area. Heavy buttressing along three of the walls suggests there was stone vaulting over the lower level, with the consequent likelihood that the principal rooms were on the first floor, which was to become increasingly common. But the picture may not be as simple as it first seems. The excavator considered that the smaller western part of this plan was a later addition, and it is also possible that the buttresses were not part of the original design, since they do not appear to be bonded in with the wall. The building may thus have started life as a single large room, possibly set at ground level, which was extended and possibly also heightened in the course of later operations.

Foundations of a number of other structures have been found attached or close to it, one of which is a rather puzzling sunken area, entered down a flight of steps immediately to its south. Other extensions were set further to the east, beyond the boundary wall of the house known as St Kierans, since substantial walls, one with a chamfered base course, have been found on the same alignment as that boundary. It can be assumed that, in addition to his hall and chamber, the abbot would eventually have had his own private chapel, chambers for visitors and a growing number of domestic offices, and some of these must be represented by the other foundations. Also closely associated with the residence was a bridge over the lade, giving access to the wider precinct to the north. In its final state the abbot's house must have been an extensive and irregularly arranged complex of structures, with the main parts rising through two or more storeys. There can be little doubt that it provided a most attractive residence, in an almost idyllic setting that looked across the valley of the Tweed on one side, and to the Eildon Hills on the other.

The commendator's house

The building known as the commendator's house, to the west of the abbot's house, has housed the site museum since the 1940s. It was extricated and recreated from the substantial post-Reformation residence known as The Priory in a programme of works that began in 1932. Once it had been realised that there was an earlier house at the core of this residence, those parts that could be identified as later additions were dismantled, leaving a basically L-shaped core, albeit with no clear indications of how it had terminated at its southern end (**92**).

At ground-floor level there was a large room at the northern end of the main block that could be interpreted as a kitchen, on the evidence of its large fireplace. South of this was a pair of barrel-vaulted chambers, entered through doorways with heavy roll mouldings from a corridor running along their east side. There was evidently another large room at the southern end of the block, on the east side of which was the projecting wing that gave the block

92 *Plan, section and elevation of the medieval fabric found within the house known as The Priory in 1932, and subsequently restored as the commendator's house.* Sylvia Stevenson/Historic Scotland

its L shape. There was also a small single-storey projection added in the northern re-entrant angle between the main block and the wing. At first-floor level the investigations in the 1930s appear to have suggested that there had been one large room at the centre of the block, which had been sub-divided at a later stage, and a room of about half its size at the north end. As with the earlier abbot's house, it is likely that this arrangement can be under-stood as a first-floor lodging of a hall and chamber. What there had been at the southern end of the range was no longer clear, but it was decided it should be re-enclosed as a room of a similar size as the supposed chamber.

The original provision for access between ground and first floors could not be determined, though it was thought there had been a stair in the east wing, and this was where a timber stair was constructed. Along the exterior of the east side of the main block a series of joist pockets was found. It was concluded these had been provided for a timber gallery reached from two blocked doorways at each end of the large room at that level, while angled pockets for timbers at the north-east angle may have been for a later forestair of some kind, although it was decided not to restore these features (**93**).

The date of the first construction of this building is by no means certain. James Richardson, who supervised dismantling of the later work and the subsequent restoration, tentatively suggested that it could have originated in the mid-fifteenth century as a more commodious and fashionable abbot's lodging. If that were the case, it is possible that it was intended to be part of a yet further extended abbatial complex stretching westwards from the earlier abbot's hall, and it certainly appears to be the case that there was a length of parallel walls between the two buildings that could have been part of a connecting pentice and gallery. Nevertheless, it is now difficult to see anything in the planning or detailing of this building that would fit comfortably with

93 *The commendator's house in its restored state, from the north-east; joist pockets thought to have been provided for a timber gallery are visible along the east face.* Historic Scotland

such an early date, while the provision of a ground-floor corridor, the form of the wide-mouthed shot holes in two faces of the wing, and the heavy roll mouldings to the internal ground-floor doorways would fit better in the sixteenth century. Indeed, there is little in the structure that is now visible which could be dated before building operations that are known to have been carried out in 1590 by the post-Reformation commendator of that time, James Douglas of Lochleven, who had acquired that office in 1569. The re-use of medieval stones in the walls also points to a post-Reformation building campaign, at a time when many of the abbey's structures had come to be regarded as a readily available source of materials.

The need for the new building had presumably resulted from Sir Walter Scott of Branxholm's destruction of the medieval 'abbotishall' in 1569 (see p.66), and Douglas's responsibility for the new building is commemorated by an inscribed lintel that was found over a window and that has been replicated and re-set over the modern entrance. This gives Douglas's initials, together with those of Mary Ker his wife, and the date 1590. An intriguing feature of this lintel is the small carved letters 'AM' in one corner. These may simply indicate that the work was carried out after the house had become an ancient monument in the care of the Ministry of Public Buildings and Works. But it has also been suggested that they could replicate a feature of the original lintel, and perhaps indicate that the house was the work of Andrew Mein, a member of a local family of master masons which later produced craftsmen, who worked on the royal building operations at Edinburgh and Stirling Castles.

The buildings of the abbey after the Reformation

Throughout the upheavals of the Reformation, part of the monastic church continued to be used for parochial worship, and it has been suggested above that part may have been a surviving portion of the west end of the original church nave (see p.88). But by 1612 costly repairs to the church that remained in use were required, and the suggestion was made that a new building should be constructed beyond the west front. Eventually, in about 1621, the decision was taken to adapt the three eastern bays of the nave that had served as the monastic choir for use as the parish church.

The extent of work that had to be carried out on the monastic choir to fit it for parochial worship is a measure of how much damage the medieval church must by then have suffered. It can only be assumed that the tierceron high vault that was designed for this part in the mid-fifteenth century would have been retained if it had survived in a sound state, and it must be concluded that the theft of the roof materials by Sir Walter Scott of Branxholm in 1569 had resulted in its collapse or severe instability. As a replacement for that vault, an altogether more utilitarian pointed barrel vault was built. Intriguingly, although the roof over that vault reached a lower point than its predecessor, as can be seen from the roof creases against the west side of the tower (62), the apex of the vault itself rose higher than the ridge of the medieval vault. This is because the stone-flagged roof of the later vault was an integral part of its outer surface, rather than a separate timber-framed structure as would have been the case with the medieval nave vault (although it should be remembered that the roof of the medieval presbytery vault had also been an integral part of its outer surface). Because of the great weight of this new vault, and on account of the difficulty of spanning the medieval nave, it was decided to reduce the width to more manageable proportions. This was done by building four massive piers of masonry to carry an arcade and an inner wall face against the north wall, virtually obscuring the whole of that wall in the process (94). On the south side the medieval arcade and clearstorey were retained but, since a barrel vault has a continuous horizontal springing rather than a series of arched junctions with the wall, the pointed heads of the clearstorey wall passage arches had to be replaced by flatter segmental heads (61). To enclose the east and west ends of the new church, solid walls were built, the latter taking the stone pulpitum as its base. Presumably once this work was complete the old church was demolished, and certainly nothing is to be seen of it in Slezer's view of 1693.

There is no doubt that the creation of a new church within the medieval monastic choir involved a massive and costly effort, and what remains of it must be accepted as a unique and fascinating illustration of one way in which a medieval monastic church could be adapted to reformed uses. Yet it could hardly be claimed as an aesthetically pleasing modification to such a magnificent building, even if allowance is made for the fact that we now see it as it was never intended to be seen, without either a plastered finish to its masonry or the furnishings which would have filled so much of it. But in fact it is likely that it never was such a satisfactory solution as had been hoped for, since major repairs were needed as early as 1653, and there was a constant problem of leaks through the vault and its roof, while the floor was nothing more than compacted earth.

There was also a problem with the furnishings. Although we are now used to the idea that the interiors of Presbyterian churches present an attractively orderly and uniform array of galleries and pews focused on the pulpit and communion table, such interiors have only been common since the later

94 *The three arches and the pointed barrel vault inserted when the monastic choir was converted into a parish church in around 1621.* Historic Scotland

95 *A late eighteenth-century view across the transept, looking south; the buttressed wall under the west tower arch, at the east end of the seventeenth-century parish church, is visible on the right, with one of the stairs that gave access to the lofts.* Stewart and Jukes

eighteenth century. Before then the provision of furnishings might be little more than a free-for-all, with the wealthier families, the burgesses and the trade guilds vying with each other to obtain the most advantageous position for their lofts or pews. Often enough, little heed was paid to the consequences for those less fortunate, who might be left to find space as best they could. Access to the higher lofts would be either from external masonry forestairs, like that to be seen in some views of the transept area at Melrose (**95**), or by internal timber stairs. By 1776 the church was described by W. Hutchinson as being 'filled with lofts in the disposition of which irregularity alone seems to have been studied; some are raised on upright beams as scaffolds, tier upon tier, others supported against the walls and pillars; no two are alike…the place is as dark as a vault….Many of the old churches of Scotland…are filthy and foul…but for uncleanliness this place exceeds them all'. Evidence for the location of some of the lofts may be seen in joist pockets in the walls and inserted piers. Some improvements were undertaken, including the piercing of a large window in the west wall, but in 1808 it was

96 *The abbey church in the late seventeenth century, from the south.* Slezer, 1693

decided to build a new church elsewhere, and following its completion in 1810, the parish congregation finally moved out of the abbey church.

It is an indicator of changed attitudes to medieval monastic architecture that it was not only the needs of the congregation that were taken into account in the decision to build a new church elsewhere. One of the factors underlying the decision was the agreement of the owner, the third duke of Buccleuch, to pay for the conservation of the abbey church once it had been vacated. This is an important pointer to the value that was increasingly being placed by informed opinion on the most impressive architectural remains of the nation's medieval history. Melrose Abbey's great beauty had probably always been recognised by an enlightened minority, even when it was most reviled for the way of life that it represented. It was certainly one of the most carefully illustrated monastic ruins in John Slezer's *Theatrum Scotiae*, when that collection of views was first published in 1693, for example (**96**). But by the second half of the eighteenth century, as the pleasures to be gained from both the picturesque and sublime qualities of such melancholically decayed reminders of the past came to be ever more cultivated by the educated public, Melrose was increasingly often represented on canvas or paper. The third duke of Buccleuch himself had commissioned a series of views of the abbey from the artist George Barret in around 1769, including one that was tellingly entitled *Part of Melrose Abbey by moonlight*. Engravings of the abbey by moonlight were to become particular favourites, especially if there was just the hint of the shadowy figure of a monk (**97**). By the late eighteenth century it would have been almost unthinkable for views of Melrose Abbey not to be included in the second part of Thomas Pennant's *Tour in Scotland* of 1772, or in the first volume of Francis Grose's *Antiquities of Scotland* of 1789. But for many it is James Ward's much-reproduced painting of 1807 that most perfectly captures the qualities of the lyrical beauty of a handsomely composed ruin within a bucolic landscape that were so dear to the Romantic mind at the turn of the eighteenth and nineteenth centuries.

At the same time that the ruined beauties of Melrose were being rediscovered, a growing group of antiquaries, of whom General George Hutton is perhaps the most important representative, was setting about systematically gathering information on Scotland's monastic history, to provide a firm basis of scholarly understanding that would complement the Romantic yearnings of others. With such a strongly gathering current of mutually compatible interests, the tide of opinion was beginning to swing strongly in favour of the preservation of Scotland's medieval abbeys. It was additionally fortunate for Melrose Abbey that there was an enlightened and wealthy land-owner who

97 *A moonlit view of the abbey in 1835.* Bower and Johnstone

was prepared to seize the opportunity of the removal of the parish church to instigate the abbey's conservation.

Melrose had yet one further massive advantage stemming from the decision of the novelist and poet Sir Walter Scott to build a Gothick house for himself at Abbotsford, a short way up the Tweed valley, with the money that he was earning from the rapidly growing sales of his publications. From the first faltering steps in 1811, a house that had started as a 'cottage' had by 1824 grown into an extensive country house, with many of its constituent elements being more or less direct quotations from the medieval buildings that Scott so much admired. Melrose, which figured prominently in his poem *The Lay of the Last Minstrel* was, naturally enough, a major contributor to the pool of ideas. One bay of the cloister wall arcading was copied for the hall fireplace; casts of a number of corbels were taken and tidied up for re-use; the transept stair tower provided a basis for the turret off Scott's study; and several other details were looked at for their possibilities. It is also highly likely that many of the carved and moulded medieval architectural fragments to be seen around the house had somehow found their way from the abbey to Abbotsford.

As Scott's popularity grew, Melrose became known to an ever wider public, becoming an essential element in almost any tour of Scotland. Needless to say, it was also an inescapable port of call for all visitors to Abbotsford, with one in 1831 being the artist J.M.W. Turner, who was called upon to illustrate Scott's works. Equally unsurprisingly, the abbey was one of the most important sources of inspiration to George Meikle Kemp in his designs for the Scott Monument in Edinburgh of 1840-6. By the mid-nineteenth century it can be suggested without too much exaggeration that Melrose had become, and has since remained, almost as much a part of the essential iconography of Scotland as Landseer's 1851 painting of the *Monarch of the Glen*.

3
THE ESTATES AND POSSESSIONS OF THE ABBEY

The abbey and its lands

It was a basic characteristic of the Cistercian order that its monasteries tended to be holders of substantial landed estates. The principle that the monks should support themselves through the cultivation of their own lands and by their own efforts, meant that initially they avoided acceptance of income from rents and other such renders, unlike other orders such as the Cluniacs and Augustinians, who possessed substantial portfolios of properties that were rented out to tenants. From the beginning, therefore, Melrose lay at the heart of a great complex of landed estates from which it drew most of the materials and foodstuffs that it needed to construct its buildings and feed its substantial community of monks and lay-brethren (**98**). An inner core of land between the river Tweed and the Eildon Hills provided the founding endowment on which the abbey itself was sited and which formed the innermost core of agricultural properties that supported the monastery. Almost immediately, however, the monks began to receive gifts of neighbouring blocks of property and rights to grazing and fishings. These early awards met another Cistercian requirement − that the property accepted should not lie further from the monastery than it was possible to travel to and return from in the same day. Most of these lay immediately north of Tweed in the hill country between the rivers Gala and Leader, and comprised a mixture of arable and pasture, but other blocks lay east of the original core in Lessudden (nowadays known as St Boswells) and in Maxton, or east of the Leader in Makerstoun, Redpath, Earlston and Bemerside.

Within about 20 years of the foundation of the abbey, the Melrose monks were beginning to accept gifts of land and rights which breached both of these strictures. Income from teinds was originally forbidden by the Cistercian rule, but by the 1150s Melrose was in receipt of these renders from

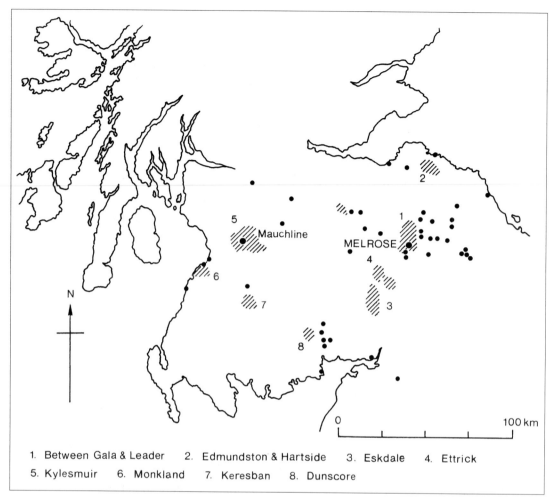

1. Between Gala & Leader   2. Edmundston & Hartside   3. Eskdale   4. Ettrick
5. Kylesmuir   6. Monkland   7. Keresban   8. Dunscore

98 *Map of the Melrose estate c.1300.* Sylvia Stevenson/Historic Scotland

Eskdale in eastern Dumfriesshire. They had also begun to acquire land in that valley, breaking the second rule concerning distance from the home monastery, but Eskdale offered the chance to acquire a very substantial block of prime sheep pasture at a time when the monks were beginning to build up their interest in wool production. Soon after, they began to build up a similar block of sheep pasture in the eastern Lammermuirs through a series of grants by the earls of Dunbar and their tenants. Here too, although these lands were described as a grange, the properties lay some two days' journey from the abbey. The biggest acquisition of this type lay in Kyle in central Ayrshire, where in the second half of the twelfth century the monks received a massive gift of land from the Stewart family, mainly pasture extending from

Mauchline and Catrine eastwards across Kylesmuir to the Lanarkshire border. This estate came to form the core of a distinct concentration of western properties running from Carrick in the south up to Barmuir and Drumclog in the north, and from the Clyde coast to the Lowther Hills. So far removed was this land from the monastery, that the monks developed Mauchline as an administrative centre from which to manage it, and it was later to be created as a distinct barony within the monastic estate.

There were other important blocks of land acquired through the later twelfth and thirteenth centuries. The abbey had, for example, a valuable series of properties in Nithsdale, centred on Dunscore but extending in an arc around the northern side of Dumfries, as well as saltpans, fisheries and grazing rights along the Solway coast near Annan. Further east, they acquired a great tract of sheep pasture in Ettrick Forest, which was fringed by further smaller arable and pasture lands in western Teviotdale. East of those, the monks gained a scattering of valuable estates down Teviotdale and through the Merse towards Berwick, as well as blocks to the north-west in central Tweeddale and south-east in the valleys running north from the Cheviots. By about 1300, indeed, the abbot of Melrose could have travelled from Berwick in the east to Ayr in the west without ever being more than about 16km from a piece of property in which his abbey had some interest.

By the end of the thirteenth century, it was not just agricultural estates that the monks possessed. In addition to arable and pasture, they had acquired a major interest in several Scottish burghs, but especially in Berwick and to a lesser extent, Roxburgh. Some of this urban land was kept as bases from which the cellarer or one of the monks' lay agents could transact business on their behalf, or where they sited stores and warehouses. Much, however, was let to rent, ignoring all the earlier prohibitions. They had also acquired a network of fishing rights in inshore waters and rivers, extending from the Clyde coast of Carrick and Kyle, up the rivers Ayr and Doon, the Solway and Esk in the south-west, across to the Tweed and the North Sea coast of Berwickshire. Coastal interests also included saltpans, which gave the monks self-sufficiency in the one bulk preservative available in northern Europe in the medieval period. Pans were acquired that served both the main monastic household at Melrose itself and also the western administrative and processing centre at Mauchline. A final item in the portfolio was control of churches, also once taboo in the rules governing Cistercian behaviour, but of increasing attractiveness to the monks on account of the income and land attached to them. Altogether, it is a rich and diverse record.

The records relating to the development of this land-holding are vast, extending to over 600 hundred charters, writs and instruments in the surviving charter books of the abbey. There are, moreover, several hundred more documents, mainly from the mid to late sixteenth century, recording the progressive dismemberment of the estate at the hands of the last pre-Reformation commendators and their post-Reformation successors, plus a superb set of records of the workings of the regality court of the abbey, including a wealth of rental information, dating from the mid–sixteenth century to the eighteenth century. Faced with this huge mass of material, it is impossible to give a detailed presentation of the build up and eventual dispersal of the monastic estate. Instead, the following sections explore a series of key areas and subjects, which will together give a flavour of the nature of the whole.

Melroseland and Lessudden

The heart of the monastic estate was the broad strip of property on the south bank of Tweed between the river and the Eildon Hills, extending from Darnick in the west round to the boundary between Newstead and Eildon and Lessudden in the east. To its south, and preventing any expansion in that direction, was Bowden, an estate that had been given by the future king David I to the monks of Selkirk, and which, by the time of the foundation of Melrose, was one of the main properties of Kelso Abbey. This tightly defined block was made up of the territories of three royal estates, Darnick, Melrose and Eildon, which were all old established agricultural communities. These were intended to provide the monks with the primary economic basis upon which they would build their later wealth. In later centuries, these estates would form the barony of Melroseland.

Expansion from this core of property was limited by the crowded nature of the land-holdings around them. Western and southern developments were effectively closed off by the presence of the Kelso estate, and north-east of Tweed was the property of Dryburgh Abbey. There were clearly disputes between Melrose and Kelso over the grazing rights in the Eildons that pertained to Bolden and to the Melrose home estate. In 1202, the *Chronicle of Melrose* records a failed attempt by the papal legate John de Salerno to mediate a settlement. It records how the legate spent over seven weeks at Melrose, and despite 'very many gifts, of gold, and silver, and also a great number of horses' given by both parties, he left without settling the issue. To the east of Eildon lay the lordship of Lessudden, now known as St Boswells, and it offered the monks some scope for expansion. Their first acquisition there was small scale, a grant of about 50 acres of arable on the east side of the old Roman road given to them by Robert de London. Further small parcels of land followed in Maxton, east of Lessudden, where Robert de

Berkeley gave them a ploughgate (104 acres) of land on the east side of Dere Street around Morridge and Lilliard's Edge, along with common pasture rights for 100 sheep, 12 oxen, six cows, three horses and one sow amongst the grazing used for Robert and his tenants' beasts, plus rights to win turf and heath as fuel. Perhaps most important for the monks, however, was his gift of the right to take stone from his quarry for building 'the house of Melrose'. Until the early fourteenth century, most new properties acquired in this area were also in the lordship of Maxton, and it was not until the early 1300s when the monks gained another 52 acres that more land was obtained in Lessudden.

During the second phase of the Wars of Independence after 1332, King Edward Balliol granted the lordship of Lessudden to Ralph Neville, lord of Raby in County Durham. As lord of Lessudden, he confirmed before 1353 a small grant of property made by one of his tenants. The trend seemed to be confirmed as one of acquiring small parcels of land piecemeal. In 1353 however, Neville made over the whole of his lordship of Lessudden to the monks, to hold in free alms after his death. Following the treaty of Berwick in October 1357, Neville confirmed his award, noting that the abbot and convent were to pay him half of the ferme of the lordship for his lifetime. This grant of the lordship of Lessudden did not mean that the monks acquired any significant new blocks of property; it was the superiority that they had received over all the various tenants of the land. There were still various portions of Lessudden that had not been held by Neville and which remained outwith Melrose's possession, in particular the Cambestoun properties of the Frasers of Frendraught, but the monks managed to secure these also in the course of the fifteenth century. By the early 1500s, the Melrose estate south of Tweed extended along the course of the river almost the whole way from its confluence with the Ettrick to Rutherford, halfway between St Boswells and Roxburgh.

Between Gala and Leader

Almost from the first foundation of the abbey, one of the most valuable components in its complex of estates lay in the hill country immediately north of the abbey across Tweed. It has been estimated that the abbey's core properties south of the river (Darnick, Melrose and Eildon) extended to around 2,150ha, but this northern block comprised 900ha around Gattonside and Gatton's Haugh, granted to the abbey outright, plus rights to pasture, to take timber for their own uses, and to pannage in over 7,100ha of upland bounded on the west by Wedale (the valley of the Gala Water), on the east by the valley of the Leader, and on the north by the lordship of Lauderdale and the Wedale estates of the bishops of St Andrews. This upland district was described as 'waste', a term which in the Middle Ages meant uncultivated land, and lay within what King David I described as 'my forest'. That label, however, does not mean that it was covered in a blanket of trees, for 'forest' referred chiefly to land reserved for hunting. Nevertheless, it appears that in the early twelfth century much of the area was covered by broken oak and birch woodland mixed with expanses of rough grassland and scrub, with willow and alder woods in the lower-lying valley fringes. Although described as 'waste', the land was already exploited routinely by those who lived around its margins, as summer pasture for cattle and sheep, a source of autumn pannage for pigs, as winter feed for the livestock left unslaughtered in November, and for building materials and fuel. There are also indications that peasant farmers in Lauderdale had begun to nibble at its eastern margins, breaking some of the east-facing slopes into cultivation, and a similar pattern had begun on the south, at Gattonside. However, these agricultural encroachments known as 'assarts', were restricted to the lower-lying southern and eastern fringes of the 'waste', with the main upland area remaining unsettled.

Unlike the gift of the lands south of Tweed and at Gattonside, Melrose had not been given outright and exclusive ownership or use of the upland. They simply had a share in the exploitation of the resources of the district, along with the inhabitants of the other settlements around its margins and chiefly in Wedale and Lauderdale. For the Cistercians of Melrose, this was an unsatisfactory arrangement that they were to work hard to change in their favour. Before the 1180s, the imprecision of David I's original grants had been skilfully exploited by the monks, but at the cost of provoking their neighbours and the other communities with an interest in the land to resort to legal action to protect their own interests. The monks were interested in developing both the arable and the pastoral potential of their properties here, so close to the abbey itself, where the produce could be exploited directly to support the monastic household. As the community grew rapidly in the 1140s and 1150s, the restrictions on agricultural expansion in this conveniently located district must have become tiresome in the extreme to the monks.

The first recorded arable developments in this area lay at Blainslie, 4km south of Lauder, and were a property called Alwin's Land (granted in the 1150s to Dryburgh Abbey), and Sorrowlessfield, 11km south-south-west of Lauder near the confluence of the Leader and Tweed. These were probably assarts into the woodland on the gentler eastern slopes of the hill country, breaking the more easily tilled fine brown forest soils of the area. These were valuable properties for Melrose, but they were immediately constrained by a prohibition on any further encroachment into the King's forest. Indeed, at Blainslie they were permitted to cultivate only that area that had been under plough at the time of its grant to them, and to expand into open areas on the edge of the woodland, but they were expressly forbidden to make any fresh assarts. Initially, their response was to acquire more properties down the western side of Lauderdale from the southern edge of Lauder itself, through Blainslie and Sorrowlessfield to Fauhope (now known as Drygrange) at the very foot of the valley, but by the mid-thirteenth century they had expanded far beyond the original cultivated area and made extensive new assarts in the forest area. Indeed, by the 1230s, the block of property running down Lauderdale, broken only by Kedslie, which was owned by the canons of Dryburgh Abbey, together with Gattonside and Eildon, had been developed into the main arable granges being run by the monks and their lay-brothers.

Their counterparts on the steep eastern slopes of Wedale, at Colmslie, Buckholm and Whitelee, were developed primarily as pastoral granges within the forest area. As they lay within the King's hunting preserve, numbers of stock and the location and scale of buildings to house them and their herdsmen were carefully regulated. Buildings and folds for the livestock were important, as the flocks and herds were driven off the hills and from the woodland at night, possibly because of the dangers from predators such as wolves in the forest territory. Permission to build was granted only after what was probably long negotiation. Shortly after 1162, for example, Malcolm IV permitted them to build a 'vaccary' or cowshed for 100 cows, together with a pen, in the lower part of Colmslie. Nearly 30 years later, William the Lion granted them permission for a new shed for 60 cows, plus a house for the monks' herdsmen within the already existing cattle enclosure at Buckholm. By the same date, the King had also granted them the right to have a shed for 120 cows *or* a sheepfold (a sign, perhaps, that the monks were starting to shift their interests towards wool production by the 1180s) at Whitelee. There, they were also allowed to build a house for their herdsmen and a store for hay, but they were still forbidden to construct anything more substantial than wicker shelters for their men within the limits of the forest.

This steady expansion of activity within the forest area through the middle of the twelfth century evidently placed considerable strain on the abbey's resources. Melrose, of course, was not the only exploiter of the forest, for the canons of Dryburgh Abbey, together with the tenants of the King, the bishops of St Andrews, and the Morville lords of Lauderdale were also seeking to maximise their rights within it. This drive to secure maximum benefit from their rights quickly produced a conflict of interests with other users, most notably the Morvilles, who were constables of the Kings of Scots and their hereditary foresters for the land between Gala and Leader. In March 1180/1, a dispute between Melrose and Richard de Morville, concerning the extent of the forest and pasture in the district, was decided in a gathering of the royal court at Haddington. Here, the conflict arose over the incompatibility of the monks' wish to extend their pasture and Morville's desire to preserve the hunting grounds in the area around Threepwood in the very heart of the forest territory. The *Chronicle of Melrose* rather smugly records that 'by God's aid, the monks retained their rights in this matter, so that possession was adjudicated to them, through the merit of their charters, and by authority of the privileges of the Roman church'. Richard de Morville also provided them with a fresh charter which more carefully defined their now extended rights to exploit the contested area as pasture, but also conceded to him his right to have a resident forester in the district to ensure that his remaining game rights were not infringed and that the monks did not exceed their rights. Ironically, Morville was only three years later to arbitrate in a similar dispute between Melrose and the inhabitants of Wedale over their rights to the pasture of the King's forest. A large gathering of nobles and clerics, together with the King and his brother, met near Crosslee on the western side of Wedale, to observe the settlement. There, they witnessed while Richard de Morville and 'twelve loyal subjects…swore with fear and trembling over the relics of our church', which the monks had brought from the abbey for that purpose, that the King's forest extended 'as far as to the road that goes to the east side of the church of the blessed Mary of Wedale (Stow); and that the pasture of the church of Melrose extended as far as the boundaries of Wedale, and as far as the stream that is called Fasseburne' and that these limits had been granted and confirmed by Kings David I, Malcolm IV and William, and also confirmed by a succession of papal bulls that set out Melrose's various privileges. Again, they received charters to confirm this settlement, but the dispute over the limits of their grazing in Wedale was not to prove quite so easy to settle.

Progressive expansion of Melrose's grazing interests in the district continued to produce conflict between the abbey and the other major landholders in the area. The main conflict was with the bishop of St Andrews, who possessed a manor-house at Stow in Wedale and a large block of property round about. Relations deteriorated to a very low level and in 1268 an unnamed abbot of Melrose and a number of his convent were excommunicated at a Church council in Perth, because 'they had broken the peace of Wedale by violently attacking the houses of the bishop of St Andrews [there], had killed a certain clerk, and left many others wounded'. Some indication of the exact cause of the dispute may lie in a mandate of 13 April 1268 from Alexander III to Simon Fraser, sheriff of Traquair and others, commanding them to go to the land of the abbot and convent of Melrose, next to the water of 'Galu', where they were to hold an inquest respecting a diversion of the course of the water. This action by the monks, presumably to improve the value of their land at the expense of their neighbours, and the simmering row over the boundary between Stow and Whitelee, had provoked violent confrontation. The Scottish Church moved swiftly to take action in this case because they had no wish for the King to involve himself in a legal process which might have led in turn to a curtailment of ecclesiastical liberties. It is probable that the abbot in question was John de Ederham, whom the *Chronicle of Melrose* records as resigning the abbacy in 1268 or 1269 after a very short reign of around two years.

The firm action taken at Perth in 1268, however, did not draw a line under the dispute, for in September 1310, Bishop William Lamberton of St Andrews and William Fogo, abbot of Melrose, drew up an agreement to settle temporarily the old controversy between them over the lands of Caitha beside the grange of Whitelee. Melrose clearly gave ground, for they accepted that the bishop should hold Caitha in common for his lifetime 'just as he has had them since the day of their creation', although the grange at Whitelee itself, and its attendant cowsheds, sheepcotes and other buildings and enclosures 'made of old' would remain in Melrose's hands. After the bishop's death, however, his successors and the abbot of Melrose could re-open the suit. The disturbances of the fourteenth century may have ensured that the case lay dormant until the early 1400s, but in 1419 the monks sought a papal mandate to commission an inquest into their rights to a piece of land called 'Yebouhous' (the Bow House – Bow lies on the north side of Caitha Hill) to the south of Stow, claiming that it had been theirs beyond memory of man, but that the bishop had asserted that it was his, had seized it, and was taking the income from it unlawfully.

Such agreements as the 1180/1 settlement were intended to attempt to strike a balance between the continued use of the forest area as a hunting ground and the desire of other users to extend their economic privileges within it. In the late twelfth century, royal hunting rights still took priority over even the rights of a favoured monastery such as Melrose, but great lengths were clearly gone to in an effort to accommodate both functions. It appears that quite sophisticated mechanisms to monitor activity within the woodland and scrub areas, primarily to preserve areas where game could shelter and feed, were set in place. Even where grazing rights were conceded, the forester still had the powers to deny access during certain specified seasons, especially the fawning period from 9 June to 9 July, and activities such as pannage and the right to make fresh assarts were permitted only under formal agreements, usually in writing. The 1180/1 settlement had been intended to regulate the use of the forest area by balancing the interests and rights of the hunters and grazers. It seems to have provided some stability for around half a century, but by the 1230s pressures were again evident to relax the restrictions. As a result, in 1236 King Alexander II gave the major concession that all their lands, and properties in which they had interests, between Gala and Leader, and also south of Tweed bounded by Lessudden on the east and by the Bowden lands of the monks of Kelso on the south and west, were to lie outwith the forest area. This act removed any residual restrictions on what the monks of Melrose could do with their lands, especially in terms of its development as either pasture or arable.

The first big expansion in the extent of the abbey's interests in the district had come shortly before the King's award, probably between around 1226 and 1234, when Alan, lord of Galloway, who had inherited the Morville lands, granted the monks the whole of his 'waste' of Lammermuir in exchange for property around Carsphairn in Galloway, reserving only rights of common pasture. The waste, meaning simply land not under cultivation but outside the forest, is not specifically located, but appears to have lain at the northern end of Lauderdale on the slopes rising up towards Soutra. This was an extensive grant, but there were strings attached. Alan stipulated that the monks could not leave their beasts on the land overnight but that they had to return each day to their own 'houses'. Nevertheless, he permitted them to build and enclose assarts taken in as cornfields or meadow on the land with ditches, banks or walls. Clearly, it was envisaged that the monks would be expanding both their grazing and arable interests in the district. In 1247, the abbey further demonstrated its determination to extend its holding in the district by its buying out of the interests in the feu of Lauder of Patrick, earl of Dunbar. By the deal, one of the many transactions undertaken by the business-minded Abbot Matthew, the monks paid 100 merks to the earl and 20 merks to his son for all their rights to pasture in Lauder. Clearly, the monks were now taking every opportunity to expand their grazing potential for sheep.

By the middle of the thirteenth century, the monks' territorial interests in the district were nearing their full extent. Freed from the restrictions of forest law, the monks had been able to exploit the property as they saw fit, developing it as a combination of sheep-runs and arable. The district was very much at the core of Melrose's land-holding, and it is no surprise that it was there that they were to achieve their first extended jurisdictional franchise which gave them almost absolute legal authority over all their tenants within the bounds of Gala and Leader. In 1358, David II granted the monks a regality jurisdiction. This grant gave the abbot the right to have all lawsuits arising from the lands covered by the franchise, except charges of treason, tried in his courts. Royal officials, such as the justiciar and the chamberlain, also had no authority within a regality. David's grant did not extend over all of the abbey's properties, but embraced only its block of land between the Gala and Leader, and that south of Tweed which encompassed Darnick, Melrose and Eildon. This was a major privilege, which could bring the abbot considerable income from the fines and forfeitures of the court but, since many of the suits tried could result in execution, the abbot could not himself preside over the assemblies. Instead, the responsibility was delegated to a baillie, who was invariably a layman and normally a member of one of the leading noble families of the locality.

The monks continued to build up their holdings between Gala and Leader into the fifteenth century. In May 1400, George Dunbar, earl of March, granted the abbey 'the whole of his firewood and woodland upon the ground or territory called Sorrowlessfield, both dead and green'. The grant may have been made in response to a pressing need for the monks to secure timber sources for fuel and building in an increasingly treeless landscape, and also to permit them to extend the area already under cultivation in this territory, where expansion beyond the original arable area and early assarts from the woodland had been prohibited.

Despite the careful regulation of earlier centuries, Melrose still found itself involved in litigation over its rights in substantial blocks of property adjacent to its main granges in this area in the late 1400s and early 1500s. The first sign of growing pressure on the land, with demand for new arable ground becoming evident, came in November 1490. In an instrument dated 12 November, Abbot Bernard Bell stated that his tenants had discovered Adam Girdwood and his son, also named Adam, with their oxen harnessed in plough, breaking pasture at Ormshill in the common of Earlston on the west side of the Leader. On questioning Adam senior, it was found that they were servants of John Hume of Earlston, who had ordered them to plough up the pasture and prepare it for sowing with grain. Bell gave proof of the monks' rights in the land and stopped the ploughing on this occasion, but the Humes were to renew their encroachment in the 1550s. Soon after the Ormshill incident, in 1506, Melrose had to defend itself against a claim of heritable right to the lands of Muircleugh, on the eastern limits of the grange of Allanshaws, brought by Robert Lauder and the town of Lauder. Muircleugh lay immediately south of the common grazings of the townsfolk, and it seems that the flocks of both Lauder and the abbey had grazed there without the boundary having been clearly defined or maintained. Melrose, however, was able to establish its right and Robert Lauder renounced all his claims in favour of the monastery. The appearance of such a challenge at this time is possibly a sign of a growing pressure on the land in the area that was to become increasingly serious in the 1520s and 1530s. Melrose controlled a substantial asset that others eyed enviously.

The attraction to others of Melrose's pasture in the area may have been heightened by the evidence for depletion of soil fertility in some of the older arable granges in lower Lauderdale. The main evidence for this comes from a series of very detailed legal instruments concerning the property of Drygrange (formerly Fauhope). The first of these, dated March 1537, records that the property had been feued to David Linlithgow at an annual rent of 10 merks. The land had been 'reducit furth of wood and forest', that is, reclaimed from woodland, in David's time, and had proven to be so fertile that an additional rent of five chalders (a dry measure for grain) of bear (Scots barley) was levied from him. These were probably brown forest soils, light, easily tilled and very fertile, but prone to exhaustion of nutrients and subject to erosion. Nutrient depletion seems to have become evident after a few years, for by 1536/7 it was noted that 'be continuall use and occupatioun yairof [the lands of Drygrange] ar becumin to sik infertilitie and unplentwisnes'. It was commented, however, that this problem was not unique to Drygrange, but that the abbey's granges at Darnick, Gattonside, Newstead and elsewhere were also suffering similarly, and that the monks were having to reduce the produce renders that they had formerly been accustomed to receive from them. As a result, a new feu-charter was drawn up in favour of David's son, William Linlithgow, and his son, John, setting Drygrange in their hands for a term of 19 years at a reduced render of three chalders of bear and three merks Scots commuted for a cash payment of £22 Scots. Three years later, the feuars sought papal ratification of the agreement, presumably as a hedge against any change in terms that the monks might yet attempt to impose.

In February 1541, William and John Linlithgow assembled a detailed case in support of their appeal. It includes a very interesting deposition by a neighbouring tenant, 66-year-old Thomas Cartar, which describes the process of reclamation undertaken by David Linlithgow, the nature of the ground, and its current condition. He tells how 'ye wod was cuttit and destroyit' and the 'stokkis and rutis' were pulled out, leaving a rich soil that bore 'mekill corne'. As a consequence, the abbot compelled David to pay an increased render of six chalders, but because the land was heavily used it shortly lost its fertility and yields declined. According to Cartar, this was because the land 'is a dry hard skalp ground and ane stanry hingand ground'. Because of this decline in productivity, the abbot granted David the same reduction of one chalder that he had given to the abbey's tenants at Gattonside, Darnick and Newstead, 'quhilkis stedingis and tounis be process of time is extreme lauborit yat yai a nocht sa fertill nor plentwuss as yai war in auld tymes'. The reduction, he claimed, had been made because otherwise the tenants would have been obliged to have left part of the land 'unmanurit or plenist' (unmanured or plenished). He concluded with the statement that three acres of arable at Drygrange now yielded what one had done when David Linlithgow had first broken it into cultivation. These statements, together with various other depositions, were produced as a dossier and finally given full legal authority by papal commissioners in February 1541.

Various pressures, including the soil exhaustion recorded at Drygrange and the price inflation of the mid-sixteenth century, which saw grain prices rise steadily, saw further inroads made into the granges between the Gala and Leader. In June 1559, Ralph Hudson, prior of Melrose, complained on behalf of the abbey's tenants over encroachment into the pasture and moorland on the west side of the Leader opposite Earlston, being made by John Hume of Cowdenknowes and his men. Hudson argued that they and their tenants had long enjoyed the right to graze their animals and cast fuel on that land, but that Hume's men had been actively preventing them from doing so. He also stated that Hume had caused a large part of the pasture to be broken into cultivation for himself.

What this last series of records shows is how by the beginning of the sixteenth century even the core of monastic properties adjacent to the abbey itself was being feued to tenants. Very little land was being retained as demesne and cultivated by the servants of the abbot and monks to supply the household needs. Instead, these were met increasingly by cash rents or renders in produce, usually grain, which could either be consumed by the monastic household or sold at market. The monks, however, appear to have attempted to retain the upland grazing, as wool still commanded a good price on the Edinburgh market, but they were finding it increasingly difficult to maintain their rights to this pasture in the face of encroachment by neigh-bouring lairds and their tenants.

East Lammermuir

Despite the strictures against acceptance of remote properties, one of the first gifts received by the abbey outside its inner zone of landed interest lay far removed from the abbey at Hartside and Spott in East Lothian. Shortly after

1153, Cospatric, earl of Dunbar, gave the monks an extensive block of moorland grazing on the eastern end of the Lammermuirs, south-west of Dunbar. It was to form the central portion of what developed into one of the abbey's main livestock granges in the later twelfth and thirteenth centuries. It was not just pasture on the moor, however, that the monks received in this district, for around the same time the earl gave Melrose a saltpan site on the coast near the mouth of the Brox Burn. Then, in the late 1150s, Walter fitz Alan, the founder of the Stewart family in Scotland, gave the first of what was to be a remarkable series of gifts of property made to the abbey by himself and his family. This gift was quite modest – four ploughgates (a measure roughly equivalent to 104 acres) of land extending to a little over 400 acres at Edmundston, a now lost settlement in the parish of Stenton in East Lothian, at the eastern end of the Lammermuir Hills. It was, as its measurement in ploughgates suggests, arable land, lying on the gentler slopes to the north-west of the pastures at Hartside and Spott. Shortly after 1198, Earl Patrick of Dunbar granted the monks a single ploughgate next to the four given by Walter fitz Alan. This was followed around 1200 by a gift of 25 acres of arable by Eva, widow of Robert de Quincy. By this time, the monks' property at Edmundston was being referred to as a grange and had been developed into an important grain-producing centre for the abbey.

The development of these East Lothian granges was to be a source of future problems for the monks, as disputes over the right to teinds from them had boiled up. In 1183, the monks reached a settlement with the rector of the parish church of Dunbar, over the teind of the two granges of Edmundston and Hartside, whereby they agreed to make an annual payment of 30s to the church in lieu of teind. This settlement was confirmed by Richard, bishop of St Andrews, who made it clear that the agreement covered not just the arable, but also the grazing at Spott. As with so many of these deals, however, disputes over the value of the teind due were to recur throughout the Middle Ages. However, it was not just teind over which dispute had arisen, for the monks were also involved in litigation with Robert de Stenton over the boundary between their land at Hartside and his properties at Stenton. This resulted in a settlement with a clearly defined boundary and an agreement that neither party would seek to extend beyond those limits at any future date.

As the monks' involvement in the wool trade grew in the late twelfth century, they began to seek to expand their grazing land to enable them to run more sheep. Hartside and Spott, where they already possessed common grazing rights on the moor, were obvious areas for expansion. Earl Patrick of Dunbar, confirming his ancestors' gifts, stated that the monks had the right to graze three flocks of sheep on the common pastures of the moor of Spott. He added to this five acres of land at its southern edge, for the exclusive enjoyment of the monks, on which they could build folds for their flocks. With the possibility of overstocking and disputes over the numbers that the monks could graze on the common firmly in mind, the earl stipulated that each flock should not exceed 500 head and that the whole Melrose flock there should not exceed 1500 sheep. It is possible that Earl Patrick was well aware of the monks' tendency to over-exploit their rights to graze, as they had done at Hassendean, and was attempting to safeguard both his own interests and also those of his tenants in the moorland grazing. Before 1214, however, Earl Patrick had added substantially to this holding, giving them a further 51 acres of land at what is now known as Friardykes, lying in one compact block near to the original five acres that he had given them. This new land was also ringed by a dyke, within which the monks were given free licence to make meadows, fields or sheepfolds, whichever was most beneficial to them. Clearly, the monks were keen to develop as much as possible in this area, which lay close to the port of Berwick, through which they were already exporting most of their goods.

Melrose was also picking up parcels of land and rights in the eastern Lammermuirs from some of the smaller landowners in the district. Alan fitz Walter, son of the man who had given them the arable at Edmundston, granted them rights of common pasture in the meadowland under Brown Rig in his lordship of Innerwick. This lay directly south of the grazing associated with Spott, and developed into a major sheep-run for the monks when Robert de Kent, one of fitz Walter's tenants in Innerwick, rented the monks a substantial block of adjacent pasture in the valleys of the Bothwell Water and Monynut Burn, where they constructed sheepfolds. Robert also gave them licence to take as much wood as they needed for their own works, either to build with or to burn, and likewise as much heather or heath as they needed. Another of Alan's tenants, Roger fitz Glai, added more pasture in the Bothwell Water valley, and common rights in the pasture of Innerwick itself. Shortly after 1204, Alan's son, Walter II fitz Alan, confirmed the various gifts made by his tenants, noting that all the land granted was enclosed by a ditch and that the sheepfolds lay beside the 'hollow road' at the head of the Monynut valley. At Spott, the monks acquired a further block of property adjacent to the ditched enclosure granted to them by Earl Patrick from one of the earl's tenants, Patrick de Withichun. At Hartside, Robert de Stenton gave them a further block of five acres of arable and associated pasture rights, while William Valence gave another block of land adjacent to the monks' existing property at Stenton. Taken together, these new grants more than doubled the original holdings in the area that the monks had acquired in the 1150s.

The development of the Lammermuir granges continued through the thirteenth century, with the monks receiving new properties on the southern side of the hills, mainly in the valley of the Whiteadder and its tributaries. Penshiel emerged as the centre of a new block of grazing (**99**), developing from an original grant of one acre of meadow and common grazing rights for 300 ewes, 30 burden cows, 24 burden horses and their issue up to two years old. Melrose was determined to build up an exclusive interest in the area. They leased the lands of Kingseat in Penshiel for an annual rent of 30s, giving them a significant holding in the area, which they bought before 1231 from their superior for 30 merks and 40d.

The monks' flocks at Penshiel proved to be the factor that broke the old agreement between Melrose and the rector of Dunbar over teind due to his church from the monks' lands. In 1291, he drew up a complaint against the monks over teind due to him, also recording his 140 hogs (sheep between their first and second shearings) taken at Penshiel, and the destruction by the monks of certain houses that ought to pertain to his church on account of the chapel at Penshiel. By 1326 the dispute had flared up again, and on this occasion the monks produced documents in court showing that a settlement had been made between their abbey and the rector of Dunbar as long ago as 1173, fixing for all time their payment in lieu of teind at 30s. In 1342, at which time Patrick, earl of Dunbar, was making the parish church of Dunbar into a collegiate church, the bishop of St Andrews produced a notarial attestation setting out the terms of the agreement once again. Despite this, in August 1442, John Middlemast, sub-prior of Melrose, and the monks' procurators met with the dean and chapter of Dunbar in an attempt to settle a fresh dispute over Edmundston, on which occasion Melrose's documents were carefully recorded to confirm their title. Three years later, however, Robert Logan, sacristan of Melrose, and the dean and chapter of Dunbar were locked in dispute over the issue of teinds. An indenture of 16 May 1453 records the further settlement of a controversy between Dunbar and Melrose over the teinds of Edmundston and Hartside, stating that in 1342, at the foundation of the collegiate church, the teinds had been assigned for the repair and maintenance of the choir at Dunbar, and for furnishing the ornaments of the choir. The 1453 composition arranged for a new cash payment of 12½ merks annually for both granges, or 6 merks 6s and 4d for one, with pro-rata reductions to apply if the monks alienated any portions of the properties. It also stipulated that if the monks chose to rent out one of the granges, all the teind of the let property would fall due to Dunbar.

99 *Melrose's grange at Penshiel.* Historic Scotland

By the end of the fifteenth century, the monks had begun to dispose of the Lammermuir granges at ferme. In the early 1490s, Edmundston Grange was leased to Robert Lauder of Edrington for an annual rent of five chalders of wheat and three of oatmeal. The smaller satellite properties on the south disappear from the records, also probably feued, while the main property appears to have been feued to the Lauders of the Bass before 1500. The abbey however, retained certain portions. One of these was the waulkmill of the grange, used for fulling woollen cloth, and clearly a legacy of the land's former importance to the monks as a wool-producing centre. In 1534, however, this asset was also feued for a period of 19 years for an annual rent of 40s. In 1541, Hartside was also feued, for the annual rent of £40. Before 1560, therefore, the whole of what had been one of Melrose's earliest and most valuable groups of granges had been effectively alienated, with the monks retaining only a nominal superior lordship over the land.

Ettrick

In 1235, the monks received one of the biggest single gifts of property and rights made since the time of their abbey's foundation. King Alexander II, one of the abbey's greatest benefactors, gave them the whole of his 'waste' of Ettrick and Glenkerry. This land comprised a huge tract of upland in western

Roxburghshire, extending west towards Eskdale and northward to Yarrow. This was probably not an outright gift of an area that had little by way of existing settlement and in which no neighbouring lords already had commercial interests, for Ettrick was royal hunting forest. As a result, the monks did not have free rein to develop it as they wished, but little information survives as to how they exploited it until the fifteenth century. The Forest, however, was one of several formerly royal properties that found its way into the hands of the Black Douglases in the course of the fourteenth century, and, despite the close relationship between the abbey and that family that developed after about 1360, it is probable that the commercial interests of both collided in Ettrick. The return in 1424 of James I from his long captivity in England brought a number of benefits to the monks, not least as a reward for the services to the King of the new abbot, John Fogo. It was to Fogo in 1425 that James granted a regality jurisdiction over Ettrick, freeing its lands there from any forest franchise exercised by the Douglases. This move may have been linked to the King's efforts to limit and contain the power of his Douglas kinsmen. In 1442, the monks' privileges in Ettrick and Rodono were confirmed by James II, and in 1446 William, earl of Douglas, confirmed that the monks, their men, household, servants and tenants were free and quit from his court within the Forest of Ettrick.

Eskdale

One of the earliest expansions of Melrose interests outwith the core around the abbey itself was in Eskdale in the hill country of what is now eastern Dumfriesshire. Some time in the 1150s, Robert Avenel, Lord of Eskdale, granted the monks the teinds from his lands there, for as long as they wished to hold them, diverting the revenue from the local parish church. The award was ratified by the bishop of Glasgow, but the issue of teind from Eskdale was to be a problem that recurred regularly down into the fourteenth century, with the parish priest attempting to assert his rights to these parochial revenues. In 1305, when the Cistercians faced the loss of their exemption from teind, the monks reached a compromise with the then parson over payment, agreeing to give 20s annually in lieu of teinds. However, the dispute was only laid to rest in 1321, when the abbey gained possession of the parish church of Wastirker, in which parish their Eskdale lands lay.

Probably in the late 1150s, Robert Avenel granted the abbey an extensive block of upland property in upper Eskdale for an annual rent of five merks. This centred on Watcarrick and Tomleuchar, bounded on the west by the Annandale lordship of the Bruces, and on the east by the Hawick lands of the Lovel family. Shortly after 1174, he extended this to a grant in free alms, cancelling the earlier rent which in any case he had remitted to the monks to pay for the lighting of the altar of St Mary in the abbey church. The new grant, however, carried certain limitations. For example, Avenel retained rights to keep deer, pigs and goats within the bounds given, without injury to the monks' rights to the hay crop. For the monks, however, the greatest irritant was probably that here, too, as in the district between Gala and Leader, the donor retained his forest rights. Only he could hunt and trap there, bringing his hunt-packs, and the monks and their men were forbidden to keep hunting-dogs, except for trapping wolves. The grant was renewed without change by Robert's son, Gervase, after his father's death in 1185, and by Gervase's son, Roger, on his death in 1219. By 1235, however, similar conflicts to those that had arisen between Gala and Leader had surfaced in Eskdale.

In April 1235, an assembly of the royal court gathered at Liston to settle the dispute that had arisen between Roger Avenel and Melrose, and to produce a friendly compromise. It emerged that Avenel had put his horses, beasts and men on the monks' lands, and that Avenel's men had destroyed houses built by the monks and thrown down or filled in their ditches and enclosures. Roger yielded considerably on the position kept by his ancestors, accepting that neither he nor his men could keep their horses, beasts, pigs, sheep or any other domestic or woodland beast within the agreed bounds, except by the monks' licence, reserving only to Roger game beasts. Roger and his heirs were to have the rights to stags and does, boar and goats, and to the nests of hawks and sparrowhawks, which the monks were ordered not to disturb. In particular, the monks and their men were forbidden to harm trees in which the birds nested, unless they had not nested there in consecutive years. The monks and their men were to be allowed to build lodges and buildings anywhere within the land as seemed best to them. The agreement represented a considerable advance on the original grant, but it still left Roger Avenel with extensive rights that impeded the monks' unlimited enjoyment of their lands.

It is unsurprising, then, to find that the disputes re-emerged towards the close of the thirteenth century, by which time the Avenel lands had passed into the hands of the Graham family. In about 1306-7, the abbot appealed to Edward I of England, asking him to protect the right and franchises of their church in Eskdale from the depredations of Sir Nicholas Graham. Sir Nicholas, and Sir John Graham, his son, had perhaps been using the political disturbances of the time to reassert their ancestral rights, for the monks claimed that they had ejected the abbey's people and imprisoned them.

Edward ordered that instructions should be sent to the Scottish chancery to give the monks remedy. It was probably as a result of this instruction that in 1309 Sir John granted Melrose unqualified possession of all their Eskdale properties with the addition of the various hunting rights that he and his ancestors had reserved for themselves. The monks could now exploit their lands as they wished, without hindrance. This agreement was confirmed by Robert I in 1316.

Further increase in their holding in this area followed in 1321, when Sir John de Soulis, to whose family Graham had sold Wastirker, died in France. The King now granted the monks their Eskdale land in free alms, but to be held with full rights of free forest, although Eskdale had never previously been designated as forest. This new grant gave them carte blanche to increase their exploitation of the property as grazing without restraint.

The western estates: Carrick and the lordship of Kylesmuir

The most significant block of Melrose's properties lay west of Clydesdale in Kyle, Carrick and Nithsdale. This is a highly surprising situation, for the development of a substantial propertied estate so far removed from the monastery proper was a flagrant breach of a fundamental principle of the Cistercian rule which prohibited its monks from accepting properties that lay further from their abbey than could be travelled to and returned from in the space of a normal day. The core of Melrose's estate met that limit, lying within a band some 8km in radius around the abbey itself. The lower Tweeddale and eastern Lammermuir properties broke that limit, the latter being on average 24 to 32km from Melrose, but the main western properties lay some 88km (around three days' journey) distant, while those in Carrick were nearer to 110km from the abbey. Melrose responded to the problems of remoteness by developing an estate centre at Mauchline from which these western lands were managed, but this arrangement still did not address the fundamental issue of the breach of the order's rule. That Melrose itself recognised the problem is clear from the ways in which they refer to Mauchline. While other outlying properties were grouped for management into farm complexes referred to as 'granges' (a term originally applied only to cereal-producing farms, grange meaning granary), Mauchline itself was never so termed and developed instead as a kind of 'super-grange' or manorial centre from which the operation of a distinct western group of granges was overseen. Quite simply, Melrose sought to overcome the problem by developing Mauchline as a semi-independent entity, a status reflected in the later creation of a barony of 'Kylesmuir' that embraced all their Ayrshire properties, with Mauchline as its administrative centre.

This development was a response unique to Melrose. What normally occurred elsewhere was that properties located remotely from the monastic core and the main complex of estates were quickly feued out or exchanged with another monastery or with a secular lord for lands located more conveniently. This, for example, was the route taken by Lindores Abbey in Fife, which had received extensive properties in the Garioch in central Aberdeenshire from its founder. These they chose to rent out from an early date and eventually feued them in return for a fixed income to the bishop of Aberdeen. Alternatively, they could have been used as an endowment for a cell or daughter-house. This was the option taken by Arbroath with its lands around Fyvie in Aberdeenshire. Melrose, however, was not prepared to take either alternative and opted instead to manage and exploit its western estates directly. Indeed, it chose to maintain this choice down to the sixteenth century and the abbey's successor, the earls of Melrose and Haddington, preserved their superiority over the Ayrshire estates into the early eighteenth century.

The reasons why Melrose chose to hang on to these distant estates are probably quite simple. They provided the abbey with resources of a kind that they either could not obtain at all closer to the abbey itself, or which they could not obtain in sufficient quantities. By maintaining control of them, they effectively signalled an interest in developing them which as a consequence encouraged further acquisition of property in the region. Once a decision had been taken to develop Mauchline as a virtually autonomous unit, there was also a need to acquire certain other lands and rights that would enable it to function as a viable, freestanding economic unit. In effect, the western lordship of Melrose achieved a critical mass that allowed it to survive and expand where a smaller enterprise would have failed.

The origin of what became the barony of Kylesmuir lay in the grant to Melrose shortly after 1165 by Walter I fitz Alan, the founder of the fortunes in Scotland of the family we know as the Stewarts, of a substantial portion of his great lordship of Kyle. Walter's rise had been rapid and spectacular. Of Breton ancestry and the younger brother of the lord of Arundel in Sussex and Clun in Shropshire, Walter had arrived in Scotland in about 1147 and entered the service of David I, eventually acquiring the office of *dapifer*, subsequently inflated to *senescallus* or steward of the King. His initial land-holding had been small scale, comprising a scattering of properties in East Lothian and Berwickshire, but he had made the first step to greatness when he received the lordship of Renfrew and Strathgryfe in what was then, and in some ways still is, the wild west of Scotland. It was a frontier lordship in a territory that marched down the western flank of the core of Scottish royal authority in the mid-twelfth century, and Walter and his family were intended from the first to play a significant part in extending that authority westward. Their success in this can be seen in the fact that it was their lordship that was the target of Somerled of Argyll's last attack in 1164, which resulted in his death at Renfrew. Walter's role as royal strong man was further underscored by the grant to him by Malcolm IV of the northern half of Kyle – a territory that came to be referred to as Kyle Stewart to distinguish it from King's Kyle, the southern portion of the district – a lordship centred on Dundonald and which stretched from the coast to the watershed with the rivers that flow north and east into the Clyde, bounded on the south by the rivers Ayr and Lugar and to the north by Cunningham.

By 1165, Walter had already begun to develop his own monastery at Renfrew, soon to be transferred to a new site at Paisley, and which was to grow into the richest abbey in western Scotland. Why he chose to direct his biggest single act of patronage to Melrose rather than to his own fledgling foundation, therefore, remains an unanswered question for which there is no obvious explanation other than his closeness to the Scottish crown and Melrose's exceptionally favourable relationship with the King of Scots. The scale of the grant was staggering. It comprised the whole of the estate of Mauchline as it then was recognised, a territory which two of his servants perambulated in the company of the representatives of the monks and whose bounds were recorded in the charter which formalised the grant. Many of the markers on the bounds can still be recognised in the modern landscape and it is evident that the property comprised most of what became the medieval parish of Mauchline, consisting of both post-Reformation Mauchline and Catrine parishes. In addition to this, he granted them the rights of pasture over the whole of his hunting forest that stretched east from Mauchline to the marches with Glengavel, Lesmahagow and Douglasdale, for an annual payment of merks, but retaining hunting rights for his own enjoyment. Furthermore, he gave them a salmon fishery at the mouth of the Ayr, and the right to 'use the river as they saw fit', that is, giving them permission to build a mill if they so chose. The grant, as mentioned earlier, contravened one basic principle of the Cistercians' rule – that of the acceptance of properties distant from the abbey – but it also broke two other fundamental principles, namely the acceptance of the control of parish churches and mills, from which revenue (teinds and multures) would be obtained. Set out so on paper, the scale of the grant is difficult to grasp, but when mapped it shows that Walter had alienated somewhere between one quarter and one third of Kyle. In terms of scale, it greatly exceeded the estates of nearby Kilwinning Abbey, and those of the earl of Carrick's later foundation at Crossraguel. In one single act, Melrose had become one of the largest landholders in western Scotland.

Walter fitz Alan's generosity was a one-off that none of his descendants were to repeat. Following Walter's death in 1177, his son and successor, Alan fitz Walter, directed most of his patronage towards Paisley, and it was not until the lifetime of his son, Walter II fitz Alan, head of the family from 1204 to 1246, that Melrose was again a beneficiary of Stewart grants. These, however, represented at first little more than a confirmation of his grandfather's awards and the clarification of the terms on which they held the rights of pasture in the Forest of Ayr. This situation was clearly not satisfactory for the monks, who were already developing their interests elsewhere in the region, and Walter was eventually prevailed upon to renounce his right to the annual payment of 5 merks and to give up his residual hunting rights in the eastern moorland of Kyle. By 1232, Melrose had undisputed enjoyment of the whole tract of hill country east of the Cessnock Water and north of the Ayr.

The monks had been active from the 1170s in consolidating the initial grant of Mauchline by securing several adjoining properties or by 'encouraging' neighbouring landholders into redefinition of disputed boundaries. Richard Wallace, tenant of the Stewarts in Tarbolton, granted them a substantial block of upland property in the east of Tarbolton parish, east of the Water of Fail and stretching to the western limits of Mauchline, known as Barmuir. Another Stewart tenant, Peter de Curry, who held property in northern Mauchline parish outwith the Melrose estate, became involved in a long and damaging dispute with the monks over the lands of Dalsangan and Bargower, a contest which he eventually lost and which saw him yield up any right over that land and assign one third of his moveable property to Melrose. A third significant addition was a block of hill country south of the Ayr between the Garpel Water and the watershed between the Ayr and Douglas waters. This grant has special interest because this land had previously been held of Alan fitz Walter by Alan 'parvus' or Little, described as a *conversus* or lay-brother of Melrose. We do not know what relationship there was between the Steward and the lay-brother, but it is highly unusual for any such individual to hold property in his own right. It does, however, confirm that Melrose was exploiting its western lands directly through employing its extensive labour force of lay-brethren to oversee or manage it. It suggests, moreover, that soon after 1177 the abbey had established an estate centre at Mauchline in which such men could be based.

Soon after 1185, the monks acquired a second significant block of property even further to the west in northern Carrick. The lord of Carrick, Duncan fitz Gilbert, was the son of one of the Scottish crown's most intractable enemies, Gillebrigte mac Fergusa, Lord of Galloway, but he was also the grandson of one of the crown's greatest supporters, Donnchad II, earl of Fife. Following the settlement of the long running dispute over the succession to Galloway, Duncan had been awarded Carrick, to be held as a feu from the Scottish crown, and was eventually to be given the title of earl. As a feudatory of the crown, kinsman of the greatest nobleman in the kingdom and a political ally of another of the crown's great servants, Alan fitz Walter, the Steward, it should come as no surprise that Duncan followed their example and directed a stream of patronage at Melrose. His first grant, made in 1193, comprised the lands of Maybole Beg, which lie to the north and north-east of Maybole, and the adjoining hill district of Beoch. It was an award nowhere near the scale of Walter fitz Alan's gift, but nevertheless represented a substantial and valuable property. It is represented today by the properties of Beoch, Grange and Monkwood, between Maybole and the River Doon. From the first, it was clearly Melrose's intention to run them as a grange, a decision facilitated by the emergence of Mauchline, which lies roughly 19km east-north-east of Maybole, as an administrative centre to which the new estate could function as a satellite.

Soon afterwards, one of Duncan's chief tenants, Roger de Skelbrooke, Lord of Greenan in the extreme north of Carrick, gave the monks an extensive property comprising a block between the ridge of Brown Carrick Hill and the coast. It was mainly upland moss and rough grazing, but the wording of the charter makes it clear that the monks intended to develop a saltpan on the coast and possibly exploit mineral rights in the hills. The possession of a saltpan would have become increasingly important to the monks as they developed the western estates, and a secure supply of salt – the only bulk preservative available in medieval Scotland – would have underpinned the viability of the Mauchline properties as an economic unit. Before 1200, Roger expanded on this original donation, giving a salmon fishery at Doonmouth, 4km south of that given to the monks on the Ayr by Walter Fitz Alan, a site for a second salt-work on the coast near Greenan, a toft on the seashore for a dwelling place for the pan operators, a second toft in the castle-toun of Greenan and, of vital importance, the right to take all the timber that the monks needed from anywhere in his demesne woods, for fuel for the salt-works and fishery, and for building their houses and shelters. The monks clearly took Roger at his word and systematically exploited their rights at Greenan, so systematically that they completely exhausted the fuel supply available to them there within about 30 years. Duncan now came to the rescue, granting the monks the sites for two new salt-works down the coast adjacent to his castle of Turnberry, plus access to new fuel sources. The economic development of the western estates had reached a level where they could not function without a secure salt supply.

Further problems, however, lay in store in relation to the Carrick properties. At Mauchline, the monks controlled the parish church and, as a result, could deal with the issue of teinds as they saw fit. As the Cistercian order was free from episcopal visitations, provided that the monks made suitable provision for the maintenance of a parish priest, they were untroubled by the intervention of the bishop of Glasgow. The Cistercians also had a privilege of exemption from payment of teind on lands that they reclaimed from 'waste' and cultivated for their own uses, a privilege that encouraged their exploitation of previously undeveloped country. At Maybole and Greenan, their lands comprised only part of the extensive parish of Maybole and seem also to have included extensive tracts of what was already considered to be developed land. As a result, the parson of Maybole, known only in the records by the initial G, began a protracted court case to try to secure the teinds, which he considered his due. Unable to gain a satisfactory result, he appealed the case to Pope Innocent III, who in 1212 appointed judges-delegate to settle the issue. It took a further nine years and a new pope, Honorius III, before a compromise settlement was finally made in 1221, whereby the monks agreed to pay the parson the substantial sum of 12s a year, a figure that indicates the comparative value of their Carrick lands. The payment implies an annual income from their lands of at least £5, which, in the early thirteenth century, was a hardly negligible figure.

The monks' defence of their financial interests over Maybole demonstrates their determination to extract the maximum benefit from their western lands and reinforces the point that they were actively building up their estates in the region in the early 1200s. The next significant component was obtained almost by default. Between either 1202 and 1206 or 1215 and 1216, Thomas de Colville, Lord of Dalmellington in King's Kyle, granted to the monks of the Cistercian abbey of Vaudey in Lincolnshire the feuferme of a great tract of upland territory extending south from Dalmellington into what is now Galloway, comprising a quarter of his lordship and covering most of the valley around Carsphairn. For an annual payment of six merks, the Vaudey monks were free to exploit the land 'for their works' as they willed. By the early 1220s, Vaudey had given up its attempt to realise its rights in Carsphairn, citing defect of discipline on the part of the brethren sent there on its business, the deceits of the barbarous inhabitants, and other unspecified perils endured. In 1223, Vaudey surrendered its possession, with the agreement of William de Colville, Thomas's son, to the monks of Melrose. In return, Melrose agreed to pay an annual of five merks to the King of Scots to quit Vaudey of its feuferme dues, plus an annual of four merks to their sister house, to be handed over at the great St Botulph's Fair at Boston in Lincolnshire. Clearly, Melrose saw something of value in this property which encouraged them to offer 50 per cent over the rate of Vaudey's original feu terms for its possession, and, moreover, they felt confident of their ability to exploit the lands directly. We have no firm evidence for what it was that they sought to exploit, but it has been argued strongly that it was the mineral wealth of the region – coal, iron and lead – that drew Melrose's interest. Certainly, the Cistercians of Newbattle and Culross were already developing the Lothian and Forth Valley coalfields in the late twelfth and early thirteenth centuries, and transporting the mined fuel to their saltpans on the Forth estuary and to meet the requirements of their households, so there is no reason why Melrose may not have intended a similar development in Carrick and Kyle. If that was their intention, it did not last long, for shortly after 1226 they exchanged their property with Alan, Lord of Galloway, for pasture in the Lammermuirs.

By about 1250, Melrose had assembled a major network of properties in central and southern Ayrshire and had developed a mechanism for their easy exploitation. The lynchpin in the operation was Mauchline, where charter evidence reveals that a small group of monks supported by a number of lay-brothers was in residence before 1200. This in itself had a number of implications, hinted at in Vaudey's abandonment of operations at Carsphairn, namely that of spiritual and moral discipline. Medieval monks were professed of the house in which they had taken their oaths and were supposed never to leave the community and have direct communication with the secular world. Some individuals such as the cellarer (responsible for the provisioning of the house) or the almoner (who dispensed alms to the poor), did, with permission of the abbot, have regular external contacts, but rarely left the monastery for more than a few days. Management of Mauchline, however, required the monks in charge there to be absent for weeks, if not months. To overcome this, Mauchline seems to have functioned almost as a cell – although it was never so termed – in which the monks and lay-brothers could live a communal life similar to that which operated in an abbey. The arrangement was a fudge that blatantly flouted the rules of the Order, but there is no evidence that anyone ever complained.

Now, the purpose of monastic estates was basically to give the community as near as possible self-sufficiency in the provision of food, fuel and basic raw materials. Agricultural surpluses could be and were traded on at market for cash, with which the monks could buy commodities that could not be produced on their own lands. In Scotland, this included such essentials as wine, which was needed for the mass as well as for domestic consumption, and the fine cloth used to make liturgical vestments and altar cloths. In general, the larger monasteries maintained land in the immediate vicinity of the abbey nucleus to provide for the daily requirements of the household and transported in bulk supplies from the outlying granges. At Melrose, this arrangement saw the produce from its granges in Tweeddale and Lauderdale supplying the main needs of the community, while the produce from its more remote properties in Berwickshire, eastern Roxburghshire and East Lothian were probably traded directly in the markets of Berwick, Roxburgh, Haddington and Edinburgh. How, though, did Mauchline and the Ayrshire lands fit in to this pattern?

After 1200, it is possible that much of the bulk produce from these western lands was disposed of through the markets of Ayr and Irvine rather than being transported overland to Melrose itself. Much of what was moved may simply have been cash remitted to the mother-house, but alternatives can also be traced. The key to what was happening in this region may lie in the nature of what was being produced on these western properties. Although the land in Carrick was termed a grange and parts of Mauchline may have been given over to extensive production of grain – usually barley and oats – the primary use of the estates seems to have been as livestock ranges. Certainly, the reference to the district as Kylesmuir points to the pastoral function of the country that stretched east to the Lanarkshire and Dumfriesshire borders. What, though, was being grazed here? We know from other sources that Melrose was a major sheep-farmer and one of the most important wool-producers in northern Europe by the late thirteenth century. Flocks of around 12,500, rising to possibly as many as 15,000 by the later fourteenth century, were run on Melrose's estates. The main sheep-runs lay in the Lammermuirs, Ettrick and Eskdale, and it is very likely that this great block of western moorland was viewed as another suitable area for grazing sheep. There is, however, an alternative – cattle.

It is often forgotten that medieval Scotland was a major producer of cattle, and that the second most important commodities after wool exported throughout this period were hides and leather. In an age before plastic, leather was the multi-purpose material that was used by all elements in society and, in parts of Europe where pastoral farming had been forced to yield ground in the face of the steady expansion of arable cultivation, there was great demand for raw and treated skins. Melrose had cattle ranches in the Lammermuirs that would have provided for its domestic needs in both leather and dairy produce, and was probably already exporting its surplus through Berwick by 1200. If Mauchline was being run as a cattle station, how was it disposing of its product?

We can assume that some proportion of Mauchline's stock was traded in local markets, such as Ayr and Irvine, and possibly also Lanark. In an age before the development of winter feeds, however, they would not have been able to maintain large numbers of beasts between November and May. The demand for salt, met through the Greenan and Turnberry pans, indicates that they were slaughtering and preserving the carcasses, possibly for transport to Melrose but, in view of the largely vegetarian monastic diet, probably for disposal on the market. We know from Melrose, too, that the monks were processing leather there on an industrial scale in the later Middle Ages, so we can infer that Mauchline may also have had a tannery as part of its complex. We can be sure that bulk products were transported – and over considerable distances – for the monks were keeping oxen as draught animals on all their estates, with six at Greenan alone. While oxen were used for pulling ploughs, they were also still the primary pullers of carts and wagons. The transport of slaughtered marts and skins, however, is not the most efficient way of moving a product that could walk for itself when alive.

Reading into the records, we can see that Melrose's primary response was cattle-droving. It is an image that we tend to think of as being typical of early modern Scotland, especially of the later seventeenth- and eighteenth-century Highlands and the trade in black cattle. That development, however, does not appear to have been a recent one, and there is strong evidence to suggest that herds were being moved over considerable distances in central and southern Scotland throughout the Middle Ages. Melrose shows itself to have been quick to recognise potential openings in the market and sought to maximise on the resources available to it to get its products to the consumers by the quickest and cheapest routes possible. Mauchline's location in relation to Melrose made it uneconomical to take the cattle to the abbey first of all, for onward movement to east coast markets. Instead, alternative routes were opened up.

In the later twelfth century, Melrose had also begun to acquire a large block of properties in Nithsdale (see pp.240–1), centred on Dunscore, 40km south-east of Mauchline, and also lands at Barnscarth and Carnsalloch near Dumfries, at Torthorwald, and at Rainpatrick on the Solway Firth near Gretna. While the Dunscore properties comprised a valuable and viable economic unit in its own right, none of the other lands amounted to much and why Melrose maintained its interest in them has always been a bit of a puzzle. The answer, however, appears to lie in one document, usually over-looked amongst the other contents of the cartulary. In 1260, John Comyn, Lord of Badenoch, permitted Melrose to rest its animals overnight on his lands of Dalswinton and Duncow in Nithsdale. The language of the document implies that the passage of these flocks and herds over his lands was a regular occurrence and had been the subject of long negotiations between Melrose and Comyn. What seems to have been happening was that Melrose was bringing stock down from Kyle to Dunscore, then driving it over the Nith through Dalswinton – where there was an important ford – then either east across Annandale to the old Roman road that ran towards Roxburgh, or down through their lands to the north-east of Dumfries to the Solway fords at Rainpatrick and Gretna. Their destination was perhaps Carlisle, where the monks had obtained a property as a business base before 1200, and where a major market had developed, through which Scottish produce was imported into England.

Despite the early promises of both the earls of Carrick and the Stewarts that the Melrose lands would be exempt from military obligations, the extraordinary crises after 1286 had seen those promises routinely breached. Shortly before his death in 1309, James the Steward issued a charter confirming the freedom of the monks' lands in Kyle from 'wapinschaws' (the periodical muster days when those between the ages of 16 and 60 had to turn out with their weapons and practise military exercises) and acknowledging that his past demands on the monks and their tenants had been in breach of their privileges. The Carrick and Kyle properties had also evidently been subjected to 'prises and captions' (the seizure of goods and materials for the King's uses, usually in time of war), for in 1326 Robert I issued a charter to the monks freeing their land from such burdens for all future time. The issue of military impositions on the abbey's western properties, however, did not end there. In 1403, when war with England was once again seeing a major Scottish mobilisation, it appears that the Stewarts, who now occupied the throne as Kings, attempted to secure military service from the Melrose properties that lay within their lordships of Kyle and Carrick. The abbot had clearly contested an attempt to have the Melrose tenants of Kylesmuir perform military service under the Stewart banner. War leadership was an important issue, for it gave the lord under whose standard the men served special legal authority over them. The monks were able to show charters from previous Stewart lords of Kyle exempting the men of Kylesmuir from service under the Stewart banner, with the result that Robert, duke of Albany, yielded the point and permitted them to lead their own men under a commander appointed by the abbot.

It was not just by the secular authorities, however, that the value of Melrose's assets in the west was threatened. In the early 1300s, the Pope began to dismantle the financial privileges that had been granted to the Cistercians in the early days of the order. The chief target was the exemption from payment of teind from their land, much of which had not been in full economic exploitation in the twelfth century. Such land, however, had been routinely developed by the monks and was generating substantial profits that were free from any secular or ecclesiastical burdens. Kylesmuir certainly fell into this category, and the Melrose monks were deeply alarmed at the threatened loss of revenue which would have been involved. As a result, they sought the aid of their sympathetic diocesan, the bishop of Glasgow, who in June 1315 permitted the abbey to constitute its Kylesmuir property as a single parish based on Mauchline. Using the poverty of the abbey as a result of the wars with England as an excuse, he permitted them to construct a chapel or church at Mauchline for the use of their tenants and indwellers within the limits of their estate. By this device, the monks were given possession of a parish church and could divert its teind directly into their own hands, with only a small deduction as a stipend for the resident priest. Now complete with its own parish church, Mauchline began to develop as a focus for settlement, and by the early sixteenth century a significant community had grown up around the buildings of the monks' grange and adjacent church (**100**).

A significant further enhancement of the abbey's position in the west came in 1425 when James I granted them a regality jurisdiction over their lands in Carrick. King James was also earl of Carrick, a title that David II had granted to the king's father, John Stewart, who became King Robert III. The gift, a sign of favour by the King to John Fogo, the newly appointed abbot of Melrose, took the large block of estates in northern Carrick, between Maybole and the river Doon, out of the jurisdiction of the royal baillie of Carrick. Together with the regality held between Gala and Leader and over the properties of Melroseland, and that given for Ettrick at the same time as the award in Carrick, these privileges gave the abbot jurisdictional powers that were the envy of many secular lords. To exercise the powers of a regality, however, the abbot needed to appoint a lay deputy as baillie, for the capital powers associated with the franchise were incompatible with holy orders. As a consequence, the office of baillie, in the gift of the abbot, emerged as a coveted prize amongst the regional nobility. Despite this privileged jurisdiction, however, the abbey's position within Carrick began to suffer from erosion and by the middle of the fifteenth century, inroads were being made into the revenues drawn by the abbey from its property there. In April 1465, for example, Abbot Andrew Hunter reached a financial settlement with James Park, the vicar perpetual of Maybole, whereby he made over to Park for life half of the vicarage teinds of the abbey's lands of Grange and Monkwood in Maybole parish. The exemption from payment of teind enjoyed by the Cistercians had been lost in the fourteenth century, but here they had clearly

100 *The tower house built by Abbot Hunter at Mauchline.* MacGibbon and Ross, Castellated and Domestic Architecture, 1889

continued to draw all the dues for themselves and Park had taken his case to the court of the bishop of Glasgow for judgement. Rather than risk the loss of all the vicarage teind to Park, Hunter had clearly chosen to make a settlement that kept half of the disputed revenues in the abbey's hands.

In Kylesmuir, by way of contrast, the monks' position appeared to have strengthened through the fifteenth century. James I had erected the Mauchline estate into a free barony, removing it from the secular jurisdiction of any sheriff, and transferring the profits of justice there to the abbey. The abbot was authorised to hold his own court within the territory and, naturally, it was at Mauchline that the barony court met thereafter. The final privilege acquired was a charter from James IV in October 1510 erecting the toun of Mauchline into a burgh of barony. This gave the right to buy and sell goods free from the overriding privileges of neighbouring burghs, such as Ayr, with a weekly market on Wednesday and market cross and an annual eight-day fair in October. It also gave the monks the power to measure out burgage plots to set heritably to their tenants, and gave the burgesses the power to elect their own baillies. Taken together, the various privileges granted in favour of the monks at Mauchline made Kylesmuir a very valuable component of the monastic estate. As a consequence, it was considered a very ripe plum to control and, when Bernard Bell resigned his claim to the abbacy in 1506, he received an assignation of Mauchline and its revenues for life. Bernard's longevity diverted a considerable portion of the monastic revenues away from the abbey for a number of years. It was to be diverted again in 1542, when it was assigned as the source of the 1,000 merk pension for life paid from the monastic lands to Andrew Durie on his promotion to the see of Galloway. It remained in Durie's hands until his death in 1558, whereupon it should have reverted to the monks, but the destination of the revenues of Kylsemuir became just one of the many sources of conflict that had arisen between them and their commendator. By 1558, however, the value of the property had already been seriously eroded by numerous feu-ferme grants made from it to monastic tenants.

Nithsdale and Dumfries

One of the monks' smaller but very strategically located blocks of property lay in Nithsdale, where it formed a 'bridge' between their holdings in Kyle and Carrick and their interests around Dumfries and along the Solway Firth. The first portion of land that they acquired there was a quarter part of a ferm-toun in Dunscore on the western side of the valley, granted to them in the 1220s by Affrica, Lady of Nithsdale. Soon afterwards, Affrica extended her grant to encompass much of the northern half of Dunscore, adjacent to the lands of the Premonstratensian abbey of Dercongal or Holywood, which lay between Dunscore and Dumfries. As well as giving the monks free rein to do with the land whatever they willed, she also granted them free rights of access and egress across any of her property for their beasts going to and from Dunscore, probably as part of the abbey's efforts to secure a negotiated drove-way for their livestock being moved south from Kyle. In 1235-6, following Affrica's death without direct heirs, Alexander II granted Melrose the now drained Loch of Dunscore and the pennyland associated with it. This grant was to provide them with rental income from which they were to receive a pittance in the refectory at Melrose every St Andrew's Day.

Also in the early 1200s, the monks were receiving a steady flow of small gifts of property around Dumfries. John Avenel, for example, granted them half a ploughgate in Torthorwald, the rents from which were assigned to the gate at Melrose to provide alms for paupers coming there. In return, the monks were obliged to give the lord of the feu a pound of pepper annually. Just to the north of Dumfries itself, at Barnscarth, Auchencrieff and Dargavel, Thomas de Aunay gave the monks an extensive tract of pasture extending into the unreclaimed moss of the Lochar. This new gift formed the next stepping-stone in the sequence of properties that extended south from Kyle.

The new acquisitions brought the inevitable dispute over teind due to the parish church of the lands in which the Melrose property lay. In 1225 they reached an agreement with the vicar of Dumfries over the teinds of Barnscarth, while in 1257 they entered a protracted dispute with the canons of Holywood over the teinds of Dunscore, resolved only in 1264. The monks' determination to secure advantageous settlements in both disputes underscores the significance of these Nithsdale properties to them. Their value was further emphasised in 1250 when the monks negotiated the right to pass through John Comyn's lands of Dalswinton and Duncow with their beasts and carts, and to graze and water there overnight. It would seem that significant numbers of animals were being moved back and forward through Dunscore.

The Nithsdale property was also developed as an arable grange. In August 1307, during Edward II's brief and fruitless foray into southern Scotland following his father's death, the English army advanced up Nithsdale. Two Melrose monks, Brothers John and Thomas, keepers of the grange of Dunscore, subsequently brought a complaint before Edward, seeking compensation for damages done by the King and his army to the grange and adjacent grain. Edward ordered payment to them of 6s 8d. Nithsdale suffered considerably during the warfare between 1307 and 1312, when Robert I and his brother, Edward Bruce, campaigned regularly in the south-west. The needs of war may also have seen heavy burdens placed on the monks' lands there, with the King demanding various forms of service and material support. It was probably on account of this that in 1327 Robert I explicitly freed the abbey's lands and tenants from all secular services in perpetuity.

Northumberland

All of the abbey's original properties and its new acquisitions through the twelfth century lay within southern Scotland. Although many of the gifts they had received were given by men who held property on both sides of the border, it was only at Carlisle that they had gained any landed interest, and that was simply a single property in the town. The monks, however, developed close ties with several Northumberland landowners, most notably the de Muschamp lords of Wooler, and it was from them that they gained a valuable estate in the northern Cheviots. In the late 1100s, the monks had acquired several properties around Hownam, Whitton and Mow in the Kale and Bowmont valleys. In the mid 1220s, Robert de Muschamp gave them a block of land at the western edge of his lordship, marching with the Bowmont valley, at Trowup and Hethpool. This was primarily pasture and lay on the edge of de Muschamp's hunting forest, within which he gave the monks rights to take building materials, as well as granting immunity from seizure by his foresters, for any of their animals that strayed into the forest area. As this was hunting ground, there would normally have been restrictions placed on the use of dogs other than by the lord and his foresters, but the monks were given the right for their shepherds to have 'mastiff dogs' for guarding their flocks, presumably against wolves, and horns for calling them together.

These lands were clearly of some considerable value, for in 1227 the monks reached a settlement with the canons of Kirkham in Yorkshire, who controlled the parish church of the area, over the level of teind due to them. Under the terms of the agreement, the monks paid the canons an annual rent of 50s and 20d, which was significantly greater than any composition over teind that they had made for any of their Scottish lands. In return, however, they gained immunity from any other claims made in respect of the parish church of Newton in Glendale.

The Northumberland properties, although a significant and valuable component of the Melrose estate, brought the unwelcome complication of a foreign legal jurisdiction and system. The abbots of Melrose were no strangers to legal disputes by the mid-thirteenth century, and in March 1269 they paid their fee to bring a case to court before the justices in Northumberland. In October 1269, Henry III ordered that the abbot be pardoned his £10 fine at the English Exchequer for his non-appearance before the justices, and instructed the sheriff of Northumberland to repay the fine, with the explanation that the abbot had actually been detained on the King's business in Scotland. Further disputes followed; in 1285 the abbot procured a writ of trespass in respect of the abbey's lands in Northumberland, while in November 1287 he secured the appointment of an assize to hear a complaint of novel disseisin brought against Walter de Huntercombe in respect of its lands at Hethpool. Despite the long periods of the fourteenth century during which the abbey was in the peace of the English crown, there is no indication that these Northumberland lands were amongst properties restored to the monks by royal mandate and they disappear from the monks' records.

Salt-works and fisheries

In much of northern Europe throughout the Middle Ages, the only bulk preservative available was salt. Whilst some meat and fish could be dried or smoked, salting was the chief means of preserving perishable foodstuffs. With notable exceptions such as Droitwich in England where mineral rock-salt was extracted, most salt used at this period was sea-salt, recovered by natural evaporation processes or by boiling sea-water in pans. As an inland monastery, Melrose had no access to saltpans of its own and presumably secured its supply through the markets of the border burghs, especially Berwick, or by exchange deals with its daughter-houses at Newbattle and Holmcultram, which possessed pans of their own by the 1150s. As the community expanded, however, and it began to require greater volumes of salt both for its domestic needs and also for industrial processing of meat, fish and leather, it became vital for Melrose to acquire salt-works of its own.

The first of the abbey's saltpans, given to them by Cospatric, earl of Dunbar in the 1150s, lay on the East Lothian coast near Broxburn, south-east of Dunbar itself. The main concentration of Melrose's early saltpans, however, was in the west on the Clyde coast of Carrick and Kyle. In the 1190s, Roger de Skelbrooke, a vassal of Duncan, earl of Carrick, granted them the right to build a salt-work anywhere that they wished on the coast in his lordship of Greenan, immediately to the south of the river Doon, plus the right to take wood for fuel from the nearest of his demesne woods. Soon after 1200, Duncan of Carrick was obliged to offer the monks sites for two new salt-works in his demesne property of Turnberry, plus land for the maintenance of the workers and pasture for their pack- and draught-animals, as their woods at Greenan had been 'completely burned and destroyed'. The implication is that the monks' men had been too zealous in their exploitation of their fuel supply rather than that the woods had been accidentally burned. Two pans to replace the one at Greenan, moreover, implies that there was pressure to produce more salt, presumably to supply the expanding cattle-production centre at Mauchline, but possibly also for shipment back to Melrose itself. Continuing problems of fuel supply may have encouraged Melrose to begin to exploit the coal resources on its lands in Kyle and, possibly, at Carsphairn.

The earliest of Melrose's western saltpans may have been acquired soon after 1174 on the Solway coast of Galloway. Roland, son of Uhtred, Lord of Galloway and husband of Helen de Morville, granted the monks a salt-works at Preston near Kirkbean in Kirkcudbrightshire, with pasture for animals, a site for a house and the right to take timber from his wood of Preston to fuel the pan. It was to be the first of several saltpans run by the monks on the sandy coast of the Solway to the east and west of the Nith estuary. Before 1200, William de Brus, lord of Annandale, gave Melrose a salt-work on the sands at Rainpatrick in Dumfriesshire. This was an area of quite intensive industrial development by this date, with other salt-works belonging to Richard de Boys and Richard Fleming lying to its east. To maintain the salt-work, he granted them the right to fuel from a nearby peatery for their salt-making and domestic use by the lay-brothers who were expected to live there during the manufacturing season. Shortly afterwards, Richard Fleming also granted his salt-work at Rainpatrick and rights to peat for fuel to the monks, reserving only an annual rent of one pound of pepper. Although remote from Melrose, the abbey exploited its rights here and seems to have transported the salt back to the abbey, possibly making use of the old Roman roadway that crossed from Annandale into Eskdale and over the hills towards Hawick and Melrose itself. Melrose worked the saltpans here for the best part of a century until 1294 when, as part of a general review of its property interests in the Solway region, it transferred its rights in them to its daughter-house at Holmcultram under a feuferme arrangement. Clearly, by that date, Melrose was able to secure its requirements from its other saltpans in Ayrshire and East Lothian.

In 1460, the abbey received an important grant of saltpan sites at 'Saltpreston', now Prestonpans in East Lothian. The donor, Robert Hamilton of Singleton, granted his three rock-cut pan-sites and a storehouse, which the monks had held at ferme for some time. He also gave the abbey the right to have a quarry for building materials elsewhere on his properties at Prestonpans. These pans were quite remote from any concentration of Melrose properties in the Lothians, but lay close to the Dere Street route southwards over Soutra and down Lauderdale. We can assume, then, that they served as the main providers of salt for the abbey and its neighbouring granges.

A fishery on Tweed within the bounds of the abbey's estates of Darnick, Melrose, Eildon and Gattonside had formed part of David I's original award to the monks. Then, as now, this would have provided a valuable source of income from the salmon-fishing. Further fisheries followed quickly. Alexander II confirmed the monks in possession of the whole fishery of Old Roxburgh, which had been given to them by David, although no earlier charter has survived. Soon after 1153, Malcolm IV granted them the royal fishing rights in Tweed at Selkirk, a net of their own and two of the royal nets at 'Berwickstream'. The Selkirk fishery, confirmed to the monks in 1247 by Alexander II, was evidently at Yare near the confluence of Ettrick and Tweed. In the 1170s and 1180s, in tandem with the build up of a portfolio of property in Berwick, the monks began to develop an interest in the fishery on the lower reaches of Tweed. In the 1240s they acquired a second net at Berwickstream from Robert de Bernham, brother of the bishop of St Andrews. They were also building up more extensive rights further up the river, with Nicholas Corbet shortly before 1228 giving them the whole of his fishery within his lordship of Makerstoun to the west of Kelso.

Amongst Melrose's early acquisitions in the west were valuable Clyde-coast fisheries. The first, at the mouth of the river Ayr, given by Walter fitz Alan, was acquired in the 1170s, while a second was granted by Roger de Skelbrooke in the 1190s on the sands at the mouth of the river Doon. About the same time, William de Brus, Lord of Annandale, granted the monks a sea-fishery in the Solway at Rainpatrick near the mouth of the border Esk, with a site to the south of the parish church on which their men could build a fishing-station, one acre of land for their support and pasture for draught oxen and four cows. He granted the property to the monks in free alms, reserving only to himself the right to take any sturgeons which the monks' men caught.

Town properties

There were two basic groups amongst the properties held by Melrose in various Scottish, and English, burghs (**101**). The first were those used for the purposes for which they had originally been given: bases from which the abbot or representatives could conduct business, both in respect of trading operations and in relation to ecclesiastical or political affairs. The second group were properties acquired speculatively or granted as pious gifts, but from which the monks drew a rental income, flagrantly breaching the original Cistercian prohibition on accepting properties of this kind. Down to 1300, the main concentration of urban properties held by Melrose lay in Berwick and Roxburgh, with a scattering through other southern burghs. After the outbreak of the wars with England at the end of the thirteenth century, Melrose began to spread its interests more widely and, whilst it recovered most of its Berwick properties and retained them down to the final loss of the town to the English in 1482, it built up a very substantial portfolio in Leith, which had emerged as Scotland's new chief outlet for wool in the later fourteenth century.

Berwick

The abbey's first property in Berwick was given to them by Walter I fitz Alan, steward of King William the Lion, shortly after 1165. It comprised a toft 'next to Tweed', possibly close to the port, and 20 acres of land in the field

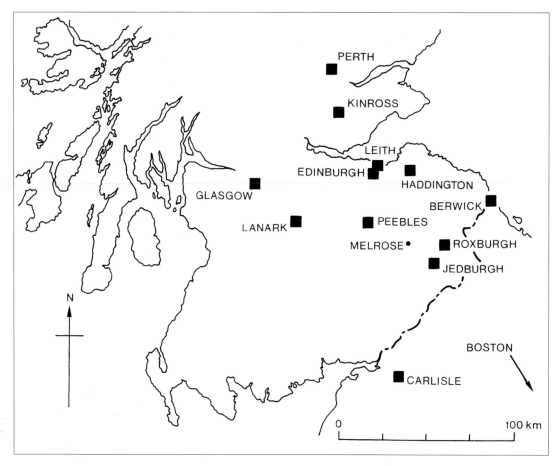

101 *Map of towns and burghs in which Melrose had a property interest.* Sylvia Stevenson/Historic Scotland

of Berwick. Between 1165 and 1177, the King added a property on the corner of Briggate, formerly occupied by one William Lunnock, that was to remain in their possession until 1482. This tenement comprised a house on Briggate and a long rig running south to the river between the land of Arnald Hanyn on the west and a property belonging to the Steward on the east. For this property, King William added, the monks were exempt from all service in times of peace or war, rendering only their prayers for his salvation. Shortly before 1200, Grim, son of Guy the Carter of Roxburgh, gave them an unlocated property in Berwick which he held of William de Somerville. The acquisition of these three properties may be linked to the abbey's greater trading activity, as already noted in the privileges granted to the monks by the count of Flanders, Berwick being Scotland's principal outlet for trade with the Low Countries at this period.

Early in the thirteenth century, Moses the Arbalaster granted Melrose 10 acres of measured land outside Berwick. This gift marked the start of another round of acquisitions in the burgh, but the new properties were mainly exploited for rental income rather than as sites for warehouses and stores for the abbey's produce. In Berwick's busy property market, there were plenty of opportunities for layers of ownership to overlap or come into conflict. In 1212, for example, Elvina, daughter of Richard son of Daniel, appears to have contested Melrose's rights in a property on the Ness and brought litigation against them but resigned her claim to the King before a judgement was given. Shortly afterwards, the abbey bought a property in the Ness from Robert de Burnham and received the gift from Adam le Vilour and Annis his wife of an adjoining piece of land. One final property was added on this date on the Snuke, the district on the east of the Ness. Quite clearly, this eastern sector of the burgh was experiencing a phase of intensive development and speculation in which Melrose was a significant player. They also took what property they could get elsewhere in the town. At the west end, they received land next to the fishpond, bounded by the castle ditch and the High Street, for which they paid an annual rent of 6d to the constable of Berwick Castle.

Scotland's booming export trade in the mid-thirteenth century may have encouraged the monks to further develop their interests in Berwick. Abbot Matthew (1246-61) is credited in the *Chronicle of Melrose* with building the abbey's 'great houses' in the burgh, the property from which the monks' business interests were run. In 1252, the monks acquired a property in the Briggate between the Red Hall (the trading centre of the Flemish merchant colony) and the land of David the Tailor. The owner of the land, Nicholas the Weaver, had granted half of the property to the monks in free alms, then sold the other half to them 'in his great necessity' for 100 merks. In return, the monks were also to give Nicholas and his wife, for life, ten bolls of marketable wheat, one chalder of barley, and half a merk of silver. Between 1273 and 1296, Alexander Jocelim, burgess of Peebles, resigned to Melrose, for payment of 140 merks 'in my urgent necessity', the properties in Briggate in Berwick that his father had held from the abbey at feuferme. This property on the corner of Briggate, which remained in Melrose's possession for another two centuries, stood on the south side of the street at its eastern corner. Jocelim's quitclaim mentioned the 'new building' of the abbot and convent, which extended from 'le stathe' as far as Tweed, on the south side of the property. A final thirteenth-century acquisition came from Mariota de Monachis, widow of Nicholas the Apothecary, who granted Melrose her property on the east side of Narrowgate on the Ness, between the tenement of the abbot of Jedburgh and that of her kinswoman, Alice de Monachis. By the end of the thirteenth century, then, the abbey held a substantial portfolio of properties in the burgh, many of them in its vibrant commercial centre. Some had been acquired through gift, others by speculative dealing, most notably through the buying up of debts or mortgages from burgesses who had got into financial difficulties. Taken together, the Berwick lands constituted a significant component in the abbey's estate, providing them with both an income from rents and also with a presence in the port through which they transacted their greatest volume of trade.

The storming and sack of Berwick by Edward I and the English army was a blow to the prosperity of the burgh from which it never recovered. Although Edward moved English settlers into the burgh to repopulate it after the massacres which traditionally accompanied the fall of the town, in August 1296 he also ordered formal restoration of the properties of Scots who had submitted to his overlordship. Amongst such men was the abbot of Melrose and it can be assumed that the abbey was restored to possession of its various properties in Berwick, along with the rest of its estate. Following the recapture of Berwick by the Scots at the beginning of April 1318, Melrose sought re-confirmations of the various charters which gave them title to their valuable properties in the burgh. In parliament at Scone in November 1318, King Robert inspected their existing deeds and confirmed to the monks 'all the tenements, burgages, rents, possessions and fishings' which they had accumulated both within the limits of the town and in the surrounding district. The monks became immediately active in the buoyant property market within the burgh, which Robert was seeking to redevelop as the kingdom's premier export centre, redeveloping their existing possessions and acquiring new ones. Soon after 1320, they rebuilt their 'great house' at 'Ledynhall' in the east of the burgh and began to expand their portfolio of properties, adding a house in Crossgate, a tenement on the Ness, and a large block of land at the south end of Ravensdean Street, all close to the commercial centre and harbour. In 1331, the monks acquired the property immediately to the south of their 'great houses' on the Ness.

On the fall of Berwick to Edward III of England in 1333, Melrose evidently was confirmed in possession of its various properties in the burgh. It retained these throughout the fourteenth century when both abbey and burgh were in English hands. The decline in English power in Teviotdale from the 1380s onwards does not seem to have compromised this position and even after the abbey was, without question, back in the Scottish allegiance, it continued to hold Berwick properties. Indeed, by 1442, it is clear that the abbey had managed to expand its interests in the burgh, gaining possession of two vacant tenements in Bridge Street that had pertained formerly to the Maison Dieu of Berwick and which adjoined one of their other possessions. These they leased to a Berwick burgess for 4s Sterling annually, with the proviso that the tenant was to build houses of 'lime, stone, oak and iron, and roofed with myrthake' on the site within 12 years of entry.

When Berwick was ceded to the Scots in 1461 by Henry VI of England in return for Scottish support for the Lancastrian cause during the civil war in England that is now known as the Wars of the Roses, the problems of cross-border property-owning might have seemed to have been resolved. Melrose seized this as an opportunity to settle disputes over the extent of its tenements in the burgh that had presumably proven difficult to pursue at law, when the town had been in English hands. In 1480, King James III gave a mandate to Sir Patrick Hepburn of Dunsyre, sheriff of Berwick, to hold an inquest into the issue, and part of the findings of the assize survives. The main property at dispute was the Briggate or Bridge Street tenement that had been leased out in 1442. The members of the assize gave a range of answers regarding its proper extent. The laird of Bass and five others considered that the houses on the corner of the Briggate should have all the land behind them running down to the burgh wall or the Tweed, as was the case with the abbey's property on the Ness. The laird of Blackadder considered that they should have the house only, while James Douglas and three others considered that they should have only the house and the backland then attached to it. Four others gave a vague response that it should have the house and a 'tale' of unspecified length. The final decision has not survived. The same inquest decided against the abbey's claim to the property at Leadenhall, which they had still possessed in the early fourteenth century, with the jurors stating that no document they had seen supported the monks' claims. The findings of the inquest, however, were rendered redundant two years later when the Scots finally lost possession of Berwick to the English. On this occasion, there is no suggestion that the abbey was able to preserve its interest in the burgh, thereby bringing to an end an association of nearly 300 years between Melrose and Berwick.

Other towns

It was not just in Berwick, nor solely in Scotland, that the monks acquired burgh properties. King William gave the monks a toft in Lanark, at that period one of the chief markets in south central Scotland. Bishop Jocelin of Glasgow gave the monks of his former abbey a toft in Glasgow, built by Ranulf of Haddington soon after the first erection of the burgh of Glasgow. The gift was made 'towards the use of the house of Melrose', either to provide rental income or to give the abbot a base at the administrative centre of the diocese in which his abbey lay. In the early thirteenth century, they acquired two tofts at the west end of Haddington, possibly on account of the substantial build up of rural properties which the monks had acquired by that date in the eastern Lammermuir Hills and which lay within the commercial hinterland of that burgh rather than Berwick. Shortly before April 1325, Robert I granted them a toft and croft in Kinross 'in the corner next to the road to Perth, on the west side of the road', with freedom to brew, bake, and sell flesh, fish, bread and other commodities. On 1 April 1325, the King ordered the chamberlain and the sheriff of Kinross to stop levying an annual ferme of 40d for the 'hostillage'. This property was always an outlier to Melrose's main interests and, although the monks did develop some further interests north of the river Forth, it must always have been inconvenient for them to administer. Eventually, in 1410, they exchanged it with Sir Malcolm Galbraith of Grenoch for a piece of land which he held in Lessudden, where the monks were attempting to consolidate their land-holding. It is not until the fifteenth century that some properties in other Scottish burghs emerge in the records. Properties in Causeygate at Jedburgh and in Selkirk, for example, were reset at feuferme in 1426. Both, however, were evidently not new acquisitions and it is likely that the Selkirk property at least had been held by the Melrose monks from an early date. None of these properties were significant in terms of scale and value in comparison to the land-holding built up in Berwick before 1296.

Melrose's trading connections, as well as its spiritual connections, brought property outwith Scotland. These properties, at Carlisle and St Botulph's (Boston, Lincolnshire), were important footholds in the later twelfth- and thirteenth-century trading network within the British Isles. The tenement in Carlisle given to them by Henry Bradfoot was of high importance, for it gave them a base from which to operate in the regional market in what, after 1157, was the chief commercial centre in north-western England. This property, however, which lay in Baker Street, was rented out but with the monks reserving the right to accommodation and hospitality there for themselves, their lay-brethren and servants when they came to the Carlisle fair. This right remained important so long as Melrose was bringing cattle south from its Ayrshire lands and over the Solway fords into Cumberland. Towards the end of the thirteenth century, when Melrose was transferring most of its interests in the Solway region over to its daughter-house at Holmcultram, this property was given to Holmcultram for an annual rent of one merk, and a continued right to hospitality there whenever the abbot of Melrose came west on his visitations of Holmcultram, or whenever he or his monks and their dependents came to the fair. Significant though the Carlisle holding was, the property in Boston which the monks were given by Thomas de Multon before around 1230 had the potential to be of even greater value. St Botulph's Fair at Boston was an event of international significance which attracted merchants from all over western Europe, primarily because of its importance as a wool-market. Melrose was certainly active at the fair in the 1220s, paying rents there to Vaudey Abbey for the lands of Carsphairn and possibly buying commodities such as grain and wine for the use of the convent. Whether they ever developed their property in Boston is open to question, as it was only ever referred to as *placea*, meaning an open space, site, plot or square. Nevertheless, it was also made over to Holmcultram by an abbot only designated as 'Frater P', probably Patrick de Selkirk (abbot from 1273 to 1296) rather than Patrick (abbot from 1206 to 1207), in view of the date of the transfer of other Melrose properties to that abbey.

Properties were also being purchased as well as received as gifts. In 1246, King Alexander II confirmed the purchases of various properties by Geoffrey, porter of Melrose, the income from which was to be used to provide alms for paupers who came to the abbey gates. Amongst Geoffrey's purchases were two burgages in King Street in Roxburgh. In Peebles, Sir William Durham bought a burgage from two burgesses and subsequently 'granted' it in free alms to the abbey. However, there is preserved in the abbey records, a receipt from Sir William acknowledging payment to him by the monks of 14 merks for the same burgage. This may be the property described as lying in the 'old' burgh of Peebles and apparently standing waste that the abbey granted in feuferme in 1492. In the thirteenth century in Berwick, the monks paid 100 merks to acquire control of a property in the commercial heart of the burgh and in 1331, they enlarged their holding by paying 10 merks to the widowed Alice Moigne and her son for their tenement which adjoined the monks' existing property on the Ness.

Leith and Edinburgh

As the political situation between Scotland and England deteriorated in the 1380s, the monks began to seek alternative outlets for their goods and to acquire holdings in burghs that were both further removed from the volatile border zone and actively involved in the same forms of trade as Melrose specialised in. It was around this time that they took the feu of a property in Perth, a burgh with a substantial wool and leather trade. It was in Leith, however, which had replaced Berwick as the principal Scottish export centre for wool and hides, and in Edinburgh, where the chief merchants active in that trade were based, that the monks began to build up a significant property interest. Their first new property in Leith, acquired in the late 1390s, was a tenement granted by Sir Robert Logan of Restalrig, superior of the burgh, to the rear of which he added a further 14ft of ground in 1415.

An important property in Leith was added to the portfolio in 1510 when Bernard Bell, one of the claimants of the abbacy, made over to Melrose the property in the burgh that he had inherited from his father, William Bell. William, burgess of Edinburgh, and his wife, Agnes, had acquired this tenement in South Leith in 1455 when it had been resigned by John Turing, another Edinburgh burgess. In 1470, William and his neighbours had their properties measured and staked out, indicating a degree of under-development in the area and suggesting that plans for building were then under consideration. By 1509, when Bernard was possessor, the forehouse of the property was described as 'waste', but was still granted in feuferme by him at an annual rent of 4 merks Scots. It was this rent and the superiority that he made over to the abbey the following year.

In tandem with the build up in Leith, the monks were adding to their holdings in Edinburgh from the early 1400s. Their first purchase, in 1408, was a property on the south side of the High Street of Edinburgh, which yielded an annual rent of 20s for the abbey. Then, in 1419 they took the wadset of all the properties of the merchant Nicholas of Wedale as security against a loan of £40. All income from Nicholas's land was assigned to the monks and 'kirkwerk' of the abbey. Even if Nicholas redeemed the mortgage within a year, he was to pay £10 to the abbey.

A degree of speculation is also evident in Melrose's building interest in Edinburgh. By the 1420s it was seeking to secure properties in the Cowgate, a district where many leading nobles and churchmen were to acquire large holdings. In 1424, Abbot John Fogo took an acre of ground on the south side of the Cowgate at feuferme from the abbot of Holyrood for an annual rent of 6s 8d. Four years later, Brother Richard Lundy, acting on behalf of the convent, took a second, larger property on the south side of the Cowgate at feuferme from the Edinburgh merchant-burgess, John Vernour, paying him 20s annually. In 1440, William Vernour renewed the feuferme for a reduced sum of 13s 4d. The Cowgate site became the location of the town house of the abbots of Melrose, described in the 1550s as a magnificent building constructed at great expense.

There were two other 'urban' communities in which Melrose had a controlling interest, Mauchline and Melrose itself. At Mauchline, the origin of the burgh lay in the grange complex developed by the monks there from the later twelfth century. The catalyst for its development into something more than an agricultural settlement, was the erection in 1315 of the monks' oratory there into a church with full parochial rights. Before then, the monks' lay tenants on the lands of Kylesmuir would have had to go to neighbouring parishes for any church service that they needed, but the creation of a parish church at Mauchline gave a focus and identity to the community. Further developments came in the fifteenth century when the monks' lands were erected into a free barony with its court place at Mauchline. Thus, by the mid 1400s, the grange had acquired spiritual and jurisdictional reality as a focal settlement. The grant of burgh status to the settlement in 1510, therefore, may simply have been the formalisation of what had been the reality for several years already.

Less can be said about the status of the community at Melrose. There were clearly secular settlements on the land upon which the abbey was founded already in existence before 1137. These do not appear to have been swept away when David I gave the property to the monks. There is, however, no evidence that any kind of settlement developed with the abbey precinct as its focus until the fifteenth century. In 1422, a prolonged dispute between the abbey and the Haigs of Bemerside over the boundary between the Haigs' demesne and the monks' lands in Redpath came to a head. On Palm Sunday that year, the monks gathered first in the chapter house, then proceeded to the chapel above the gate, and finally to 'the cross before the gate', where they issued solemn notice of their intention to excommunicate their opponent should he not cease from his harassment of the monks and their men. It has been assumed that this 'cross before the gate', presumably the main, that is the south, gate of the abbey precinct, was the market cross of a community that had grown up at the principal approach to the monastery. Certainly, settlements developed in this way at the gates of several other Scottish monasteries, such as Whithorn, Paisley, Kelso or Arbroath, but in all those instances there was a formal charter from the King permitting its establishment. There is no evidence for any such charter from the crown, even to highly favoured abbots such as John Fogo or Andrew Hunter. The likelihood is that the powerful local interests of Roxburgh in the twelfth to fourteenth centuries, and of the other borders burghs subsequently, prevented any formal status being given to any settlement at Melrose's gates.

A civil settlement did exist at Melrose by the later medieval period. The area in front of the main gate to the precinct did become the location of the market of the burgh founded in 1605, which provides circumstantial evidence in support of an earlier community with the 'cross before the gate' as the symbol of its market. House plots had already been laid out along the road running up to the gate, and extending back to the precinct wall, before the middle of the sixteenth century. For example, in March 1556, John Clennen and Agnes Watsoun, his spouse, were infefted in a tenement 'before the front door of the monastery of Melrose', between two other tenements and with 'the High Street on the West and the garden of the monastery called the Prentyse yairds on the East'. Various tenancies, however, had also breached the precinct wall by that date and it is clear that even before 1560 there were numerous burgage-like holdings laid out within the old circuit. Therefore, the creation of the burgh of barony of Melrose in 1605, was simply the formal recognition of a much older development.

Churches

As part of their driving principle of finding stability, order and spiritual perfection on earth, free from worldly distractions, the original Cistercians had rejected accepting control of the patronage of parish churches, or of parish revenues, as these elements would of necessity have required them to be involved in the affairs of men. Not least of their concerns was that Cistercian monks should not be involved in the 'cure of souls', that is, in dispensing sacraments, receiving confession and offering absolution to laymen. This principle, however, stood in contrast to the general reformist argument within the western Church, which argued that it was improper for laymen to control the patronage of churches, and to possess the churches as property, especially where the cure of souls was concerned. Lay patrons, indeed, were being encouraged to grant away their rights to a religious corporation of some kind, and some monastic orders, especially the Augustinian canons, had received many gifts of this type. By the 1130s, the prohibition against controlling parish churches was being adhered to less rigidly, and in the founding grant to Melrose possession of the parish church was implicit. This was to be the case in several other of the earlier twelfth-century Cistercian foundations in Scotland, such as Dundrennan and Newbattle, although in those cases also, there was no explicit grant made. Various devices were employed to overcome the prohibition before the end of the twelfth century, as the lure of parish revenues became increasingly difficult to avoid, especially where the monastery already held a right to receive the teind from land which it controlled or developed in a parish. At Mauchline, for example, Melrose prevented the church from acquiring parochial status until the early fourteenth century, thereby side-stepping the issue. At Kirkgunzeon in Galloway, held by Melrose's daughter-house of Holmcultram, the monks were accused in the thirteenth century of having 'degraded' a previously parochial church to a mere chapel and having evicted the lay population to turn the whole vill into a monastic grange. By the 1190s, the Cistercians were being less coy about accepting the patronage of a parish church, but were still careful, as at Hassendean, to have the terms on which the church was held spelled out very clearly. After around 1300, all pretence was over and control of parish revenues was actively sought as a means of replacing or supplementing incomes disrupted by warfare and economic depression.

At one time or other, Melrose possessed, or claimed to possess, up to 11 parish churches, although it never controlled all of them simultaneously (**102**). The following list gives them in date order of acquisition, and outlines their fate in Melrose's hands.

Melrose

In the early twelfth century, the church of Melrose was held by the Benedictine monks of Durham Cathedral-priory, or by their dependent cell at Coldingham in Berwickshire. This arrangement was of probably some antiquity, probably arising from Durham's status as successor to the monastery of Lindisfarne, which had controlled Melrose in the seventh and eighth centuries. Perhaps in preparation for the founding of the Cistercian abbey, David I gave Durham the church of St Mary of Berwick-on-Tweed in return for Melrose, which was then given to the monks. From the outset, therefore, despite the prohibition on control of parish churches, the abbey church itself also served a parochial function. As a consequence, lay folk would have required access to the monastic precinct to attend parish services, which were probably housed originally in the western porch of the abbey church. In 1234, Pope Gregory IX granted the monks the privilege of serving the cure with one of their own monks, thereby allowing all of the parish revenues to be diverted to the uses of the abbey. Probably from the fourteenth century, when the bulk of the nave was no longer required to house the choir of the lay-brethren, the parishioners may have moved into the nave of the church. Certainly, the parish congregation was housed in the 'gret church' in the sixteenth century, and they perhaps continued to use what survived of the old church nave while the new church was under construction to its east after 1385.

Hassendean

This was the first of the churches acquired by Melrose in the twelfth century (**103**). The simple entry in the *Chronicle of Melrose*, recording that Jocelin, bishop of Glasgow, had in 1193 given the monks 'the church of the bishop

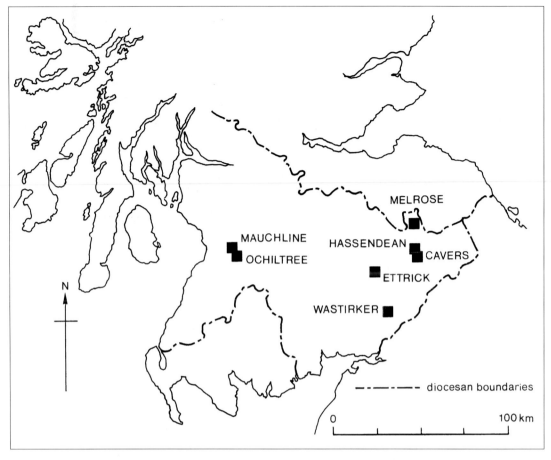

102 *Map of parish churches appropriated to Melrose.* Sylvia Stevenson/Historic Scotland

St Kentigern at Hassendean' in perpetual alms, masks a deeper controversy between the bishop and King William, to which Melrose had added its own irritants. At the outset, there seems to have been a dispute between bishop and King over which of them had the right of patronage in the church. The King appears to have surrendered any right that he had into Jocelin's hands, but only on the condition that Jocelin then made the church over to Melrose. Jocelin's original charter does not survive, but it seems to have made over the church to the abbey for the maintenance of the poor and pilgrims coming there. The latter may allude to the increasing numbers coming to the tomb of Abbot Waltheof, whose cult Jocelin had done much to foster. Having gained possession, Melrose chose to exploit the rights previously enjoyed by the parson in the vill in which the church was situated, and in particular his grazing rights on the common land. The result appears to have been serious over-stocking and damage to the grazing, which led the inhabitants of Hassendean, who were tenants of the King, to take their complaint to the royal court. There, faced with claims by his tenants that Melrose's actions were threatening their ability to pay their rents, King William decided on strong action, driven especially by the argument that the bishop was effectively making a grant of land, hidden in the guise of a grant of a church. In consequence, Jocelin was forced to rescind his 1193 grant and, following a major assembly in 1195 of both the royal court and a church synod at Melrose, a new formula was agreed. The new charter, carefully confirmed by the King, again granted the church to Melrose for the support of the poor and pilgrims, but stipulating that its revenues must be put to no other use. It also stated that the extent of the grazing rights associated with the church would be settled by an assize, which assigned pasture for 200 ewes, 16 oxen and four cows. Finally, to secure the compliance of the chapter of Glasgow, who had evidently balked at the alienation of the church by their bishop, it was agreed that Melrose would pay an annual rent of 20s to the canons.

103 *The remains of Hassendean Church by Archibald Rutherford, drawn in 1776.* Reproduced courtesy of the National Galleries of Scotland, D163

From 1195 onwards, the parsonage revenues of Hassendean were annexed to Melrose and a vicarage established to provide for the spiritual needs of the parishioners. In 1315, using claims of poverty on account of the wars with England, the monks succeeded in having the vicarage revenues also annexed to the abbey for an agreed period of 20 years. Although this settlement was challenged in 1326, Melrose won the dispute. At some point in the fourteenth century, the temporary annexation was made permanent and both the parsonage and vicarage revenues remained united to Melrose until the Reformation.

Mauchline

When Walter fitz Alan had made over the extensive tract of land in eastern Kyle that later developed into the Melrose lordship of Kylesmuir, it had not been served by an independent parish church, but by the chapel of St Michael at Mauchline. It is likely that Mauchline would have developed into a full parish had it not fallen into Cistercian possession at this time but, adhering to the prohibition against accepting control of parochial churches, the monks prevented this from happening. As the Cistercian order was exempt from payment of teind from its lands, there was no pressing need in any case to regularise Mauchline's status, and it remained a chapel serving the estate centre there into the early 1300s. In 1315, however, with the order about to lose its privilege of exemption from payment of teind, the abbey had to move swiftly to gain full parish status for their dependency, or face the loss of a substantial amount of revenue to whichever parish church on which Mauchline was regarded as dependent. Using the supposed poverty of the abbey caused by the wars with England as a pretext, Robert, bishop of Glasgow, permitted them to establish Mauchline as a parish church with full rights of baptism and burial, and confirmed them in possession, effectively handing them undisputed rights to all teind revenues.

This peculiar development of the church at Mauchline, despite Bishop Robert's charter, caused long-running friction between the abbey and subsequent bishops of Glasgow, who regretted the loss of a valuable source of potential revenue. In their eyes, Robert's grant had been far too generous, as it had given away all episcopal rights in the new parish, and by the late fourteenth century there was an attempt to deny that parish status had been granted. In 1402, the Pope attempted to settle a dispute over the status of the 'church or chapel' there, in which Melrose claimed that it was exempt from visitation by the bishops of Glasgow by the terms of the old agreement, while Bishop Matthew Glendinning had denied that such an exemption existed and had threatened the monks with excommunication if they attempted to obstruct his visit. The case was eventually settled in the monks' favour in August 1404, when the Pope confirmed Bishop Robert's charter to Melrose. There was no further challenge to the monks' possession of the parish, with all its revenues being diverted to the uses of the abbey with a pensionary vicar being installed to serve the cure.

Hounam

Melrose began to build up a landed interest in Hounam in the course of the twelfth century, but the parish church remained a free parsonage until sometime after 1185. In the 1230s, Melrose and Jedburgh abbeys were involved in a dispute over conflicting claims to the patronage of the church. Melrose lost the suit and in 1237 formally renounced all rights which it had, or claimed to have, in the church.

Ettrick

In 1235-6, Alexander II granted Melrose his waste of Ettrick, which the monks began to exploit systematically as primarily sheep pasture. There was clearly a dependent population on its extensive lands there, but there is no early indication that they were served by a parish church. In the mid-fourteenth century, David II granted a church of the Blessed Virgin of Ettrick Forest to the canons of Dryburgh, but this was certainly not a church serving Melrose's estates there. In the mid-fifteenth century, however, a vicarage of the church of St John the Baptist is mentioned, and in the early sixteenth century the parsonage and vicarage teinds of the New Kirk of Ettrick are mentioned as being annexed to the abbey. Although there is no hard evidence to support the idea, it is probable that Melrose's Ettrick properties, like Mauchline, were served only by a chapel in the thirteenth century. Teind could then be diverted to the abbey, but on the removal of that privilege in the 1310s Ettrick had been elevated into a separate parish so that these revenues could remain in Melrose's hands.

Dunscore

Melrose had begun to acquire a landed interest at Dunscore in Nithsdale in the 1220s and '30s. This property was developed as a separate grange by the monks and remained a distinct block in its possession into the sixteenth century. In 1257 and 1264, Melrose reached agreements with the Premonstratensian abbey of Holywood in Nithsdale over teinds in Dunscore, and it is clear that Holywood possessed the church by the earlier of these dates. Pope Benedict XIII ordered an inquest into this agreement in 1411, described specifically as relating to the right of patronage, to ensure that it was not prejudicial to the interests of the papacy. While these settlements, or compositions, clearly arose from a dispute between the abbeys over control of the parish church – and in the mid-sixteenth century Melrose still enjoyed half of the parsonage revenues – teind lay at the heart of the controversy. Indeed, it may have been the development of Melrose's grange of Dunscore and the order's exemption from payment of teind on its lands running up against Holywood's desire, as patron and possessor, to extract full teind, that had prompted a challenge to Holywood's rights.

Ochiltree

The parish of Ochiltree lay to the south-west of the great block of Melrose properties centred on Mauchline in Kyle and was, through the thirteenth century, in the possession of the Colville family. Towards the end of that century, there was prolonged litigation within the family over the patronage of the church, which Sir John de Colville attempted to grant to the Knights Hospitaller of Torphichen to prevent it from passing to his younger brother, William. Eventually, in 1316 the Colville heiress, Eustacia, granted the patronage to Melrose, who swiftly secured confirmations of the gift from King Robert I and the bishop of Glasgow. From the outset, both parsonage and vicarage revenues were annexed to the abbey, and a vicar pensioner was installed to serve the cure.

Wastirker

The relationship between Melrose and John de Graham, Lord of Wastirker in Eskdale, had not proven to be a smooth one, and in the early 1300s they had been involved in protracted litigation over land and rights in his lordship. Graham had lost the dispute and down to 1317 he issued charters effectively yielding up the rights at the centre of the conflict. Possibly in a move to win the monks' favours after so many years of hostility, shortly before 1321 he made over his rights in the church of Wastirker to Melrose. The monks moved quickly to secure their possession, and between April and September 1321, received a series of confirmations from the King, the bishop of Glasgow, and the chapter of Glasgow. Melrose had possessed the right to teinds in upper Eskdale since the mid-twelfth century, and in 1305 had struck a deal with the rector of Wastirker over ecclesiastical dues from their lands around Watcarrick in the parish. This new deal, however, allowed them to extend these rights over the whole parish, Bishop John of Glasgow permitting them to serve the church with a vicar perpetual and divert the bulk of the teinds to the uses of the abbey. Although there is no indication that this position was ever challenged subsequently, the monks' experience at other churches in their possession prompted them in 1404 to secure a belated papal confirmation of their rights. Wastirker remained in Melrose's possession down to the Reformation.

Tarbolton

The patronage of this parish remained in the hands of the secular lord of Tarbolton down to the 1330s. In 1335, Sir John de Graham gifted the patronage to his kinsman, Robert de Graham of Walston, but three years later made it over instead to the Trinitarian community at nearby Fail, only to cancel that grant by 1343 on account of some fraud on the part of the friars. Sir John then reconfirmed his original award to Robert de Graham, who in 1342 had already granted the right of patronage to Melrose. Fail, however, received a confirmation of its rights from John Stewart, earl of Carrick (the future King Robert III) in 1368. Following the death of the incumbent priest in 1404, John Stewart of Darnley, Melrose and Fail all claimed the patronage, and in 1414 accepted the King's arbitration. Melrose, despite its charters, lost the case and never succeeded subsequently in making good its claim.

Wilton

The parish church of Wilton was a late and temporary addition to the Melrose portfolio. After a dispute over control of its patronage in the early 1200s, it had remained as an independent parsonage down to the 1340s. At that time, patronage of the church was attached to half of the barony of Wilton, which was held by Gilbert de Maxwell. In 1342, in what appears to have been a mortgage arrangement, Maxwell made over his half of the barony – and the right of patronage – to Melrose, but the loan was evidently redeemed soon after and the abbey permanently lost possession.

Cavers

The continuing shaky condition of Melrose's finances in the period after the Anglo-Scottish treaty of 1357 was used as a further excuse to secure additional revenue by the annexation of parish churches to the abbey. In 1358, William, first earl of Douglas, who was rapidly establishing a position as protector and patron of the abbey, granted it the parish church of Cavers in Teviotdale, securing confirmation of the award by his superior lord for the barony of Cavers, Thomas, earl of Mar, from King David II, and from the bishop of Glasgow. The bishop's agreement was given in return for the guaranteed establishment of a vicarage perpetual to fulfil the parochial duties in the church, and in 1363 he issued a precept to his dean of Christianity in Teviotdale to give possession to Melrose.

Firm possession of Cavers, however, was not that easily secured and 40 years later they faced a sustained challenge to their right to the church. On 25 November 1402, the monks' case was recited at length in a papal letter. This described how the abbey had been ravaged by war and, as its revenues were insufficient to meet the cost of repairs, Pope Clement VII had annexed the revenues of the parish to Melrose for a period of 10 years from the death or resignation of the incumbent rector. On learning of the sack of the abbey in 1385, Clement had authorised a permanent annexation, but this had not been put into effect by the time of Clement's death in 1394 and his successor, Benedict XIII, had annulled all such grants. It had taken another eight years of lobbying, but now Benedict was permitting the union to proceed on the understanding that the abbey would install a perpetual vicar to provide parochial services, guaranteeing him a sufficient income from the parish revenues. Two years later, in 1404, they sought and secured two confirmations of the award following the death of the incumbent priest, and later in the same year the pope also confirmed their possession of the patronage of the church. His mandate narrated how the patronage had been granted to Melrose by William, first earl of Douglas, patron of Cavers, and confirmed by Thomas, earl of Mar, superior lord of the barony, and also by Kings David II and Robert II. Melrose's title seemed absolute.

On 11 March 1405, Pope Benedict ordered the induction of Roger of Edinburgh, priest of St Andrews diocese, as rector of Cavers following the promotion of the former rector to the bishopric of St Andrews. His mandate stated that Melrose had detained possession of the church for over a year and named its patron as Isabella, countess of Moray, not the monks of Melrose. The dispute rumbled on, and in May 1406, another mandate was issued which described the conflicting claims to the church of David Binning, abbot of Melrose, who claimed that Cavers had been united to his house, and Simon de Mandeville, archdeacon of Glasgow, who claimed that the parish had lain vacant for so long that the right to appoint a rector had devolved on the Pope. The archdeacon made over his rights to a third party, James Walterson, canon of Glasgow, vicar of Innerleithen and chaplain of Dalkeith, who in September 1406 received a papal mandate permitting him to hold Cavers in conjunction with his other charges. James, using the same arguments as the monks, had claimed that the revenues of all his benefices had been so diminished by warfare with the English that he needed to hold them conjointly to make a decent living. In 1408, however, James was promoted to the archdeaconry of Teviotdale and, seizing their chance, the monks claimed that the parish was now vacant and sought, and again received, papal confirmation of the agreed appropriation of its revenues to the abbey. Any hope that this confirmation might have ended the dispute over Cavers was dashed in 1418 when William Croyser, a rising Scottish cleric at the papal court, re-opened the case before Pope Martin V. Croyser stated that Melrose's claim to the church was fraudulent and ought to be cancelled and, to ensure that the parish was properly served, he should be appointed as rector, regardless of his other benefices. After another round of litigation, Melrose finally received what was to prove to be a firm confirmation of its rights and the revenues of the parish were to remain annexed to the abbey until the Reformation.

Trade

Probably as early as the 1150s, when the monks began to acquire properties remote from their main concentration of estates around Melrose itself, the abbey had begun to trade its agricultural surpluses through the developing burgh markets of south-east Scotland. Of course, it had presumably always been obliged to trade through these markets to secure some of the basic commodities that it required to function but which could not be produced on its own land. The most obvious of these commodities was wine, required as a central component of the mass. The monks, however, quickly discovered that there was an almost insatiable market in mainland Europe for their wool, a commodity which had not originally been one of their main products. By the 1180s, however, it was clear that they had responded to the demand, lured by the high profits to be made, and had begun actively to seek out opportunities to expand their flock. The scale of their trading interest can be seen in the privilege that the monks secured in the early 1180s from Philip, count of Flanders, who granted free passage through his land and ports for the monks' goods, with no tolls to be levied on them. He also guaranteed them his protection should disputes arise between English and Flemish merchants. At around the same time, King William the Lion reaffirmed an earlier grant by David I which exempted the monks from payment of tolls at any market in his kingdom. Clearly, the monks' business operations were reaching a level where it was advantageous for them to negotiate and secure such protection.

Count Philip's grant of privileges referred only to the monks' goods and injury done to the interests of the abbey, not to the agents or men of Melrose themselves. It seems likely, then, that the monks were trading through intermediaries at this time, men who would negotiate a sale for commission and purchase the abbey's needs to order. This dependence on intermediaries was largely dispensed with in the thirteenth century, with the monks either selling direct to foreign merchants at source or trading overseas using their own men and ships. The monastery was trading actively for itself by the 1220s and possessed or had hired its own vessel. In August 1224, Henry III of England granted a licence at the request of King Alexander II for the men of the abbot of Melrose 'in charge of his money to parts beyond the sea', to pass safely through his dominions. The following April a more specific licence permitted the abbot to send a vessel to Flanders, laden with wool and other merchandise, in charge of William de Led and Brother Thomas of Boulden, while in April 1230 he received a licence for his ship in the charge of Brother William de Bueldon, laden with goods and merchandise, to pass through Henry's lands for a year.

Important though Continental trade was to the monks, much of its trade was probably carried out through England in the twelfth and thirteenth centuries, capitalising on the existing Cistercian network there. Their properties at Carlisle and Boston gave them access to the important fairs held at these centres. At Carlisle they were probably delivering the produce of the western estates to the growing livestock market of the city. It, however, was a smallscale operation when compared to the great fair at Boston. St Botulph's Fair was an event of truly international significance. It attracted foreign merchants, principally through its importance as a wool-market. Melrose was dealing through the fair in the 1220s, paying its rent to Vaudey Abbey for the lands of Carsphairn, probably with cash received from the sale of its wool, and possibly buying grain and wine for its household needs. The monks were also active traders at other fairs closer to home, especially the St James' Fair at Roxburgh, which was held in late summer shortly after the sheep-clip. It was at this fair that the monks received many of their 'peppercorn' rents on feued property, such as cinnamon, obtained from the foreign merchants who came to Roxburgh, lured by the wool of Teviotdale.

Although the monks possessed their own vessel and traded directly with continental ports, they also continued to deal through foreign merchants. At the end of the thirteenth century, for example, they may have been selling their wool at source to Italian merchants, such as Francesco Balducci Pegolotti, whose notebook records the quality and volume of the wool produced at most Scottish monasteries. In 1306, they were dealing with two Italian merchant houses, the Pulici and Rembertini, whose goods, personal property in England and debts due to them were arrested on the orders of Edward I, as they owed substantial amounts to various English nobles and merchants, but had defaulted on payment and fled. Two Scottish abbeys were noted by Edward's clerks as owing money to the Pulici and Rembertini:

Coupar Angus owed 180 merks, and Melrose owed 130 merks; and the English authorities ordered that their property be distrained to satisfy the amounts owed.

Melrose's ability to trade became complicated as the Wars of Independence progressed. As discussed above (see pp. 248–9), Melrose retained its interests in Berwick despite its several changes of hands after 1296, and was encouraged by the King of England to keep its wool flowing out through the port there. When Berwick was back in Scottish hands between 1318 and 1333, the Scots had likewise encouraged that trade, but after the fall of the burgh to Edward III of England they attempted to divert most of the trade of south-eastern Scotland to the port of Leith or the new burgh at Dunbar. In 1360, following the Treaty of Berwick of 1357 which suspended hostilities for the duration of the 10-year period in which David II was to pay his ransom to Edward III, the Scottish King recognised the difficult position of Melrose and permitted it to trade with the English since 'their place and monastery is located in the dominion of the English upon the marches'.

There are some indications that in the thirteenth century Melrose was acting as a collection centre for the wool of other Scottish monasteries. This may have been an arrangement of convenience which gave the monastic cartel better bargaining power with merchants, or which got the wool of some smaller producers at locations far from the main wool market in Berwick closer to the buyer. It did not, however, serve all Scottish monasteries, nor even all the Cistercian abbeys, for Flemish merchants were actively buying up wool in Moray in the early 1300s and using Valliscaulian Pluscarden Priory as a collection centre and store, whilst Cistercian Sweetheart was shipping out its own product and was storing some at Holmcultram. Nevertheless, it may have been with Melrose's former role as a middleman in the Scottish wool-trade in mind that Richard II granted them the extraordinary privilege of a customs reduction on up to 1,000 sacks of wool per annum exported through Berwick. That grant, however, did not succeed in funnelling either Melrose's or other Scottish wool through the declining English-held port for long, and it was, in any case, revoked after only three years. By the fifteenth century, Melrose was exporting primarily through Leith, from which port it also obtained the bulk commodities it needed for its household uses that could not be obtained on its own lands, although it also continued to deal directly with foreign craftsmen and traders for specialist goods, such as church furnishings. The volume of trade, however, declined steadily through the 1400s as the expanding Castilian wool export trade replaced Scotland as a source of cheap, bulk materials for the Flemish cloth industry, but even in the early sixteenth century Melrose wool was listed separately amongst Scottish commodities imported through Bruges.

The end of the abbey

By the late fifteenth century, the great complex of property that had been so carefully assembled over the previous 300 years was beginning to be disposed of by the monks. At first, a process of rationalisation may have been in operation, with small, remote or unprofitable pieces of land or rights to resources being sold off or exchanged for ones that lay closer to other more substantial blocks of Melrose interests. The process, however, had begun to accelerate after the disappearance in the course of the fourteenth century of the lay-brothers from the Cistercian order generally. In their place, Melrose, like other Cistercian houses, could employ paid servants to work the main granges of the home estate, but elsewhere there was a growing trend towards renting out the property to secular tenants. Even the right to collect teind was let at ferme, with the secular collectors agreeing a cash rent with the monks, then collecting the renders in kind and disposing of them at market for a profit, or collecting money payments direct from the abbey's tenants and parishioners. By the later fifteenth century there were further burdens on the land which saw the temporary loss of large blocks of property to furnish pensions for former abbots or failed candidates for the abbacy, such as Bernard Bell, who received Mauchline for life.

In the sixteenth century, the process changed character with an increasing move towards the feuing of property to secular tenants (**6**). This was a legal device which preserved the nominal superior lordship of the donor, and reserved for him some legal rights over the property, but which gave the tenant secure possession in return for an annual money payment that was fixed in perpetuity. It was at first possibly employed as a means of rewarding individuals for their loyal service to the abbey, as in the case of David Linlithgow at Drygrange, who received his feu-charter in recognition for his defence of the abbey's properties against English raiders and Scottish brigands. It was, however, also a good way to inject large sums of money into the monastic coffers, for there was usually a larger payment made on first entry to the property, and the annual payment thereafter brought in regular rental income. Such a device was very useful as a resort in times of financial crisis, but it simply provided short-term funds and the abbey effectively lost control – and economic value – in the feued property thereafter. Furthermore, as inflation rose in the sixteenth century, the real value of money rents fixed in the past diminished sharply.

The feuing of the Melrose estate that started in the late 1400s gained pace in the sixteenth century as the Church became increasingly exposed to economic pressures from the crown. James IV sought to extract more and more revenue from the Church and negotiated taxes. To provide the money to pay the crown, many Church lands were feued. The process accelerated sharply after about 1530 as James V began to collect regular taxation from the Church in Scotland, supposedly to fund the College of Justice that he established in 1532, but in reality to support his lavish court and building programmes. At Melrose, the abbacy of Andrew Durie witnessed an explosion in feuing, mostly in response to the King's taxation but also to win favour with the King and important nobles. In May 1535, for example, Durie issued a charter to James Stewart, the King's eldest bastard son, who would later replace the abbot at Melrose, giving him the feu of the lands of Rodono – part of the great lordship of Ettrick – at an annual rent of 50 merks. As usual, an explanation had to be offered for this alienation of ecclesiastical property, and Durie claimed that the lands had 'for many years lain waste and uncultivated on account of the wars, disorders and disquiet of the realm', with the result that no benefit had been gained from them. Now, however, he anticipated that much benefit would flow to the monastery from 'the help, counsel, favour and protection' that 'this noble and illustrious young man' could offer. In May 1534, James Stewart had been appointed to the commendatorship of Kelso Abbey, and by August 1535 had also received that of Melrose. The 'noble and illustrious young man' was 5 years old!

Durie presided over the wide scale alienation of the monastery's resources. Outlying properties were amongst the main subjects of feuferme grants. The eastern Lammermuir territories had already largely been set at feu by the early 1500s, and it was to be the turn of the western properties from the 1520s onwards. Direct control of the Ayrshire lands of the abbey had been slipping away gradually since the late fifteenth century when Kylesmuir had been used as a 'pension' source for bought-off, unsuccessful claimants to the abbacy. Individual blocks of property were steadily alienated at feu to sitting tenants or to influential local lairds whose support and protection the monks sought in the increasingly unstable politics of sixteenth-century Scotland. In 1527, Mossgiel in Kylesmuir, valued at 6 merks 40d in the abbey's rental, was feued to William Hamilton of Maknaristoun. In March 1533/4, Over and Nether Sorn were feued to William Hamilton of Sanquhar and his wife, with reservation to the monks of the glebe and peat banks. In 1535, it was Gilmuliscroft, Glenschamroch and Kamis, that were feued to Alexander Farquhar. Hamilton of Sanquhar benefited again in 1547 when the administrators of the abbey for the 17-year-old commendator, James Stewart, began to feu land with the excuse that the moneys so gained would be used to repair and rebuild the monastery after its recent 'wasting and burning' by the English. On this occasion, Hamilton gained properties in Kylesmuir, Barmuir and further west around Ayr.

Control of the abbey provided a vital source of patronage and revenue for the embattled Regent in 1559. To secure the support of Sir Hugh Campbell of Loudon, sheriff of Ayr and one of the key figures in the regional nobility of south-western Scotland, she arranged the lease to him of the abbey's lordship of Kylesmuir and Barmuir, including the revenues of the church of Mauchline and the teinds of the whole district, four meal mills and a waulkmill, with power to grant leases to tenants. The lease, which was to last until a new commendator was appointed, but with the proviso that any new appointee was to grant Campbell a 19-year lease, was held at a rent of 1000 merks per annum, payable quarterly. Clearly, Sir Hugh recognised this as a good deal and could expect to return a substantial profit from the land. In 1565, Michael Balfour, commendator of Melrose, still using the pretence that the feu was to raise money for the rebuilding of the abbey, set the land to Matthew Campbell of Loudon and his heirs. Theoretically, safeguards were built in to the grant that could permit the recovery of Kylesmuir at some future date, but the reality was that the property had been effectively alienated with only superiority retained.

The other western properties also disappeared as feuferme grants in the early sixteenth century. In Carrick, the lands which the abbey had held since the 1190s, comprising the so-called grange of 'Monkland' to the north of Maybole, were alienated piecemeal. In 1553, for example, Isabella Kennedy of Cloncaird and John Blair received the feu of Fisherton on the coast, for an annual rent of six merks and three suits of court at Monkland, while in 1555 it was her kinsman, Gilbert, Earl of Cassillis, who acquired a charter of Monkland itself, valued at 20 merks. The rest of the property there followed suit between the 1560s and 1580s, mainly into the hands of Cassillis and his tenants. In Nithsdale, it was the Maxwells who began to acquire portions of the Dunscore grange, with Glengunzeoch and the Grange Mill falling into the hands of Robert Maxwell of Porterrack in 1555. The remaining constituents of Dunscore were feued to their sitting tenants in 1565. Here, too, little more than notional superiority was retained.

The extensive Ettrick estate had begun to be broken up in the 1530s, but it was dismantled with great rapidity from the 1550s onwards. Rodono, which James Stewart himself had received in feuferme in 1535, was the subject of more traditional alienation in 1557 when James, as commendator, sold the land to John Lamb, an Edinburgh burgess. Several other Ettrick properties were alienated in the 1560s, with Robert Scott of Thirlstane acquiring a substantial block of land from Michael Balfour in 1568. Nearer to Melrose, in 1539, the monks confirmed an earlier alienation of the lands of Drygrange to one of their faithful servants, David Linlithgow (see pp.220–1). It represented the start of the large-scale erosion of the estates between Gala and Leader and Melroseland itself. In March 1540, for example, Arthur Sinclair received the feu of Lessudden, with some minor reservations, for an annual rent of a little over 80 merks. In 1546, the Scotts of Branxholm began to build up what was to become a major property portfolio composed of Melrose estates. Their first acquisition was various properties around Galashiels. Sir Walter Scott coveted the monks' property at Hassendean in Teviotdale, in particular the tower there that had been kept in the monastery's hands. Although he had acquired much of the abbey lands at Hassendean before 1560, it was only in 1562 that he acquired the 'Munkis-toure'.

The alienation of Hassendean Tower was just part of a flood of feuferme grants that followed the Reformation of 1560. The feuing proceeded apace after that, with properties in Melroseland figuring largely in the charters of Michael Balfour, the commendator. In 1564, it was Eildon, one of the three original properties granted by David I that was alienated, given to John Stewart, while in 1565 it was Darnick, granted to Queen Mary's Secretary of State, James Maitland of Lethington. In March 1568, shortly before he lost control of the commendatorship, Balfour attempted to make over what remained of the abbey's properties to his kinsman, Alexander Balfour of Denmiln, and in April issued a precept that sasine be given to him.

It was not just outlying properties that were being nibbled away, for by the 1560s the core of the abbey complex itself was under assault. The disappearance of the lay-brothers in the course of the fourteenth century had ended the spiritual seclusion of the monks at Melrose, for they needed to replace the *conversi* with lay servants who represented a worldly intrusion into the isolation of the precinct. Of course, that ideal isolation had never been fully achieved, for there had always been comings and goings of visitors, pilgrims and other travellers, and the abbey's tenants would have required entry to the precinct to deliver their rents in kind to the cellarer. None, however, had established a permanent presence within the monastic enclosure. The Reformation in 1560 removed any obstacle in that direction, and the commendators began to dispose of portions of the area within the precinct in the same manner as they had alienated the outlying granges.

The break up of the precinct moved with great rapidity after 1560, aided by the commendator's intention to extract the maximum potential revenue from his charge. Whilst before the Reformation it had been the abbey's lands and properties outwith the precinct that had been alienated for cash payments, through the later sixteenth century it was the precinct itself that was progressively broken up and rented out or granted away at feuferme. Some of the grants were quite substantial. On 15 December 1584, for example, Alexander Young was given the tack of the Bakehouse Yard, which lay within the 'mantill wall' (**7**). It was described as bounded on the north and west by the precinct wall, with the mill and mill dean on the south, and the common way to the river (Annay Road) on the east. Young also took the tack of a second yard within the precinct, which had formerly been the portion of one of the monks. It had the mill dean on the north, the precinct wall on the west, the 'hie streit that passis to the…abbay' on the south (St Mary's Road), and the 'baikhous grein' on the east. With these, he also received the adjacent bakehouse itself, already in 1584 described as 'ruinus and decayit', and its green, bounded by the mill dean on the north, his own yard on the west, and the 'hie passage to the said abbay' on the south and east; and another piece of ground on the south side of the 'hie passage' bounded on three sides by yards, also feued to lay tenants. Altogether, this placed most of the north-west quadrant of the precinct in the hands of one man.

The fabric of the abbey, already under assault from laymen in the 1550s, proved an irresistible lure once fear of ecclesiastical sanction by the monks had been removed after 1560. The records of the Court of Session in April 1573 noted that from January to April 1569, Sir Walter Scott of Branxholm, baillie of the abbey, and his men had indulged in the

> 'wranguis violent and maisterfull casting doun demolitioun and tyrving … of the principale abbay and kirk of Melros … alsweill inner kirk quier vter kirk and stepill and croce kirk of the samin And for the wranguis spoliatioun detening avaytaking withhalding and disponing of the stanis tymmer leid irne and glas of the said kirk and stepill … and for the wranguis etc breking up … of the durris of ane hous of the said place callit the platform alias abbotishall and tua inner chalmeris within the samyne all the saidis housis being thekit with leid and breking up of the durris of ane hous callit the west loftis entering thairin etc hewing doun and disponing of the stanis tymmer irne and glas insycht of the saidis houses chalmeris and yard of the said abbay…'

This was a comprehensive assault on the main complex of buildings, involving the removal of masonry and lead-work, as well as salvageable iron, timber and glass from the abbey church and the old abbots' residence especially.

The cloister itself, which had never recovered from the sack of the abbey in the 1540s, seems also to have succumbed to a sustained attack on its integrity. A letter of tack of 2 July 1587 in favour of John Knox, minister of Melrose, confirmed his possession of 'the chalmer and gairdene' to the north-east of the cloister which he already occupied. Its bounds were given as the kirk and kirkyard to the south, a dyke between its garden and the property occupied by John Watson, one of the monks, with a dyke dividing the infirmary lengthwise in halves as far as its 'comoun foir entrie' on the east, a newly-built dyke on the north, and the 'auld ruinus wallis' on the east side of the cloister on the west. From these references, it appears that the east range of the cloister was wholly ruinous by the 1580s, and that the infirmary, occupied by the monks in the 1550s, was also derelict, with the remaining monks having moved into separate accommodation scattered around the precinct.

Although the circuit of the precinct remained discernible in the property boundaries at Melrose, and the old precinct wall remained an upstanding feature for much of the seventeenth century, its role as a physical boundary between the sacred and profane had ended with the Reformation. By the 1580s, when the existence of a 'convent' at Melrose was little more than a legal fiction preserved in the charters of the commendators, there was no distinction between the world within and the world outwith the monastic enclosure. The emerging burgh of Melrose had already spilled into the south and west of the precinct, developing into streets along the main roads leading to the west end of the church and cloister. Long before the formal winding up of the abbey as a religious corporation in the early 1600s, the old complex had been overwhelmed by the community that had grown up in its shadow.

APPENDIX

The building stones of the abbey

One of the memorable aspects of Melrose Abbey is the range of the stone types used in its construction. The abbey church itself, as rebuilt after 1385, is built of large blocks of sandstone ashlar which are cut and jointed throughout with exquisite precision, and this stone permitted carving of the highest quality. It varies in colour from a deep reddish, almost purple pink to a buff or yellow hue. The variations in the colour of the stone used in the different parts provide one of the clues to the sequence of building, although, assuming that masonry of such extremely high quality would not have had a lime wash applied over it, it might seem rather strange to modern eyes that such colour changes might be considered acceptable when so much care was being taken over the cutting and laying of the stone.

By contrast with the church, much of the rest of the complex is built of rubble masonry with only minimal freestone dressings and, even without the evidence which shows this was the case, there could be little doubt that such stonework was intended to be rendered over with a coating of lime both internally and externally.

At the time of the clearance excavations of the abbey, in the years between the First and Second World Wars, a report was prepared on the building stones by R.J.A. Eckford and F.W. Anderson of the Scottish Office of the Geological Survey of Great Britain. They identified four main types of stone as having been used.

Agglomerate is a rock made up of angular fragments resulting from volcanic eruption. Rocks of this kind, which are datable to the Lower Carboniferous age, are found to the south-west of Melrose, and there is evidence of quarrying at Quarry Hill (NT 541 337), amongst other locations. This stone

104 *The quarry workings at Bourjo, on the lower slopes of the Eildon Hills.* Fawcett

was used for many of the earlier conventual buildings of the abbey in the twelfth and thirteenth centuries, including the east, north and parts of the west claustral ranges, and the walls of the drain. Agglomerate continued to be used throughout the abbey's history, though it has been suggested that in the case of the commendator's house this may have been because the materials were re-used from other buildings (**93**). But re-use cannot have been the explanation for the relatively late employment of agglomerate in other cases, including parts of the webbing of the transept vaults, which can be dated to the mid-fifteenth century.

Trachyte and **felsite** are also igneous rocks, but are generally more finely grained and have a rather unpredictable cleavage. The Eildon Hills are largely composed of this type of rock, and it is likely that it was from there that such stone used at the abbey would have been brought, although it was perhaps mainly gathered as fieldstones rather than quarried. Parts of the walls at the north end of the later lay-brothers' range are of trachyte, and some of it is used along with other stones in the abbot's house and along the walls of the drain. Small quantities of felsite are also found amongst other materials in the original part of the west range.

Greywacke, perhaps more commonly referred to as whinstone, is a hard sedimentary rock of the Silurian period, and is found extensively around the site of the abbey itself. Large blocks of this stone were used for the lintelling of the drain. This stone was also used in the form of river-washed pebbles along much of the floor of the drain, parts of which perhaps perpetuate the earlier channel of the Tweed on which the abbey was located.

Sandstones represent the finest of the building materials used at the abbey. Those found at Melrose are probably of Upper Devonian age, and belong to the Upper Old Red Sandstone lithofacies. They are characterised by considerable variation in both texture and colour, varying from finely-grained to gritty, and from yellow through red to purple. A nearby source of these stones is the lower levels of the Eildon Hills, where there is considerable evidence of early quarrying activity, for example at Bourjo (NT 548 327) (**104**) and at Ploughlands (NT 633 307). It was the finer varieties of these stones that were used for rebuilding the church after 1385, and they are also found in the mid-thirteenth-century west front of the chapter house (**87**) and as dressings in other buildings, including the commendator's house. In addition, sandstone is used in parts of the extension to the lay-brothers' range, though this may be associated with the secondary insertion of vaulting and the piers to support that vaulting.

BIBLIOGRAPHY

Primary Sources

Hutton Papers in the National Library of Scotland: Adv MS 9A, 1-20; 19.1.22; 20.3.1-9; 20.5.5-7; 20.6.6; 22.1.13; 22.2.1-4; 29.4.2; 29.5.5-8; 30.5.1-28; 33.4.17

Official Ministry of Works files now in the National Archives of Scotland:

MW.1.335 (Finds and gifts of exhibits 1921-39)

MW.1.337 (Setting up of abbey museum)

MW.1.1284 (Finds and gifts of exhibits 1940-46)

DD.27.1035 (Finds and gifts of exhibits 1946-69)

DD.27.1037 (Setting up of abbey museum)

Historic Scotland drawings collection 138/214

Printed Primary Sources

'Accounts of the King's Pursemaster 1539-40', ed. A.L. Murray, *Miscellany of the Scottish History Society*, x (1965), 11-51

Accounts of the Lord High Treasurer of Scotland, eds T. Dickson and J. Balfour Paul (Edinburgh, 1877-1916)

'Bagimond's Roll: Statement of the Tenths of the Kingdom of Scotland', ed. A.I. Dunlop, *Miscellany of the Scottish History Society*, vi (Scottish History Society, 1936), 1-77

John Barbour, *The Bruce*, ed. and trans. A.A.M. Duncan (Edinburgh, 1997)

Calendar of Documents Relating to Scotland, eds J. Bain *et al.*, 5 vols (Edinburgh, 1881-1985)

Calendar of the Laing Charters, ed. J. Anderson (Edinburgh, 1899)

Calendar of Entries in the Papal Registers, Letters, eds W. Bliss *et al.*, (London, 1893-)

Calendar of Papal Letters to Scotland of Clement VII of Avignon 1378-1394, ed. C. Burns (Scottish History Society, 1976)

Calendar of Papal Letters to Scotland of Benedict XIII of Avignon 1394-1419, ed. F. McGurk (Edinburgh, 1976)

Calendar of Scottish Supplications to Rome 1418-1422, eds E.R. Lindsay and A.I. Cameron (Edinburgh, 1934)

Calendar of Scottish Supplications to Rome 1428-1432, eds A.I. Dunlop and I.B. Cowan (Scottish History Society, 1970)

Calendar of Scottish Supplications to Rome, iv, *1433-1447*, eds A.I. Dunlop and D. MacLauchlan (Glasgow, 1983)

Calendar of State Papers Relating to Scotland 1509-1603, ed. M.J. Thorpe (London, 1858)

Calendar of State Papers Relating to Scotland and Mary, Queen of Scots 1547-1603, eds J. Bain *et al.* (Edinburgh, 1898-)

The Chronicle of Melrose (Facsimile Edition), eds A.O. Anderson *et al.* (London, 1936)

Early Sources of Scottish History AD 500 to 1286, ed. A.O. Anderson, 2 vols (Edinburgh, 1922)

Exchequer Rolls of Scotland, eds J. Stuart *et al.* (Edinburgh, 1878-1908)

The Hamilton papers, letters and papers illustrating the political relations of England and Scotland in the XVIth century, ii (Edinburgh, 1892)

Historical Manuscripts Commission, Twelfth Report, Appendix, Part VIII, The Manuscripts of the Duke of Athole, KT and of the Earl of Hume (London, 1891)

Historical Manuscripts Commission, Fourteenth Report, Appendix, Part III, The Manuscripts of the Duke of Roxburghe; Sir H.H. Campbell, Bart; The Earl of Strathmore; and the Dowager Countess of Seafield (London, 1894)

Ledger of Andrew Halyburton 1492-1503, ed. C. Innes (Edinburgh, 1867)

The Letters of James the Fourth 1505-1513, eds R.K. Hannay and R.L. Mackie (Scottish History Society, 1953)

Letters and Papers, Foreign and Domestic of the Reign of Henry VIII, eds J.S. Brewer *et al.* (London, 1864-)

The Letters of James V, eds R.K. Hannay and D. Hay (Edinburgh, 1954)

Liber Sancte Marie de Melros, ed. C. Innes, 2 vols (Bannatyne Club, Edinburgh 1837)

The Orygynal Cronykil of Scotland by Androw of Wyntoun, ed. D. Laing, ii (Edinburgh, 1872)

Regesta Regum Scotorum, i, *The Acts of Malcolm IV*, ed. G.W.S. Barrow (Edinburgh, 1960)

Regesta Regum Scotorum, ii, *The Acts of William the Lion*, ed. G.W.S. Barrow (Edinburgh, 1971)

Regesta Regum Scotorum, v, *The Acts of Robert I*, ed. A.A.M. Duncan (Edinburgh, 1988)

Regesta Regum Scotorum, vi, *The Acts of David II*, eds B. Webster *et al.* (Edinburgh, 1982)

Register of the Privy Council of Scotland, eds J.H. Burton *et al.* (Edinburgh, 1877-)

Registrum Honoris de Morton, 2 vols (Bannatyne Club, Edinburgh, 1853)

Registrum Magni Sigilli Regum Scotorum, eds J.M. Thomson *et al.* (Edinburgh, 1882-1914)

Registrum Secreti Sigilli Regum Scotorum, eds M. Livingstone *et al.* (Edinburgh, 1908-)

Rotuli Scotiae in Turri Londiniensi et in Domo Capitulari Westmonasteriensi Asservati, eds D. Macpherson *et al.*, 2 vols (1814-19)

Scotichronicon, eds D.E.R. Watt *et al.*, 9 vols (Aberdeen and Edinburgh, 1987-98)

Scottish Annals from English Chronicles, ed. A.O. Anderson (London, 1908)

Selections from the Regality Records of Melrose, ed. C.S. Romanes, 3 vols (Scottish History Society, 1914-1917)

Tours in Scotland 1747, 1750, 1760 by Richard Pococke, Bishop of Meath, ed. D.W. Kemp (Scottish History Society, 1887)

Secondary Sources

G.W.S. Barrow, *Robert Bruce and the Community of the Realm of Scotland*, 3rd ed. (Edinburgh, 1988)

M. Brown, *James I* (Edinburgh, 1994)

M. Brown, *The Black Douglases* (East Linton, 1998)

G. Coppack, *Fountains Abbey* (London, 1993)

G. Coppack, *The White Monks* (Stroud, 1998)

I.B. Cowan, *The Parishes of Medieval Scotland* (Scottish Record Society, 1967)

I.B. Cowan and David E. Easson, *Medieval Religious Houses, Scotland*, 2nd ed. (London and New York, 1976)

J. Curle, *A Little Book about Melrose* (Edinburgh, 1936)

E.P. Dennison and R. Coleman, *Historic Melrose* (Edinburgh, 1998)

M. Dilworth, *Scottish Monasteries in the Late Middle Ages* (Edinburgh, 1995)

D. Ditchburn, *Scotland and Europe: the Medieval Kingdom of Scotland and its Contacts with Christendom, 1214-1560* (East Linton, 2001)

A.A.M. Duncan, *Scotland: the Making of the Kingdom* (Edinburgh, 1975).

R. Fawcett, *Scottish Architecture from the Accession of the Stewarts to the Reformation* (Edinburgh, 1994)

P.C. Ferguson, *Medieval Papal Representatives in Scotland: Legates, Nuncios and Judges-Delegate, 1125-1286* (Stair Society, 1997)

P. Fergusson, *Architecture of Solitude* (Princeton, 1984)

P. Fergusson and S. Harrison, *Rievaulx Abbey* (New Haven and London, 1999)

A. Fraser, *Mary, Queen of Scots*, rev. ed. (London, 1994)

J. Gilbert, *Hunting and Hunting Reserves in Scotland* (Edinburgh, 1979)

J. Gilbert, *Melrose, its Kirk and People* (Melrose, 1991)

A. Grant, *Independence and Nationhood: Scotland 1306-1369* (London, 1984)

F. Grose, *The Antiquities of Scotland*, i (London, 1789)

A.J. MacDonald, *Border Bloodshed: Scotland, England and France at War, 1369-1403* (East Linton, 2000)

N.A.T. MacDougall, *James III: a Political Study* (Edinburgh, 1982)

N.A.T. MacDougall, *James IV* (East Linton, 1997)

D. MacGibbon and T. Ross, *The Ecclesiastical Architecture of Scotland*, 3 vols (Edinburgh, 1896-7)

A. Milne, *A Description of the Parish of Melrose* (Edinburgh, 1743)

M.G. Newman, *The Boundaries of Charity: Cistercian Culture and Ecclesiastical Reform* (Stanford, 1996)

R. Nicholson, *Scotland: the Later Middle Ages* (Edinburgh, 1974)

C. Norton and D. Park (eds) *Cistercian Art and Architecture in the British Isles* (Cambridge, 1986)

T. Pennant, *A Tour in Scotland*, ii (London, 1776)

F. Pinches, *The Abbey Church of Melrose* (London, 1879)

J.S. Richardson and Marguerite Wood, *Melrose Abbey*, 1st ed. (Edinburgh, 1936)

Royal Commission on the Ancient Monuments of Scotland, *An Inventory of the Ancient and Historical Monuments of Roxburghshire*, ii (Edinburgh, 1956)

D. Robinson, *The Cistercian Abbeys of Britain* (London, 1998)

The Statistical Account of Scotland, ix (Edinburgh, 1793)

The New Statistical Account of Scotland, iii (Edinburgh, 1845)

J. Slezer, *Theatrum Scotiae* (London, 1693)

D.E.R. Watt, *Medieval Church Councils in Scotland* (Edinburgh, 2000)

D.E.R. Watt and N.F. Shead (eds), *The Heads of Religious Houses in Scotland from Twelfth to Sixteenth Centuries* (Scottish Record Society, 2001)

Articles and Essays

G. Coppack, C. Hayfield and R. Williams, 'Sawley Abbey: the Architecture and Archaeology of a smaller Cistercian abbey' *Journal of the British Archaeological Association*, clv (2002), 22-114

J. Curle, 'Melrose: the Precinct Wall of the Monastery and the Town', *History of the Berwickshire Naturalists' Club*, xxix pt.i (1935)

O. Delepierre, 'Documents from the records of West Flanders relative to the stalls of Melrose Abbey', *Archaeologia*, xxxi (1846), 346-9

R. Eckford and F.W. Anderson, 'Report on the Building Stones Used in the Construction of the Abbey of St Mary at Melrose', *History of the Berwickshire Naturalists Club*, xxx (1938-46)

A.A.M. Duncan, 'Roger of Howden and Scotland, 1187-1201' in B.E. Crawford (ed.), *Church, Chronicle and Learning in Medieval and Early Renaissance Scotland* (Edinburgh, 1999)

D.E. Easson, 'Foundation Charter of the Collegiate Church of Dunbar, AD 1342', *Miscellany of the Scottish History Society*, vi (Edinburgh, 1939)

J. Gilbert, 'The Monastic Record of a Border Landscape 1136 to 1236', *Scottish Geographical Magazine*, icix (1983), 4-15

R. Gilyard-Beer and G. Coppack, 'Excavations at Fountains Abbey, North Yorkshire', 1979-80, *Archaeologia*, cviii (1986), 147-88

A. Grant, 'Acts of lordship: the records of Archibald, fourth earl of Douglas', in T. Brotherstone and D. Ditchburn, *Freedom and Authority: Historical and Historiographical Essays Presented to Grant G. Simpson* (East Linton, 2000)

D. Laing, 'A contemporary record of the Earl of Hertford's Second Expedition to Scotland and of the Ravages Committed by the English Forces in September 1545', *Proceedings of the Society of Antiquaries of Scotland*, i (1854)

G. Neilson, 'The Feuing of Drygrange from the Monastery of Melrose', *Scottish Historical Review*, vii (1910), 355-63

C. Norton, 'Medieval floor tiles in Scotland', in John Higgitt (ed.), *Medieval art and architecture in the diocese of St Andrews* (British Archaeological Association Transactions for 1986) (Leeds 1994), 137-73

R.D. Oram. 'Prayer, Property and Profit: Scottish Monasteries *c*.1100-*c*.1300', in S. Foster, A.I. Macinnes and R.K. MacInnes (eds), *Scottish Power Centres from the Early Middle Ages to the Twentieth Century* (Glasgow, 1998)

J.S. Richardson, ' A Thirteenth-Century Tile Kiln at North Berwick, East Lothian, and Scottish Medieval Ornamented Floor Tiles', *Proceedings of the Society of Antiquaries of Scotland*, lviii (1928-9), 281-310

M.H.B. Sanderson, 'The farmers of Melrose', in M.H.B. Sanderson, *Mary Stewart's People* (Edinburgh, 1987)

W.W. Scott, 'Abbots Adam (1207-13) and William (1215-1216) of Melrose and the Melrose Chronicle', in B.E. Crawford (ed.), *Church, Chronicle and Learning in Medieval and Early Renaissance Scotland* (Edinburgh, 1999)

G.G. Simpson, 'The Heart of King Robert I: Pious Crusade or Marketing Gambit?' in B.E. Crawford (ed.), *Church, Chronicle and Learning in Medieval and Early Renaissance Scotland* (Edinburgh, 1999)

J.A. Smith, 'Notes on Melrose Abbey, especially in Reference to Inscriptions on the Wall of the South Transept', *Proceedings of the Society of Antiquaries of Scotland*, ii (1854-7), 166-75 and 295

W.B. Stevenson, 'The Monastic Presence: Berwick in the Twelfth and Thirteenth Centuries', in M. Lynch, M. Spearman and G. Stell (eds), *The Scottish Medieval Town* (Edinburgh, 1988)

K.J. Stringer, 'Acts of Lordship: the Records of the Lords of Galloway to 1234' in T. Brotherstone and D. Ditchburn, *Freedom and Authority: Historical and Historiographical Essays Presented to Grant G. Simpson* (East Linton, 2000)

K.J. Stringer, 'Reform Monasticism and Celtic Scotland: Galloway, *c*.1140-*c*.1240', in E.J. Cowan and R.A. McDonald, *Alba: Celtic Scotland in the Medieval Era* (East Linton, 2000), 127-65

INDEX

Figures in bold denote illustration numbers

If you are interested in purchasing other books published by Tempus, or in case you have difficulty finding any Tempus books in your local bookshop, you can also place orders directly through our website

www.tempus-publishing.com

or from

BOOKPOST, Freepost, PO Box 29, Douglas, Isle of Man IM99 1BQ
Tel 01624 836000   email bookshop@enterprise.net